MARGUERITE DE NAVARRE'S
HEPTAMERON

To Jocelyn and Marc

MARGUERITE DE NAVARRE'S *HEPTAMERON*: THEMES, LANGUAGE, AND STRUCTURE ❧ ❧

Marcel Tetel ❧ *Duke University Press Durham, N. C. 1973*

© 1973 by the Duke University Press

L.C.C. card no. 72–88735

I.S.B.N. 0–8223–0279–9

Printed in the United States of America
by Heritage Printers, Inc.

Contents

00418

Acknowledgments

This book could not have been written without the trustful generosity of the John Simon Guggenheim Memorial Foundation and the Duke University Research Council. In its manuscript form, it owes much to John Dowling and Susan Dyer. To these institutions and individuals, I remain ever grateful.

MARGUERITE DE NAVARRE'S
HEPTAMERON

1. MARGUERITE DE NAVARRE RE-CAPTURED

A<small>N</small> exemplary figure of her age, Marguerite de Navarre remains elusive. And as long as critics persist in narrowly fixing her thought and religion, she will continue to elude them. If there is one assured resemblance linking the three major French prose writers of the sixteenth century—Rabelais, Marguerite, and Montaigne—it is that each leaned toward several philosophical or religious points of view without ever totally accepting any one and kept evolving toward another. Thus a fervent syncretism marks the thought and religious attitudes of all three. In the case of Marguerite de Navarre, of late, this elusiveness has been stressed, and yet rejected, by the adoption of another synthesizing formula. On an ideological level, her syncretism presupposes a free will that dominates choices and actions, strongly buttressed by an empirical view of life; on a literary level, it inevitably produces composite, amorphous works that on the surface defy the Aristotelian concept of order.

Written as they were in a century of spiritual ferment and exploration, it is no surprise, and almost inevitable, that Marguerite de Navarre's works reflect varying, even contrasting, tendencies. Thus Saulnier can assert: "Ondoyante, Marguerite s'est laissée tenter par toutes les formules de croyance."[1] And of the many religious labels that have been attributed to her, not one need be erroneous; they merely represent the momentary assimilation or convergence of spiritual strains into a literary corpus which reflects the changing moments of her intellectual journey through life.[2]

1. Marguerite de Navarre, *Théâtre profane*, ed. V. L. Saulnier (Geneva, 1963), p. xv.
2. "Marguerite catholique, évangélique, protestante, luthérienne, calviniste, mystique, spirituelle, sceptique . . . toutes ces étiquettes . . . engendrent d'abominables anachronismes de pensée; ou bien prétendent enfermer en

For the queen, religion was not an abstraction, but a living organism setting forth practical and attainable standards for human conduct;[3] if her position cannot be fixed, it is precisely because in trying to bridge the gap between theological theses and the experiences of life she finds in herself an unresting spiritual mobility. As a result, she is doubtless a moralist, but in the French seventeenth-century sense of the word; that is, she observes and carefully depicts human behavior and the experiences of life much more than she judges.

The result, of course, is pessimistic, though faith remains, the one indestructible constant: "foy seulement peut montrer et faire recevoir le bien que l'homme charnel et animal peut entendre" (XIX, 134).[4] Marguerite's religion, however, is of her own making and necessarily a composite. This infallibility of faith creates a certain a-religion, an indifference toward the established church and conventional morality, which in turn leads to a freedom of expression and honest depiction of life.[5] Observations and experiences of life domi-

deux mots toute la vie et toute l'oeuvre, infiniment variées, d'une femme qui vécut cinquante ans de la vie la plus pleine et la plus riche; ou bien encore visent à l'emprisonner dans tel état d'esprit qui put être le sien pendant un an ou deux—mais elle ne saurait l'avoir gardé intact et sans changement de la trentaine à la cinquantaine. . . ." L. Febvre, *Autour de l'Heptaméron: Amour sacre, amour profane* (Paris, 1944), p. 154. "Bien qu'elle ait explicité sa pensée dans de nombreuses œuvres, on lui a imposé les étiquettes les plus diverses, catholique, évangélique, luthérienne, calviniste, mystique en accord avec les libertins spirituels. Seules les qualifications de déiste et d'athée lui ont été épargnées." R. Lebègue, "Le second *Miroir* de Marguerite de Navarre," *Comptes-rendus de l'Académie des Inscriptions et Belles Lettres (1963)*, p. 51.

3. "The queen's interest in religion was part of her personal search for values—not just rules—to live by, and to make it the exclusive concern of her life is to misconstrue her nature. Neither a theologian nor a philosopher, but a moralist deeply concerned with human experience, she confined her vision to the limits of heart." J. Gelernt, *World of Many Loves: The Heptameron of Marguerite de Navarre* (Chapel Hill, N.C., 1966), p. 18.

4. Marguerite de Navarre, *Nouvelles*, ed. Yves Le Hir (Paris, 1967). All further citations from the *Heptameron* will be from this edition. The roman numerals refer to the novella and the arabic to the page.

5. This notion is aptly suggested but not sufficiently developed by E. Meylan, "La Date de *L'Oraison de l'âme fidèle* et son importance pour la bio-

nate her outlook and constantly erode and undermine the bastion of faith. A reconciliation between an absolute and true faith obtained through grace and the relativistic and fluid condition of life is naturally quite impossible.

Traditionally, criticism of Marguerite de Navarre has tried and even succeeded in harmonizing her idealism or spiritualism with what is vile and earthly. The formula is rather simple: dejected and disillusioned by the ugly world, she rises to a purifying reunion with the spiritual world and seeks refuge in it; or again, faulty earthly love is the necessary step toward the love of God, perfection, the Platonic Idea.[6] Biographical facts can substantiate this point of view; the queen did retire into a monastery during the last year of her life. The net result is a Platonico-Christian quietism. That there exists such a strain in her works is beyond any doubt; but the question arises of what role it plays and under what light it should be seen.

Certainly in the past the importance of Platonism has been quite inflated, perhaps even to the point of obsession. In two ponderous studies at the turn of the century Abel Lefranc gave the main impetus to criticism along Platonic lines.[7] Oddly enough, Lefranc never actually proved his thesis by means of incontestable textual confrontations; he mostly catalogued individuals, especially from the fifteenth and sixteenth centuries, whose works propounded the Platonic philosophy of love and God. Naturally, similar notions and

---

graphie morale de Marguerite de Navarre," *Modern Language Notes*, 52 (1937), 565.

6. "Elle y a trouvé d'abord une psychologie de l'amour qui répondait à ses désirs de rénovation morale et qui exaltait ses aspirations mystiques: 'La Coche,' 'Les Quatre Dames,' 'La Distinction du vray amour,' 'Chansons spirituelles,' 'Les Prisons,' tout l'*Heptaméron* en sont des preuves éclatantes." R. Marichal, ed., *La Navire; Ou Consolation du roi François I à sa sœur Marguerite* (Paris, 1956), p. 33.

7. "Le Platonisme et la littérature en France à l'époque de la Renaissance," *Grands écrivains de la Renaissance* (Paris, 1914), pp. 64–137; and "Marguerite de Navarre et le Platonisme en France," ibid., pp. 139–249.

even textual references are to be found in Marguerite de Navarre. But does this presence justify calling her a Platonic writer? Renaudet neatly divides her spiritual formation into two periods but without any real basis: the first, from 1521 to 1540, in the shadow of Briçonnet and Lefèvre, during which she seeks the abnegations of the self in God, and the second, from 1540 until her death in 1549, during which her chief study was Plato through Ficino's commentaries.[8]

Moreover the substitution of one ism for another is not particularly helpful:

> On a trop parlé du platonisme de Marguerite de Navarre; il faudrait dire ficinisme: un ficinisme tout christianisé par les fréquentes références aux Epîtres du Nouveau Testament. Pour Marguerite l'amour de la créature est une étape vers l'amour du Créateur. Aussi voyons-nous souvent dans l'*Heptaméron*, les amoureux infortunés entrer au couvent, et y trouver enfin la satisfaction de leur coeur. Mais trop d'amoureux, au gré de l'auteur, ne se contentent pas de "l'honnête amitié" et satisfont leurs appétits charnels; d'autres quoiqu'ils restent chastes, aiment trop la créature au détriment du seul parfait amour, qui est l'amour divin.[9]

The main significance of this passage derives from its last lines, which bring forward a discrepancy between the thesis of ideal love and a more dominant thesis emphasizing carnal

8. A. Renaudet, "Marguerite de Navarre, à propos d'un ouvrage récent," *Revue du Seizième Siècle*, 18 (1931), 287–88. Of course, Renaudet, excellent historian though he is, does not claim to be a literary critic.

9. R. Lebègue, "Les Sources de l'*Heptaméron* et la pensée de Marguerite de Navarre," *Comptes-rendus de l'Académie des Inscriptions et Belles Lettres* (1956), p. 472. P. Jourda, in his monumental but sometimes prolix two-volume study, wisely devotes only a few pages specifically to Platonism (901–3), in the same vein, however, as his colleague: "Est-ce là simplement la doctrine de Platon? Il semble qu'il s'y mêle des idées chrétiennes,—et qu'à l'influence du disciple de Socrate s'ajoutent celles de Ficin et des moralistes italiens, celle surtout de l'Evangile." M. d'Angoulême, *Duchesse d'Alençon, Reine de Navarre (1492–1549). Etude biographique et littéraire.* II (Paris, 1930), p. 903.

love. Although this discrepancy is noted, it is not explained, for fear that the effort to explain it might bring down the Platonic edifice. Such an assertion has finally been made following the same train of thought: "Perhaps the most conclusive evidence of the fact that the *Heptameron* is not essentially Neoplatonic is the ambiguous nature of what I have called, for lack of a better term, Christian love, where a frustrated relationship causes one or both parties to retreat from the world and turn to God instead."[10]

The myth of a Platonic Marguerite de Navarre becomes difficult to substantiate even from a reading of all her works. Traditionally her poetry provided a good source for the Platonic thesis, for it is intensely lyrical, emotional, and personal. It depicts, for the most part, the flight from the ugly and earthly to the beautiful and spiritual. The essential point missed, however, is that Marguerite does not deprecate the earthly; on the contrary, she indicates her disillusionment with it. This interpretative difference then becomes quite significant because it reveals a tortured soul, still firmly held to the ground, instead of a soul abnegating itself for a union with God.

As for Marguerite's theater, it is sharply divided. In the tradition of the medieval *débat*, it sets forth contrasting abstracted moral or religious concepts of an uncompromising kind. In the *Comédie de Mont-de-Marsan*, for example, La Mondainne and La Supersticieuse, on the one hand, and La Ravie de l'Amour de Dieu, on the other, do not convince; but La Sage does. Marguerite de Navarre did not have to introduce La Sage; she created the character to advocate wisdom, moderation, and reason, the deified trilogy of the humanists. The importance of moderation and reason, although often implied, in Marguerite de Navarre is not sufficiently stressed or known.[11] The personal theater, e.g., the *Comédie*

10. Gelernt, p. 69.
11. The point, however, is quite well made by E. Telle: "Pour la première

sur le trépas du Roy, like her personal and highly emotive poetry, results from the tragedies in her life, the loss of children, of her two husbands, of her brother; the death wish in these works reflects much more a love of persons than the precepts of a quietist. At first suffering and sorrow dominate, but they are soon rationalized into a somewhat pessimistic view of the human condition.

In the *Heptameron*, the question of Platonism and quietism, or Platonico-Christian love, appears finally in its proper perspective, in spite of some critical efforts to maximize it. Dagoucin, one of the narrators and participants in the discussions following each novella, is the chief exponent of Platonic love; although he never changes in the course of the discussions, his stories toward the end of the *Heptameron* do not necessarily illustrate the omnipotence or desirability of perfect and ideal love. Parlamente, considered Marguerite's mouthpiece, begins by relating stories that deal with the failure of ideal love, and toward the end her stories contain heavy dosages of coarseness and cruelty. Oysille, identified with Louise de Savoie, Marguerite's mother, is the incarnation of faith and the untiring champion of the Gospel; her position remains steadfast throughout the narrating of the stories. If these three narrators reflect varying degrees of idealism—all at the beginning but not all toward the end—there remain seven narrators, three women and four men, who tell stories and discuss them strictly along unrestrained, but always empirical, lines. And these seven voice Mar-

fois, la Raison apparaît dans le débat entre hommes et femmes, et il fallait que ce fût une femme . . . qui enseignât cette leçon aux hommes de son siècle. C'est ce qui fait de l'*Heptaméron* une oeuvre *moderne*." *L'Œuvre de M. d'Angoulême, reine de Navarre et la Querelle des Femmes* (Toulouse, 1937), p. 147. Recently a whole book has been devoted to the usage of the word *reason* in Marguerite de Navarre. Although it demonstrates easily the capital importance of this word, the work appears more as a catalogue of every mention of *raison* than an interpretative study; see H. Vernay, *Les divers sens du mot "raison" autour de l'œuvre de Marguerite d'Angoulême, reine de Navarre (1492–1549)*, (Heidelberg, 1962).

guerite's opinions just as much as do the other three. To choose and emphasize the opinions of the first three, without even noting the developing ambivalence of two of them, and not to give equal importance to the opinion of the other seven is to distort the text. The form of Platonism that really pervades the *Heptameron* in every part is that of the Socratic banquet, the expression of the unfathomable multiplicity of human conduct without any fixed conclusion. Only marriage offers an immutable synthesis to the multifarious and evanescent nature of love: "il faut que les personnes se soumettent à la volonté de Dieu, ne regardans ny à la gloire, ny à l'avarice, ny à la volupté, mais par une amour vertueuse et d'un consentement desirent vivre en l'état de maryage, comme Dieu et nature l'ordonnent" (XL, 240).[12]

Platonic love, ideal love, Christian love, whatever it may be called, always contrasts enormously with everyday observable life; in fact, an abyss exists between these spiritualized forms of love, which fail even as they are attempted, and the carnal norm of human behavior. Even marriage fails in the *Heptameron* because "amour vertueuse" remains a rare commodity among men. And on the few occasions that marriage does seem to triumph, often after infidelities on the part of husband or wife, neither party need necessarily have reformed. Hence further abuses of marriage remain a definite possibility, indeed a constant threat.[13] In the final

12. This kind of statement appears more than once, always with the notion of order: "Dieu a mis si bon ordre, dit Oysille, tant à l'homme qu'à la femme, que si l'on n'en abuse, je tien le maryage le plus bel et plus seur état qui soit en ce monde" (XXXVII, 231).

13. "Hircan, Géburon, Symontault et Saffredan jurèrent qu'ilz s'étoient mariez en pareille intention, et que jamais ne s'en étoient repentys. *Mais quoy qu'il en fut de la vérité*, celles à qui il touchoit en furent si contentes, que ne pouvans oÿr un meilleur propos à leur gré, se levèrent . . ." (240–41, italics ours). This passage is particularly significant because it comes at the end of the fourth day of storytelling during which several novellas ended with a seemingly happy marriage or reunion, but the queen's comment stresses the very probable falseness of such a condition in life, that is, in the narrators' marriages.

analysis, both a spiritualized love outside marriage and a faithful ("virtuous") love within marriage become abstract ideals, by definition unattainable.

In the *Heptameron*, Marguerite de Navarre does not present an optimistic view of man. For the most part, he is weak and a prey to the pleasures of the flesh; when he resists them, he appears over-saintly and therefore no longer human in the eyes of others. It has often been said that the queen offers the reader a pessimistic panorama of life to strengthen the positive didactic aims of her work. True; but the fact remains that she thinks pessimistically of the human condition. Only true faith can save man, but few are eligible, or even have the capacity, to receive the grace of God. Faith and the grace of God then become another unattainable ideal, given the basic weakness of man. Marguerite postulates a set of ideals—Platonico-Christian love, marriage, faith—that should provide a guideline for living; life about her, however, appears totally different. There results obviously a tragic discrepancy, between life as it is and as it should aim to be, that reflects the troubled and insecure mind of Marguerite the observer.

A most felicitous formula by Saulnier sums up Marguerite de Navarre's mind: "Sa religion, le quiétisme? Tout le contraire. L'inquiétisme, si l'on veut."[14] Disquietude indeed dominates her thinking and urges her on into manifold spiritual and intellectual explorations in search of a constant to cling to. It could be said that her pessimistic restlessness stems from her strong evangelical tendencies, especially as it brings her to the Pauline view of human weakness. But following the norms of psychological behavior, it is much more natural to assume that she was attracted to evangelism because of her frame of mind; she saw in it a substantiation of her own spirit. Again the tragedies of her life, her experiences, and her observation of the life about her, notably

14. Saulnier, *Théâtre profane*, p. xvii.

at the court, made her conscious of the flux in human nature.[15] She did not need to discover from without what already pervaded her entire being from within. As a matter of fact, in more than one story, Marguerite marks the downward turn of events with a formula stressing an implacable fate: "Au bout de quelque tems la félicité de ce monde qui avec soy porte une mutabilité, ne peut durer en la maison qui étoit trop heureuse" (XLVII, 267).[16]

One way of dominating a fluid world is to retreat into one's-self with a kind of stoicism; Rabelais certainly saw some advantages in this weltanschauung, especially toward the end of his life, and Montaigne, of course, incorporated it in varying degrees of intensity during his creative years. Marguerite considers the advantages of stoicism in specific cases, but remains dubious of its lasting value. At first glance, stoicism offers some positive assets because it imposes self-control and moderations:

> Car ils ont une joye en leur cueur, et un contentement si modéré, que nul accident ne les peut muer. Qui sont ceus là? dit Hircan. Les philosophes du tems passé, répondit Géburon, desquelz la tristesse et la joye n'étoit quasi point sentie, au moins n'en montroient ilz nul semblant, tant ilz estimoient grand'vertu se vincre soy mesme et ses passions. [XXXIV, 218][17]

15. "Elle refuse de détourner son regard de son deuil pour le tourner vers la félicité céleste qui l'attend; avec une sorte de joie farouche, plus proche du désespoir que de la résignation chrétienne, elle ne veut sentir çà-bas qu'adversité." R. Marichal, *La Navire*, p. 7.

16. When the Grace of God does intervene, it is to reveal to the protagonists an ugly truth, here that the man the daughter married is really a monk inducted in this role by his superior; one may even detect a wry smile emanating from Marguerite de Navarre, the omniscient narrator: "Mais ainsi que la bonté de Dieu a pitié de ceus qui sont trompez par bonne foy, aveint de sa grace et misericorde, qu'un matin preind dévotion à cette dame et à sa fille d'aler oÿr la messe à Saint Françoys, et visiter leur bon Père confesseur, par le moyen duquel elles pensoient ettre si bien pourveues, l'une de beau fiz et l'autre de mary" (LVI, 298).

17. In a later story, the same argument recurs when Parlamente advocates

Soon, however, the line of demarcation between stoicism and masochism (or mortification) becomes blurred in the course of discussion, although Oysille in the preceding story had attempted to resolve the paradox by declaring, in keeping with her spiritual character, that faith alone "peut mortifier notre cueur, sans mutation ne ruyne de notre cors" (XXXIII, 215). Furthermore the discussion focuses on Diogenes the Cynic, an exponent of stoicism, and Plato. Interestingly enough, Plato is derided for his pride, that is, the vanity of giving so much importance to the power of love. On the other hand, it is argued that Diogenes' scornful attitude toward life is just as vainglorious (p. 218).

Hence stoicism and Platonism contain the seeds of their own decay in the form of vanity. The extremes meet, in that both are rejected because the self-control or abnegation they produce rests on an invalid precept, a cardinal sin. Once again the concept of man's weakness emerges, since he cannot dominate himself. At this point, a form of naturalism could bridge the gap; Marguerite, through her most naturalistic mouthpiece, Saffredan, rejects it outright. "Suivre son naturel" entails a measure of freedom which man is not capable of exercising or which others will not allow him to exercise: "Pleut à Dieu, dit Saffredan, que cette loy apportat autant d'honneur qu'elle fait de plaisir" (XIV, 103).

In the final analysis, ideologically and religiously, Marguerite de Navarre finds herself in a no-exit situation; every new avenue she explores or would like to explore turns out to be a dead end. No wonder then that disquietude best sums up her frame of mind, with ambiguity its inevitable correlative. Indeed, the whole thematic chorus converges on ambiguity, as will be amply shown. The *Heptameron* stresses the relativism of truth and the difficulty people have in com-

---

emulating the heroine: "Je vous prie qu'à son exemple nous demeurions victorieuses de nous mesmes. Car c'est la plus louable victoire que nous puissions avoir" (XLII, 252).

municating with one another because of the impossibility of discerning the real facts or motivations behind human behavior. Marguerite then feels that she is facing a universe that cannot be grasped, where everything is falsified and disintegrating. In addition, the mercurial nature of time contributes generously to the instability and fragmentation of society and life: "car ils dérobaient le tems, comme fait le larron une chose précieuse" (XXI, 142). The obvious consequence is the search for an order which will provide a constant to seize upon, even if only temporarily and illusorily.

Marguerite wishes that love could provide this coalescent order; instead it causes a state of saturation and oppression. To further express this feeling the queen sketches a metaphoric vocabulary. The image of weight could have positive implications but, given the nature of man and woman, produces negative ones:

Car il n'y a fes si poisant que l'amour de deux personnes bien unies, ne puisse doucement supporter. Mais quand l'un faut à son devoir, et laisse toute la charge sur l'autre, la poisanteur est insupportable. Vous devriez doncq, dit Géburon, avoir pitié de nous qui portons l'amour entière sans que vous y dégnez mettre le bout du doigt, pour la soulager. Ha, Géburon, dit Parlamante, souvent sont différens les fardeaus de l'homme et de la femmes. [XXI, 153][18]

Not only does this combined weight-scale-balance image accentuate the precariousness of man-woman relationship with a suggested criticism of the proverbial double standard

18. Two more examples of this image are particularly noteworthy because they crytallize its meaning: "Car qui a bien poisé le fes de maryage, il ne l'estimera moins facheus qu'une austère religion" (LXIV, 329); "Car la passion plus aveuglante est amour, et la personne la plus aveuglée, c'est la femme qui n'a pas la force de conduire sagement un si grand fes" (LXIX, 337). Indeed, in this last story a wife had used a drug to regain her husband's favor but "sans y garder doze, pois ne mesure" (LXIX, 337).

of the sexes, it also reveals a certain malaise, a constant suffering. The "faubourg de la mort" (XL, 239) describes the region (life) where one scorns and at the same time wishes death; the "ottelleries où ilz ont plus cryé que reposé" (XL, 239) relate to the precise and intense moments of suffering. Both of these expressions contain a conscious internal contradiction in that while they describe a spiritual crisis or torment, the words *faubourg* and *ottelleries* denote calm or restful places, the calm at the storm's eye, so to speak. Again the fact contradicts the wish. Furthermore the word *ennuy* occurs more than once with the gamut of meanings that it has nowadays. A revealing usage strikes the reader toward the end of the *Heptameron*: "Mais sa femme, qui étoit sage, en fut avertye, dont elle porta une si grande angoisse qu'elle en cuyda mourir d'ennuy" (LX, 312).[19] Without abusing the text or extrapolating the meaning, it can safely be stated that Marguerite in this instance transfers to the word *ennuy* a tragic intensity which she may have felt herself. This one example, and the above metaphoric expressions, are mere indicators of the Marguerite that will emerge from this study.

A frank depiction of the world of sham she saw about her leads to a fatalistic viewpoint. In fact, a study of the language of the *Heptameron* (see chapter 3) reveals this world of sham, the contradiction between intent and action, between thought and expression, to the extent that words offer their multifaceted, often contrasting meanings in order to unveil the duplicity and multiplicity of thought and action. As a result, an outwardly superficial, simple, and poor language assumes rich metaphorical overtones. Such a linguistic dimension contributes to the dismissal of the myth of a Marguerite nonartist-but-above-all-moralist.

As will be demonstrated, the *Heptameron* is well orchestrated and structured, and Marguerite de Navarre has the

19. For other occurrences of *ennuy* see, among others, novellas XXI, XXIII, XXIV, XXV.

gift of storytelling. The novellas are not only tightly connected by outer links but also by inner thematic ones. Although the *Heptameron* remains an unfinished work, the main prologue and the short prologues to each day further seal thematically the novellas into a solid entity. Marguerite knows how to compose a tale so as to stress one viewpoint over another. She experiments with the whole gamut of short narrative, from the medieval *exemplum*, whose dryness she avoids every time by adopting snappy dialogues or a sharpened metaphoric language, to the flowing novella, and even novelette, dominated by eloquent and sometimes ironic discourses to express emotional outpourings. The queen's multifarious outlook on life converges into a narrative technique that juggles and purposely confuses the concepts of fiction and reality into a Pirandellian interplay.

A craft of fiction does, then, pervade the *Heptameron* and is closely integrated with the didactic aims of the work. There remains of course the problematic question of the relationship between didacticism and entertainment in a short story or a collection of them, even if the two functions of moralizing and amusing are closely integrated and serve each other. Although each reader has to untie this knot for himself, no critic should conclude that Marguerite de Navarre is above all a moralizing author.

2. THE LANGUAGE OF LOVE

THE subject matter of the *Heptameron* is first and foremost love, which in turn becomes the catalyst for an exposition of human behavior. In the discussion following each novella, the language of love hovers at a theoretical and argumentative level and because of the contrasting points of view never quite settles on any one opinion. Here appear the idealistic definitions of conduct, always shaded or contradicted by one or more opposing opinions. In the short stories themselves, ideal love and virtue, with very few exceptions, fail and sometimes end up assuming unnatural proportions, whereas carnal desires are rampant. The idealist viewpoint, therefore, is definitely undermined, if not eliminated, by the discrepancy between the facts of life and rhetoric, as well as by the conscious contradictions within the discussions. To express these conflicting notions, Marguerite de Navarre adopts, on the one hand, a traditional Petrarchan vocabulary and forges, on the other hand, a metaphoric erotic language that through its frequency and above all its creative verve gives a dominant importance to earthly love. In fact, she merely uses verbal platitudes and rhetoric to depict sentiment and emotion, transformed to her own ends of course, but invention and fantasy intervene to describe the weakness of flesh and the bestiality of man. This metaphoric language can certainly not be regarded as just prudish periphrasis.

The first theoretical presentation of Platonic love occurs in the discussion following the eighth story; Dagoucin introduces the image of the androgyne to illustrate his thesis that two halves, man and woman, constantly seek each other out to re-form a perfect union, but in life, love is of a different nature:

> Mais je [Dagoucin] suis ferme en mon opinion, que celuy qui ayme n'ayant autre fin ne desir que de bien aymer, laissera plus tot son ame par la mor, que cette forte amour saille de son cueur. Par ma foy, dit Symontaut, je ne croi pas que jamais vous ayés été amoureus. Car si vous aviez senti ce fœu comme les autres, vous ne nous pindriez point icy la République de Platon qui s'écrit et ne s'expérimente point. [49]

Furthermore, Saffredan, the naturalistic voice, remarks that an abyss separates fiction from reality: "J'ai tant oÿ parler de ces transis d'Amour, mais encore n'en vi-je jamais mourir un" (50). Although Dagoucin is entitled to his point of view, his opinion is soon neutralized and put in perspective; it simply becomes one of several. This discussion occurs after a story of the fabliau type: a husband sends his friend to sleep with his wife, thinking she is the maid. The novella entertains; the discussion is supposed to elevate the mind. In this instance, Marguerite means to give just as much if not more importance to the discussion (two pages) as to the story (three pages).

The theory of perfect or ideal love states that man and woman seek each other out for the sake of the beauty and perfection in one another. If their union does not succeed according to such criteria, or if it does, then it has served as the useful and necessary step toward the one and ultimate perfection—God.[1] However, the one ingredient needed to complete this spiritual process is faith, a commodity not equally or evenly distributed among men. In the nineteenth tale, Parlamente, Marguerite's fictitious incarnation, offers an explicit definition of this concept of love which combines the Platonic version, the school of the "dolce stil nuovo," and "fin amors."[2] She presents perfect love as a theory which

1. For the concept of Platonic love, see such notable studies as: J. Festugière, *La Philosophie de l'amour de Marcile Ficin et son influence sur la littérature française au XVIe siècle* (Paris, 1941); P. O. Kristeller, *The Philosophy of Marsilio Ficino* (New York, 1943); J. C. Nelson, *Renaissance Theory of Love* (New York, 1958); E. Garin, *Studi sul platonismo medievale* (Florence, 1958).

2. "J'appelle perfetz amans, répondit Parlamente, ceus qui cerchent en ce qu'ilz ayment quelque perfection, soit beauté, bonté, ou bonne grace, tousiours tendens à la vertu; et qui ont le cueur si haut et si honnette qu'ilz ne voudroient, pour mourir, le mettre aus choses basses, que l'honneur et la conscience répreuvent. Car l'ame qui n'est créée que pour retourner à son souverain bien, ne fait, tant qu'elle est dedans ce cors, que desirer d'y pervenir. Mais à cause que les sens par lesquelz elle en peut avoir nouvelles, sont obscurs et charnelz par le péché du prémier père, ne luy peuvent montrer que les choses visibles plus approchantes de la perfection, apres quoy l'ame court, cuydant trouver en une beauté extérieure, en une grace visible et aus vertus morales, la souveraine beauté, grace et vertu. Mais quand elle les a cerchées et expérimentées, n'y trouvant point celuy qu'elle ayme, elle passe outre, ainsi

she proposes at this moment, as an ideal to try to live by in order to bring moments of nobility to human relationships, because life is quite different. Indeed two of the narrators, fictitious exteriorizations of the author's frame of mind, cast some questioning aspersions on Parlamente's discourse: "Mais, dit Ennasuyte: *Quis est ille, et laudabimus eum,* aussi perfet que vous le dites? . . . Ceus là, dit Saffredan, sont de la nature de la camalercite [chameleon] qui vit de l'air" (XIX–XX, 134–35). As in the eighth tale, the definition of perfect love follows a tale that illustrates both its failure—the inability of the man to overcome or subdue the physical nature of his love after entering the monastery in despair—and the mercilessness of the woman in uselessly testing the man's love, as well as her continued vanity after he enters the monastery.[3] Such a contrast between theory and fact undermines further the practicality and possibility of perfect love. And the abstract fideism of the discussion counteracts but does not suffice to contradict the bad faith that causes the young nobleman to enter the monastery.

If Marguerite/Parlamente (or /Dagoucin) ever tried gropingly to posit perfect love as an eventual code of behavior, it was never done convincingly nor was she ever completely

que l'enfant selon sa petitesse ayme les poupines, et autres petites choses que son œil peut voir les plus belles, et estime richesse d'assembler de petites pierres, mais croisçant ayme les poupines vives, et amasse les biens nécessaires pour la vie humaine. Puis quand il connoit par plus grande expérience qu'ès choses transitoires n'y a nulle perfection, ne felicité, desire cercher la fonteine et source d'icelles. Toutesfois si Dieu ne luy ouvre l'œil de foy, seroit en danger de devenir d'un ignorant, un infidèle philosophe. Car foy seulement peut montrer, et faire recevoir le bien que l'homme charnel et animal ne peut entendre" (IX, 134).

3. ". . . son pauvre serviteur qui entendoit mieus ce son là [her cough] que celuy des cloches de son monastère . . ." (132); "Puisqu'il ne pouvoit plus avoir d'elle autre chose en ce monde que la parole, il se tenoit bien heureus d'ettre au lieu, où il auroit toujours moyen de la recouvrir, et qu'elle seroit telle, que l'un et l'autre n'en pourroit que mieus valoir, vivans en un état d'une amour, d'un cueur, et d'un esprit . . ." (133); Poline had already told him "Si mon honneur eut permis qu'aussitot que vous je me fusse ausé mettre en religion, je n'eusse tant attendu" (132).

convinced herself. If there was ever any doubt on her part about the feasibility of this ideal concept, Parlamente finally states explicitly its shortcomings and her cynicism toward it:

Ma Dame, répondit Parlamente, il y a assez d'hommes estimez hommes de bien, mais d'ettre hommes de bien envers les Dames, garder leur honneur et conscience, je croi que de ce tems ne s'en trouveroit point jusques à un. Et celles qui s'y fient le croyant autrement s'en trouvent en fin trompées, et entrent en cette amytié de par Dieu, dont bien souvent elles saillent par le Diable. Car j'en ai assez veu, qui sous couleur de parler de Dieu, commençoient une amytié dont à la fin vouloient se retirer, et ne pouvoient, pour ce que l'honnette couverture les tenoit en sujétion. Car une amour vicieuse de soymesme se défait, et ne peut durer en un bon cueur. Mais la vertueuse est celle qui a les lyens de soy si deliez, que l'on en est plus tot pris qu'on ne le peut voir. [XXXV, 224]

Although Parlamente continues to exalt "virtuous" love at the end, she expresses a profound disillusion with the perversion of it everywhere about her. She postulates utopic conditions, but shows that man falsifies them and brings them down to his own needs. She may protest; but in fact, she begins to lose faith in perfect love, if she has not lost it already. In the two preceding theoretical presentations she had allowed two other narrators to advance counter-arguments; here Parlamente herself voices doubt and a certain helplessness before the weakness of man.

Finally there appears an ethereal definition of perfect love completely divorced from daily life. Interestingly enough, Oysille expounds it. She is, it should be remembered, from a religious viewpoint the most fundamentalist of the narrators; if she is the most respected in the group, it is just as much for her age (she is the oldest) as for her strong and blind faith. There definitely exist generational differences between her and the rest of the audience. She maintains that just as those who seek perfect knowledge forget about eating and drinking so do those who love perfectly forget about the desires of the flesh because "quand le cors est sujet à l'esprit, il est quasi insensible aus imperfections de la chair" (LXIII, 325).[4] As for such behavior in the story, Hircan had termed it "miraculous," and Géburon chides her that she is setting forth saintly examples.

Parlamente tacitly agrees with the gentlemen and will show her agreement by telling the next tale, the sixty-fourth. Although this novella purports to demonstrate that one should take advantage of the present because the future may change matters to the worse, it really constitutes a criticism of perfect love depicted as a "mortification de son extrème passion" (328). The female protagonist refuses to marry because "ou cuydant trouver mieux ou voulant dissimuler l'amour qu'elle luy avoit portée, en feit quelque difficulté" (326). The net result is that after having subjected himself to many rebuttals and having patiently proved his love for her, the gentleman flees to a monastery in desperation. When she comes to him in the monastery, it is too late: "Vous voyez, mes Dames, quelle vengeance preind le gentilhomme de sa rude amye, qui en le pensant expérimenter, le desespéra de sorte que quand elle voulut, elle ne le peut recouvrer" (329).

A sensible deterioration or downward movement of the concept of perfect love develops, then, in the course of the *Heptameron*. At first, the two theoretical definitions by Da-

4. ". . . ceus qui ont mis leur cueur et affection à cercher la perfection des sciences, non seulement ont oublyée la volupté de la chair, mais les choses nécessaires, comme le boire et le manger. Car tant que l'ame est par affection dedans son cors, la chair demeure comme insensible. Et de là vient que ceus qui ayment femmes belles, honnettes et vertueuse, ont tel contentement d'esprit à les voir, ou à les oÿr parler, que la chair est appaisée de tous ses desirs" (325).

goucin and Parlamente are presented as valid ideal concepts, although others downgrade them and even strongly contradict them. Later, in the thirty-fifth novella (i.e., about halfway through the work), there occurs a partial shift in Parlamente's attitude toward perfect love—a very significant point because she is considered Marguerite's mouthpiece; she pictures this love as being falsified and perverted about her and indicates thereby a pronounced disenchantment with it. The belittling process takes one more step forward when Oysille gives a definition of perfect that borders on self-flagellation and maceration. And when Parlamente to illustrate this point narrates a tale that depicts the acute martyrdom of a man before his lady, she takes the final step into an anti-perfect-love position. Not only do some narrators assert the divorce between reality and fiction about the validity and practicality of ideal love, but Marguerite / Parlamente herself takes pains to demonstrate the infeasibility of such a concept even on a fictitious level.

Virtue, like virtuous love, is rare. To stress this rarity metaphorically, Marguerite uses the symbol of the Roman Lucretia raped by Tarquin; in fact, such mention occurs only twice. On the first occasion it appears in relation to a maiden of a lower social level, Françoise, who repeatedly refuses the prince's advances: "Car ceux qui ont tant loué leur Lucrèce, l'eussent laissée au bout de la plume pour écrire bien au long les vertuz de cette cy" (XLII, 252). The majority of the audience doubt Françoise's absolute virtue and claim that only a fear for her reputation restrains her. The second time she is mentioned, this paragon of virtue takes on a much more absolute meaning:

Dea, dit Géburon, quel péché avoit-elle fait? Elle étoit endormye en son lyt, et il la menaçoit de mor et de honte. Lucréce tant louée en feit bien autant. Il est vray, dit Parlamante, je confesse qu'il n'y a si juste, à qui il ne puisse méchoir; mais quand l'on a pris grand plaisir à l'œuvre, l'on en prend aussi en la mémoire, pour laquelle effacer Lucréce se tua, et cette sote en voulut faire rire les autres. [LXII, 322]

On either side of this metaphoric paragon of virtue, the language of love belongs either to the Petrarchan tradition or falls into the physical and erotic domain. Following typical Petrarchan lines, this language personifies and mythologizes love, depicts it as a malady and a war, adopts the life-death interplay, makes an abundant use of fire imagery, in addition to common hyperboles drawing on the metaphoric senses of the heart and tears. *Petrarchan* is a useful term here because it sums up a whole composite tradition of love while implying at the same time conceptual and stylistic abuses that followed it. Furthermore, this term in its pristine meaning stands for a tension within the writer between the material and the spiritual; the same tension besets Marguerite. Ultimately this dichotomy results from an existential position, a helplessness before the insignificance and weakness of man in the universe, a malaise which holds for both Petrarch and Marguerite, even if this critical attitude has not been yet taken toward the latter.[5] Stylistically the internal tension manifests itself through the usage of key words that take on now a positive meaning, now a negative or anomalous one, and thereby attain a metaphorical level. Thus an inner thematology can emerge from a given frequency of multi-meaning words.

Written with a capital initial, the personification and deification of love appears many times. Because of its frequent occurrences in the literature of the age, the personification does not offer any particular significance. It inserts itself in a Petrarchan tradition, continues the medieval allegorical lit-

5. For Petrarch, see for example the introduction to a recent French translation of the *Canzoniere* by Gérard Genot, *Le Chansonnier* (Paris, 1969), pp. 15–40.

erature culminating with the *Roman de la Rose*, and reflects the strong position of emblematic literature in the sixteenth century. A cataloguing of the numerous mentions of *Amour* in the *Heptameron* would serve no real purpose. It is obvious, however, that through a characteristic frequency of mention, Marguerite wants to emphasize the overwhelming dominance of love, here in its physical sense—Cupid—over man, and his helplessness and weakness before it; the connotation remains quite negative and the eulogy, if it occurs, ironic:

> L'histoire . . . est pour vous faire voir comment Amour aveuglit les plus grans et honnettes cueurs. [XII, 82] . . . ce petit dieu qui prend plaisir à tormenter autant les Princes que les pauvres, et les fortz que les foibles. [XIII, 86] Mais il n'y a si grand Prince en ce monde, combien qu'il eut tous les grands honneurs et richesses que l'on sçauroit désirer, qui ne soit sujet à l'empire et tyrannie d'Amour, et semble que plus le Prince est noble et de grand cueur, et plus amour fait son effor de l'asservir souz sa forte main. Car ce glorieus dieu ne tient conte des choses communes et fidéles et ne prend plaisir sa majesté que de faire tous les jours miracles d'aucuns, comme d'affoiblir les fortz, fortifier les foibles, donner intelligence aus ignorans, oter le sens aus sçavans, favoriser aus passions, détourner la raison; et en telles mutations prend plaisir l'amoureuse divinité. [XXV, 176][6]

Of course, the technique of the personification / deification of love becomes more meaningful when Marguerite trans-

6. One reason for choosing this particular quote is that Le Hir, the editor of the edition we cite, gives its source as St. John 11:25 ("Jesus said unto her, I am the resurrection and the life: he that believeth in me, though he were dead, yet shall he live"). Although such a reminiscence can exist and insert itself in Marguerite's evangelism, it can probably be argued more convincingly that such expressions had become long before an integral part of the poets' language.

forms it creatively to her own needs. The term then leaves the abstract allegorical domain and attains a concrete metaphorical plane that expresses one of her favorite leitmotifs: "Combien qu'Amour s'estime si fort et puissant, qu'il veut aler tout nu, et luy est chose ennuyeuse et à la fin importable d'ettre couvert, si est ce que bien souvent ceus qui pour obéir à son conseil, s'avancent trop de le découvrir, s'en trouvent mauvais marchand" (XXIII, 169). Although the point of departure remains the visual commonplace of Cupid's shameless nudity, with the interplay between *nu, couvert,* and *découvrir,* Marguerite molds this metaphorical complex in such a way that it ends up introducing the theme of the secrecy of love: in order to succeed (if it is ever to do so) perfect love needs to be kept secret from others—a near impossibility, owing to human nature. Furthermore, the whole imagery vibrates around the two-dimensional *découvrir* (uncover and discover) and culminates ironically upon the common *marchand,* which imparts to love the meaning of a vulgar commodity constantly changing hands; both will be recurring images, the former, however, more important than the latter.

Because *Amour* lends itself to ambivalent contrasting meanings, the eighteenth and the nineteenth novellas illustrate Marguerite's method of applying a different sense to either side of the same linguistic coin. Hircan narrates the eighteenth story, which deals with the extreme tests to which a lady subjects a man; she demands that he sleep with her but without making advances; and she further tries him with one of her young ladies in waiting. Rightfully one of the narrators wonders if the protagonist belongs to those "qui sont compris au titre *De frigidis et maleficiatis*" (125). Hircan tells the whole set of events with tongue in cheek so that he undercuts the whole notion of perfect love: "Mais avant qu'Amour s'essayat de vincre ce gentilhomme par la beauté de cette Dame, il avoit gangné le cueur d'elle, en voyant les perfections qui étoient en ce seigneur. Car en beauté, bon sens, bonne grace et bons propoz, n'y avoit homme de quelque état qu'il fut qui le passat" (122). Irony here is rampant and quite mordant. In Hircan's hands the personfication of love not only destroys the notion of perfection and ideal love but becomes a sheer pastiche of Petrarchism.

In order not to unmask herself totally, Marguerite in the very next novella gives to *Amour* its most elevated sense, the love of God: "Car si vous avez du bien, j'en aurai ma par, et si vous recevez du mal, je n'en veuil ettre exente, et par tel chemin que vous irez en Paradis, je vous veuil suyvre, étant asseurée que celuy qui est le vray, perfet, et digne d'ettre nommé Amour, nous a tirez à son service, par une amytié honnette et raisonnable . . ." (XIX, 132). To counteract a derision of deified love in the eighteenth tale, Marguerite offers in appearance the very opposite, because in the nineteenth, perfect love in the name of God will fail and frustrate both protagonists, as we have already seen. Thus the brittleness of human relationships is shown through conscious ambivalence in the personification / deification of love. Assimilation and transformation of this literary *topos* have thus taken place.

In the literary language of love, intentional confusion and inversion of the meaning of life and death occur to depict the torments and ecstasies of the protagonists. Such linguistic hyperboles and distortions are commonplace in the *Heptameron*, and had already in the sixteenth century entered the realm of clichés. Thus when a lover refers to "celle qui étoit sa vie et sa résurrection" (IX, 51) or to the one "entre les mains de laquelle je metz ma mort et ma vie" (XXIV, 170), absolutely no originality can be claimed for such usage, even if a conceptual complexity is introduced in a more typical Petrarchan vein: "racontez une histoire de quelqu'un qui soit suscité de mor à vie pour connaitre en sa Dame le contraire de ce qu'il désiroit" (XX, 135).

Once again it takes a metaphorical stamp to give new facets to trite expressions. Through the narrator Saffredan, Marguerite slily undermines men who satisfy their desires only with appearances: "Et l'on dit qu'il n'y a rien que les femmes hayent plus que de toucher les mortz" (LVII, 302); in other words, women do not like to deal with effete men. In the course of the same discussion, Symontaut takes the metaphor a step further when he tells of a woman who was found at four in the morning "baisant le cors mort d'un gentilhomme" with whom she had sinned, in order to do penitence for the past (303). If morbidity may here appear predominant, one discerns as well a willful *rifacimento* of traditional images or expressions. She gives this task here to Symontaut, Saffredan, and Hircan, whose very wry and caustic smile pierces the thin veil of appearances and delineates traces of anti-Petrarchism.

A marked hyperbole weighs upon the usage of the traditional wound image symbolizing the suffering caused by love; such a distortion would further indicate a derisory attitude toward accepted means of poetic expression. A man undergoes a phlebotomy to be cured of what is believed to be "une opilation [occlusion] de foye" (L, 276), in reality unrequited love. Finally when his lady grants him a meeting, the beneficial effects of her promise are taken to be those of the bloodletting, so that when the long awaited moment arrives, "ayant pour s'amye mis en oubly soy mesme, ne s'apperceut de son bras qui se débanda, et la playe nouvelle qui se veint à ouvrir rendit tant de sang, que le pauvre gentilhomme en étoit tout baigné. . . . Et pour la grande effusion de sang, tomba tout mort aus piez de s'amye" (277). The wound, image of fatal love, is not an act of Cupid, but man-made by a doctor; the lover does not appear as a hero but as a wretched victim. The blood bath implies a scornful view toward both the cold lady and the blind nobleman. The blood here stands for a foolish blindness of love with no regard to a minimal reason. Quite an abyss separates the slight wounds of Cupid's arrows from this sanguinary surgery. Again morbidity occupies a very secondary role; in the foreground looms a criticism of the excesses brought about by unrequited love, and the transformed image of the wound and blood constitutes the artistic core of the novella formulated to transmit this message.

In the realm of the language that depicts suffering and torment, love assumes the role of a sickness; an exterior physiological anomaly reflects or conceals an interior spiritual stress. Before reaching Petrarch, this metaphorical representation of love had its roots in an Ovidian tradition and in "fin amors."[7] In Marguerite's hands the concept of love sickness becomes the center radiating toward other themes. It is linked, for example, to the life-death interplay: "une maladie, donnant tel contentement, que la guérison étoit la mor" (XXIV, 171). Or it brings forth the notion of dissimulation and feint, so prevalent in the novellas, as will be seen: "souvent il tomboit malade" (XIII, 89); "Mais le plus fort étoit que le médecin de ses douleurs étoit ignorant de son mal ... et comme ignorant sa maladie, luy demanda la cause de son mal. Elle luy répondit que c'étoit un catarre" (XXXV, 220, 222).

Ultimately love is also equated with a malady, a spiritual disorder, causing a depressed state completely beyond human cure or reason; here fever acts as the central metaphoric core related to the black humor, melancholy: "preind une fiévre continue causée d'un humeur melencolique, et tellement couverte, que les extrémitez du cors luy veindrent toutes froides, et dedans incessamment bruloit. Les Médecins en la main desquelz ne pend pas la santé des hommes, com-

---

7. Some of the better studies on this topic still remain Denis de Rougemont, *Love in the Western World*, trans. M. Belgion (New York, 1956); M. Valency, *In Praise of Love, An Introduction to the Love-Poetry of the Renaissance* (New York, 1958); and C. S. Lewis, *The Allegory of Love, A Study in Medieval Tradition* (New York, 1958).

mencérent à douter si for de sa maladie, à cause d'une opilation qui la rendoit extrémement mélencolique" (XXVI, 188).
Because it conveys a malaise, the adaptation of the love dis-
ease into a love malady image remains the closest to the
queen's temperament. Even if this particular imagery does
not contain any striking originality in its multiple meanings,
it serves a useful purpose in further exposing some basic
themes. Above all, the frequency of *maladie* makes the reader extremely aware of the acute scarcity of the word *santé*,
an important factor in discerning the mood of Marguerite's
thought. And when the word *remède* occurs, it may have an
initial reassuring impact, but in the course of the novella
proves to be self-defeating.

In the Petrarchist tradition, the image of war expresses
above all the inner turmoil between body and spirit. In a
totally different writer like Montaigne the image of war
will assume metaphysical proportions and depict his assertion over himself and his universe in order to attain his fullest
dignity. In contrast, Marguerite brings the metaphor down
to a very earthy level; to her war means the conquest of
woman by man and the incessant confrontations between
the two in order to effectuate this conquest. Of course some
Petrarchan usages do occur, but they are not predominant.[8]
Usually war is carried out to seek victory and enjoy the spoils
of conquest: "Car il n'y avoit gentilhomme en la cour qui
menat plus la guerre aus Dames que cetuy là" (LVII, 305);
"avoir part au butin" (VIII, 45); "Car oncque place ne fut
bien assaillie qu'elle ne fut prise" (IX, 54); "esperoit avoir la
victoire de celle qu'il avoit estimée invincible" (XII, 84);
"cercer tous moyens pour en avoir la victoire" (XVIII, 126).
Therefore this image in its essential role reflects the bestiality
of man and his incessant carnal desires.

Furthermore the metaphor of war points to a no-exit no-

8. To cite an example, "ne pouvant porter la guerre que l'honneur et
l'amour faisoient en son cueur" (XXVI, 188).

tion in the sense that it is used as a means of escape from an untenable situation, only to fall into another: "Car il n'y a rien qui face plus saillir l'homme hors de sa maison, que d'ettre maryé, pour ce que la guerre de dehors n'est pas plus importable que celle de dedans" (LXX, 355). Even when the hero is not buffeted from one hell to another, war continues to appear as an escape, here from sinful guilt, paradoxically enough: "car il ne désiroit autre chose qu'après la jouyssance de s'amye s'en aler à la guerre" (XXX, 200). Eventually war offers an outlet for the death wish born out of the frustrations of love (see the tenth and thirteenth novellas, for example); although the hero would like to see this act as an apotheosis, Marguerite makes it appear to be an undertaking that always brings either repentance or absurdity. The prowess of war, accompanied by foolish heroism and even treachery and hypocrisy, offers a weak substitute for success in love. No longer does the nobleman go to battle to prove his courage and valor to his lady so that she will accept him as her lover and master. Instead, he flees to war out of disdain and scorn toward her; thence the war assumes the same role as the monastery in some novellas. This reversed situation certainly knocks some of the glory out of the concept of war. However, as in most collections of tales, war is as much or more a narrative accessory as it is a moral or political concept.

The image of war meaning the confrontation between man and woman, though it appears throughout the *Heptameron*, is most salient and is sustained at greatest length in the tenth novella. In fact, Marguerite in this tale and others uses the verb *guerroyer* to denote the verbal and psychological combat between the two protagonists. Stripped to its essential nature, the tenth tale amounts to a series of confrontations between Floride and Amadour; the technique takes on all the more importance because this novella is the longest of all (about twenty-five pages in the edition we use), the one that Marguerite took the most care to develop fully and not for sheer prolixity. She wants to focus on love as a testing ground, and the results are never encouraging. Having discounted marriage because it can never take place, Amadour tries spiritual love, but eventually seeks to possess only Floride's body; at first she contains him to test the genuineness of his intentions, and then, of course, she needs to protect herself from savage advances. In this offensive and defensive climate, a military vocabulary imposes itself and transforms lady and love into mere matter, an object to be captured at all costs: "Mais, ma dame, tout ainsy que la nécessité en une forte guerre contrainct faire degast du propre bien, et ruyner le blé en herbe, à fin de paour que l'ennemy n'en puisse faire son profit, ainsi pren-je le hazard d'avancer le fruyt qu'avecq le temps j'espéroie cueillir, à fin garder que les ennemys de vous et de moy n'en peussent faire leur profit de vostre dommaige (61)."

Since Marguerite had informed the reader from the very outset that Amadour's chief trait is "hardiesse," it ensues naturally that this characteristic should manifest itself both on the battlefield and in his mind when he is before a woman. To undermine the hero she juxtaposes the battlefield of sentiments, the boudoir ("Toutesfoys, il guangna la bataille, tant qu'elle luy promeit . . ." [64]) and the literal one to which Amadour dashes off to reassert himself after sentimental defeats: "Or, advint que le Roy de Thunis, qui de long temps faisoit la guerre aux Espaignols, entendit comme les Roys de France et d'Espaigne faisoient la guerre guerroyable sur les frontieres de Parpignan et Narbonne" (65). As a result the two are reduced to a single and futile common denominator. The stress falls on aggressiveness and victory by any means.[9] To defend herself, Floride counters with a weapon that in

9. "Au bout de deus ou troys ans apres avoir fait tant de belles choses, que tout le papier d'Espagne ne sçauroit contenir, imagina une invention tresgrande, non pour gangner le cueur de Floride, car il le tenoit tout perdu, mais pour avoir la victoire de son ennemye, puis que telle se faisoit contre luy" (73).

the end has become rather meaningless, her virtue; in fact even in one of the last stories, Marguerite makes use of this very image: "Votre accusateur . . . ne porte autres armes que sa chasteté" (LXX, 344). Because Floride to a great extent misuses her virtue and miscalculates her actions, she brings upon herself her own misfortune.

As a consequence, each frontal encounter reflects in turn a conflict within each protagonist which surfaces explicitly. Floride is torn between her honor, her virtue, and her love for Amadour until he reveals strictly carnal desires toward her; but on the other hand her ambivalence is largely responsible for his change in behavior; her flight to the monastery at the end is a sign of defeat for herself and her code of behavior. As for Amadour, he alternates between his confrontations with Floride, constantly frustrated, and his flight to battles where his valor and dignity remain intact. If after many trying years he finally abandons, out of sheer despair, the battle for ideal love, only Floride's repeated refusals bear this responsibility. Or were Amadour's attempts at ideal love mere sham? The one certainty about him centers on his belligerent but self-defeating "hardiesse."

In theory the image of war conveys a sense of conquest and victory in the realm of love; in practice it leads to setbacks or checkmate situations. When success there is, it occurs to bring love down to a materialistic level. Therefore this metaphor contains intrinsically a negative meaning. Even if such a usage could insert itself in a Humanistic antiwar context, a bit farfetched in this case, it indicates above all a failure of love on all levels because the word *guerre* with all its linguistic dependents is stripped of any attribute whatsoever.

Like war, fire has always been a word in the language of love. Although on many occasions associated with passion, fire actually has a dual and contrasting role. On the positive side, it provides heat and sustenance, it purifies; on the negative side, it destroys.[10] This dichotomy appears throughout the *Heptameron*, since it lends itself perfectly to Marguerite's ambivalence in order to achieve the complete truth. Of course, in the process of this search, the usual composition of the dichotomy can be reversed; out of destruction, for example, can come revelation. Furthermore, the image of fire refers to an interhuman level as well as to a divine one.

Fire as a metaphor of love is scattered widely through the novellas—as a matter of fact, in at least half of them. The frequency of *feu*, *flamme*, and *brûler* can easily have contributed to labeling Marguerite preclassical or pre-Racinian.[11] However, such attributes, even if they may help to define her, often do so at the expense of completing our understanding of the image itself and its various usages. In the positive sense, fire is an image of perfect or ideal love: "La royne qui étoit femme de grand' vertu, mais non du tout exente de la flamme qui moins est connue et plus brule" (XXIV, 169); "impossible étoit que le fœu si longuement continué en leurs cueurs ne se ralumat plus fort que devant" (LXIV, 328). The first quotation leaves some doubt, once again, as to the true nature of perfect love, because of the inherent contrast between "grand' vertu" and "flamme." But the tradition of the code of courtly love could be invoked here to remove any discrepancy; "fin amors" does not forego possession of the body.

Transferred to the realm of chivalry, the image of fire illustrates further the devotion of servant toward master, in this instance the governor of a province toward his king: "brulant de l'amour de son maitre" (XVII, 119–20). Ulti-

10. At this time it would probably seem appropriate to cite Gaston Bachelard (*La Psychanalyse du feu* [Paris, 1938], and *L'Eau et les rêves* [Paris, 1947]) who has contributed sensibly to the study of primordial elements in literature, but what we state needs no theoretical support, just as what Bachelard proclaims is often self-evident.

11. See P. Jourda, "L'*Heptaméron*: Livre préclassique," *Studi in onore di Carlo Pellegrini* (Turin, 1963), pp. 133–36.

mately, the love and the Word of God assume definite beneficial effects, following a biblical or evangelical tradition: "[avoir] en son cueur le fœu qui brule toute crainte" (XVI, 119); after hearing a reading of Saint John's Epistles, the narrators, "tout enflammez de ce fœu s'en alèrent oÿr la grand' messe" (LXXI, 357). Or what has come to be regarded as a typical Petrarchan *concetto* is used by Saffredan, a sardonic narrator who deliberately perverts the biblical language: "alumer le fœu de charité en vos cueurs de glace" (XXXVI, 228); this casuistic game implies and sharply criticizes the interpretative distortions that the Gospel undergoes in the hands of dishonest preachers on both sides of Christianity.

When in a negative context, the image of fire as love brings forth a concept of hell; fire tortures and consumes the body. Significantly enough, this particular meaning of the metaphor occurs much oftener than the positive one. Of course, it depicts carnal desires and shows their intensity, and in this context cannot claim any originality; yet its extreme frequence adds much weight to the predominance of this concept of love. To explain away such a view by asserting that it intends to impose a high moral purpose and elevate the reader's spirit, although true to some extent, appears much too facile. In addition to torture and consumption, fire takes on a very impure consistency or a dissimulating capacity to express the low nature of this love:

Ce méchant fœu qu'il avoit en son cueur ne cessa de le bruler jour et nuyt. [XXII, 157] ... Car le fœu le bruloit si for qu'il ne sçavoit de quel coté se tourner. [LXVIII, 337] ... brulant d'un fœu non clair comme celui de ginevre, mais comme d'un gras charbon de forge. [XXVII, 193] ... Ainsi ce fœu souz titre de spirituel fut si charnel que le cueur qui en fut embrasé brula tout le cors de cette pauvre Dame. Et ainsi qu'elle avoit été tardive à sentir cette flamme, ainsi elle fut pronte à enflammer et sentit plus tot le contentement de sa passion. [XXXV, 220]

In another instance, the same Petrarchan *concetto* accentuates a transfixing intensity: "ses contenances qui étoient assez ardentes pour faire bruler une glace" (LXX, 341).

The metaphor of fire is highly developed in the twenty-sixth novella and therefore attracts special attention; it occurs about ten times in the last three pages. Here a figurative fire is opposed to a literal one that immediately assumes another dimension. Fire supposedly represents perfect love, but since a sardonic Saffredan narrates the tale, an ironic overcast permeates it. Monsieur d'Avannes obtains through a subterfuge a "maternal" kiss from his lady, which produces "le fœu que la parole avoit commencé d'alumer au cueur" (187). In order to move in with his "adopted parents," he sets fire to his own house. Then "le mary, ayant donné ordre au fœu" of d'Avannes's house, invites him to remain with them. In such circumstances, the language instantaneously leaves the literal plane and alternates between the ironic and the figurative. In d'Avannes's love declaration, fire assumes a purifying role; but in view of his hypocritical aims, the apparent exalting connotation of the metaphor falls flat: "croyez, qu'ainsy que l'aur s'épreuve à la fornaize, ainsi un cueur chaste au mylieu des tentations se treuve le plus fort et vertueus, et se refroidit tant plus il est assailly de son contraire" (187). Only when on the threshold of death does the lady admit that she loved him all along. And then he embraces the dead body that had been denied him during life, with so fierce an impetuosity that the husband in an admirable understatement declares: "Monsieur, c'est trop" (190). At this point, the corruption of fire, latent before, becomes flagrant.

In keeping with Marguerite's fundamental trait of wanting to expose both sides of the medallion, fire appears both as a genuine purifying agent, and as a revealer of truth. A wife, upon finding her husband in bed with the maid, sets a fire under the bed, and as the smoke is about to suffocate him, she wakes him up shouting; "Au fœu, au fœu!" (XXXVII, 230). At one point in the comments following the novella, two of the lady narrators give a perfect metaphoric résumé that elucidates the meaning of fire and its derivatives: "Et trouvez vous grand patience à elle, dit Nomerfide, d'aller mettre le fœu souz le lyt où son mary dormoit? Ouy, dit Longarine. Car quand elle vid de la fumée elle l'éveilla, et par avanture ce fut où feit plus de faute. Car de telz marys que ceus la, les cendres seroient bonnes à faire la buée" (231). On a metaphoric level, setting fire and waking up become equivalent to bringing the husband back to reason, while the smoke takes on its traditional warning connotation. In addition, the purifying element is reinforced by the notion of washing and cleaning with soap, a fire-derivative at the time. Finally in this story, fire ends up having a conciliatory or mending role because husband and wife are reunited and live happily thereafter, it is hoped.

The combination fire-smoke-ashes further denotes traits of human character. To indicate that good or evil will somehow show through a person, Marguerite renovates the fire-smoke image: "Je n'ai guéres veu grand fœu, duquel ne veint quelque fumée; mais j'ai bien veu de la fumée où il n'y avoit point de fœu" (VII, 45). The fire-ashes metaphor occurs to discuss the jealousy which perverts love just as ashes kill a fire: "Et qui dit que le soupçon est amour, je luy nye. Car combien qu'il en sort (comme la cendre du fœu) aussi le tue il" (XLVII, 268–69). Upon reading such a statement, Proust's *Un Amour de Swann* comes to mind; although Swann blinded himself to the truth, Odette would readily agree with, but certainly not admit, the validity of the above metaphor, since she purposely created situations to engender jealousy. And what did not necessarily happen, Swann imagined.

Not only does the image of the candle relate directly to fire but it offers a springboard for a further development in handling a metaphoric language and gives a first glimpse into structural patterns of the novellas. Thematically the image of the candle brings again to the fore a negative attitude toward perfect love, best illustrated in the sixty-fifth novella. In the following quotation, one sees a fusion of the language of love and religion with a sprinkle of the chivalrous (the italics are ours); a backstage smile resulting from the heroine's foolishness humanizes the altar of love with its fixed and insensitive liturgical paraphernalia:

> Un *soldat* se promenant en *l'église au tems d'été*, qu'il fait grand chaut, luy preind envye de dormir, et regardant cette chapelle obscure et fresche, pensa d'*aler dormir au sépulcre* comme les autres. . . . Or aveint une *bonne vieille for dévote* y arriva au plus fort de son sommeil . . . tenant une *chandelle ardente* en sa main la voulut attacher au sépulcre . . . mais la *cyre* ne peut tenir contre la *chair de l'image*, luy va *mettre le fœu contre le front* . . . pour y faire tenir sa bougie, mais *l'image qui n'étoit insensible* commença à s'écrier . . . *regarder d'ores en avant à quel saint vous baillerez vos chandelles.* [330]

In case there is any doubt about the metaphoric value of this language and its meaning, Marguerite has the narrators fix it and clarify it: "Est-ce mal fait, dit Nomerfide, de porter des chandelles aus sépulcres? Ouy, dit Hircan, quand on met le fœu au front des hommes" (330–31). In other words, is it wrong to worship love instead of loving a man? Yes, answers Hircan, if man and his dignity are hurt and abused, because man is not to be confused with an insensitive and cold statue or a saint; he is alive and not dead. The sixty-fifth novella is a short one, the story not quite a page, the discussion only half a page. This compactness, however, does not constitute a defect; on the contrary, it lets us focus on a language that at first vacillates between the figurative and literal until its metaphoric meaning finally emerges out of the vulgarity of daily usage. Thus the discussions following the novellas acquire a double dimension. They serve as a round table for an exposition of ethical and religious values that produces fluid opinions, but on a linguistic level the discussions often stabilize new meanings of words.

On a structural level, one notes that the image of the candle has already been introduced two novellas before, in the discussion to the sixty-third. Oysille tells of a gentleman who held a burning candle for three nights without feeling any burns to prove his perfect love for a given lady; Géburon retorts that he would never have endured such useless pains unless the reward were high.[12] The sixty-fourth story then proceeds to exemplify a case of perfect love that fails because of the lady's dubious motivation, and the gentleman, tired of "holding the candle," retires bitterly to a monastery. The sixty-fifth novella, a highly metaphoric *exemplum* as we have seen, revolves entirely around the image of the candle that somewhat derides perfect love and warns against its dangers. Thus the sixty-fourth tale develops Oysille's contention but does not succeed in substantiating it; whereas the sixty-fifth one proves Géburon's point. In the final analysis,

12. "Et j'ai connu un gentilhomme qui pour montrer avoir plus fort aymée sa Dame que nul autre, en avoit fait preuve à tenir une chandelle les doigtz tout nuz l'espace de troys nuytz contre tous ses compagnons. Et regardant sa dite Dame teint si ferme, qu'il se brula jusques à l'os. . . . Il me semble, dit Géburon, que le dyable dont il étoit martir en devoit faire un saint Laurent. Car il y en a peu de qui le fœu d'amour soit si grand, qu'ilz ne craindent celuy de la moindre bougie. Et si une Dame m'avoit laissé tant endurer pour elle, j'en demanderoie grand' récompense, ou j'en retireroie ma fantaisie" (325).

what seems to be a succession of unrelated tales coalesces about the metaphor of the candle.

If Marguerite makes an abundant and varied use of the metaphor of fire, the same does not hold true for its counterpart, water. As a rule, when the image of water or its derivative, cold, does occur, it depicts a vulgar, even perverted passion—here an incestuous relation between mother and son: "Et tout ainsi que l'eau par force retenue a plus d'impétuosité quand on la laisse aler, que celle qui court ordinairement, ainsi cette pauvre Dame tourna sa gloire à la contrainte qu'elle donnoit à son cors" (XXX, 199). When an unfaithful wife waits outside in the night to rejoin her canon lover, an inner infernal fire is juxtaposed with the intense cold of the night in such a way that the "froidure" becomes the equivalent of her unfaithfulness: "Et qui ne sçauroit comme le fœu d'enfer échaufe ceus qui en sont remplis, on deveroit trouver étrange comme cette pauvre femme saillant d'un lyt chaud, peut demeurer tout un jour en si extréme froidure" (LXI, 318). On the other hand, running water as a purifying or edifying element assumes a more traditional role in depicting wifely patience: "il y a bien peu de marys, que patience et amour de la femme ne puissent gangner à la longue, ou ilz sont plus durs que pierres, que l'eau foible et mole par succession de tems vient à caver" (XXXVIII, 233). And, of course, Marguerite does not fail to adopt, though rarely, the time-worn metaphor of the thirst at the fountain to denote the lover's suffering before his lady.[13]

The paucity of water imagery may need some explanation. During the first half of the sixteenth century from Jean Lemaire de Belges to the young Ronsard, water expresses the harmony and beauty of nature and, on a human level, a real

13. "Et me semble que ce soit folie ou cruauté à celui qui garde une fonténe, de louer la beauté et bonté de son eaue à un qui languit de soif en la regardant, et puis le tuer quand il en veut prendre" (XL, 240).

or imagined happiness and joy of living and loving. During the second half of the century, in the late Ronsard, in Montaigne, or in poets such as du Bartas or d'Aubigné, water represents the flux of everything about them, the disintegration of a universe they constantly try to seize and embrace. By temperament, Marguerite would tend naturally to the same position, but since this so-called baroque usage of water imagery did not surface in her time, its rarity is understandable. And its hedonistic overtones in her day would have no place in her work. Since water does not lend itself very readily to a negative concept of love, she prefers fire, which has flexibility and a long tradition that she takes pleasure in deriding on occasion.

The downgrading attitude appears again in Marguerite's manipulation of an integral component of the language of love, the heart. She underlines its weakness through a verbal play on the very word *cœur* and some of its derivatives; while at the same time the fortress image for the heart itself comes under an ironic light: "à la fin la forteresse du cueur, où l'honneur demeure, fut mynée de telle sorte que la pauvre dame s'accorda en ce dont elle n'avoit point esté discordé" (XVIII, 122). The same undercutting result can be obtained through an overprecious language worthy of that attacked by Molière: "Ma Dame, recevez le cueur qui veut rompre mon estomach pour saillir en la main de celle dont il espère vie, grace et miséricorde" (LVII, 302). It would be sheer distortion to assert that Marguerite gives only a derogatory view of the heart; in many cases the heart remains simply the unadorned depository and concretion of sentiments, but in this role it does not draw and hold much attention except as a counterpart to the slighting viewpoint. In fact, at the very beginning of the *Heptameron,* in a sincere and eloquent moment of the second novella, the heart of a common woman plays the role of a "gendarme" against the bestial advances of a valet; the wounded woman prefers to bleed to death rather than give in.[14] This "gendarme" image contrasts directly with the fortress metaphor just mentioned. However, no conceptual contradiction or weakness in narrative composition results, only a very conscious ambivalence serving to accentuate the discrepancies and variety in human behavior.

Indeed, Marguerite asserts herself and escapes platitudes with heart imagery when she centers on differentiating what the heart feels and what the body does. A case in point is the seventieth novella, one of the last ones and also one of the better-known stories, since it is an amplified *rifacimento* of the widely diffused medieval tale, *La Chastelaine de Vergi*. Here the essential metaphoric theme alternates between having and not having a heart, with chiasmic effects due to the protagonists' deception or ignorance. On the very first introduction of the novella's evil character, we know that "La Duchesse . . . n'avoit pas cueur de femme" (340). She has set her sights on a young man who does not want to reveal to her that he loves another: "Si jamais douleur saisit le cueur de loyal serviteur, elle preind celuy de ce pauvre gentilhomme" (346). To induce her husband to find out whom the young man loves, she feigns pregnancy, in highly emotive terms saying to the alleged father that she has part of him in her heart.[15] When she learns the other woman's identity, "elle feit semblant d'ettre for contente, mais en son cueur pensoit bien tout le contraire" (349). Finally the soliloquies uttered

14. "Car tout ainsi qu'un bon gendarme voiant son sang, est plus échauffé à se venger de ses ennemys, et aquerir honneur, ainsi son chaste cueur se renforça doublement à courir, et fuyr des mains de ce malheureus, en luy tenant les meilleurs propos qu'elle pouvoit, pour cuyder par quelque moyen le réduyre à reconnoitre ses fautes" (26).

15. "Je le di, Monsieur, pour un tel gentilhomme, nommant celuy qu'elle hayssoit, lequel étant nourry de votre main, élevé et traité plus en parent et en fiz qu'en serviteur, a ausé entreprendre chose si cruelle et misérable, que de prouchasser à faire perdre l'honneur de votre femme, où git celuy de votre maison et de voz enfans" (343).

by the young nobleman and his beloved Madame du Verger before their self-inflicted death are dense with references and counter-references to each other's hearts, as embodying good or bad sentiments, real or imagined, of their minds.[16]

Thus in the seventieth novella, the heart is the symbol around which revolve various and contrasting meanings of the word, ranging from the physiological to the spiritual, from the literal to the figurative. It evokes the heartfelt: acute pathos and pity; the heartless: cruelty and egoism; the heart: possession or loss of love; hypocrisy and honesty, truth and lie. It takes all these elements to form a valid symbol; the extraction of one falsifies the whole: "Doncques, dit Hircan, s'il n'y avoit poinct de femmes, vous voudriez dire que nous serions tous marchans, comme si nous n'avions cueur que celuy qu'elles nous donnent" (355). The basic importance of this symbol to the understanding of the novella has not been noted before; only an admiring reader contemporary to Marguerite discerned it clearly. When Bandello gave his own version of the Dame du Verger tale, he had the duchess eat the nobleman's heart to punish her for her perfidy.[17]

16. "Celuy qui a . . . le cueur plus ingrat que nulle beste . . . Helas, mon cueur, je sçai bien que vous n'en pouvez plus. . . . Et à Dieu, amy, duquel le nom sans effet me créve le cueur . . ." (350, 351); "O mon cueur trop craintif de mor et de banissement . . . . Car votre cueur pur et net n'a peu porter sans mor de sçavoir le vice qui étoit en votre amy. O mon Dieu, pour quoy me créates vous homme ayant l'amour si légère et le cueur si ignorant?" (352).

17. Mentioning Bandello in relation to Marguerite de Navarre is like opening Pandora's box. Much ink has flowed on the subject, especially when source studies were so prominent at the turn and the beginning of the century. The two opposite positions are probably best illustrated by P. Toldo, *Contributo allo studio della novella francese del XV e XVI secolo* (Rome, 1895), or P. Lorenzetti, "Riflessi del pensiero italiano nell'*Heptameron* di Margherita di Navarre," *Athenaeum*, 4 (1916), 266–308, who saw Italian sources everywhere, and by P. Jourda, *M. d'Angoulême . . . étude biographique et littéraire*, II: 747–49, 757–59, who minimized them. One of the better recent studies on the subject, though a bit prolific, remains that of J. Frappier, "La Chastelaine de Vergi, Marguerite de Navarre et Bandello," *Mélanges de la Faculté des Lettres de Strasbourg*, 2(1946): 89–150. Cf. also K. H. Hartley's monograph, *Bandello and the Heptameron. A Study of Compara-*

Tears are a final element of what we have been calling a Petrarchan language of love. Although crying occurs in plausible and sincere circumstances in the *Heptameron,* an ironic tone created by the narrator of a tale or known only to the omniscient reader can easily deride such acts and therefore assume an antitraditional role. A hyperbole achieves a similar aim in a more explicit way. An enormous outflow of tears can reflect a highly emotive intensity, but when a hyperbole goes beyond all reason, a smile on the author's part becomes at least perceptible: "luy disant à Dieu avec une telle sueur, que non ses yeus seulement, mais tout le cors jetoit larmes" (XIII, 90). Furthermore, in given situations tears are abused and become synonymous with hypocrisy. Again the seventieth novella offers an excellent example of this technique, using an identical vocabulary. The duchess's false tears in trying to persuade her husband to achieve her treachery contrast with the nobleman's genuine tears over the Dame du Verger's dead body: "embrassa et baisa son mary arrosant tout son visage de ses larmes avec telz crys et soupirs" (349); "embrassant le cors de s'amye, l'arrosa longuement de ses larmes" (352). Even on the nobleman's part, the genuine intensity of emotion may reach an hyperbolic level that casts a shadow on Marguerite's sincerity: "Puisqu'avec mes larmes, j'ai lavé votre visage" (353). Is she smiling at the medieval model?

Thus Marguerite renovates the metaphoric commonplaces of the language of love by either imparting to them a different meaning or an opposite one from the usual acceptation. This rejuvenation of worn-out words in turn reveals an anti-perfect-love pose, often struck, or accentuates contradictions that deride literary traditions. At the same time, words that acquire new dimensions in meaning flirt with their own disintegration; these linguistic traits in fact cor-

tive Literature (Melbourne, 1960), and A. Lomazzi, "Recenti interpretazioni della 'Châtelaine de Vergi,'" *Studi di Letteratura Francese,* 2 (1969), 268–73.

respond formally to a view of an unfathomable diversity in human motivations, with a resulting parallel of a gloomy human condition.

In formulating an erotic language, Marguerite adheres a great deal to the process of juxtaposing the edifying or spiritual connotation of a word and a vulgar one. She likes to strip a word of its dignity, so to speak, in order to make evident the discrepancy between man or society as it should be and as it actually is. In forging an erotic vocabulary, Marguerite also creates a strictly new metaphoric language that has no model in the lofty love literature of the age. And the third category of this sexual vocabulary gravitates about the realm of animals in order to underline the bestiality of man.

Food, a concept often touched on in the *Heptameron*, lends itself naturally to service as an emblem of the sexual needs of the body; moreover, it evidences a willful ambivalence by suggesting the opposite: spiritual needs. To denote this concept of food, Marguerite uses both *viandes* and *nourriture*. Not until after the middle of the projected *Heptameron* does *viandes* appear in a spiritual context contrasted with its literal meaning; at the end of the fifth day, the narrators, "Veppres oÿes, s'en alèrent souper autant de paroles que de viandes" (278); then in the prologue to the sixth day, after hearing readings from Saint John by Oysille, "La compagnie trouva cette viande si douce . . ." (280).

However, most of the occurrences of this word show an erotic meaning, or sometimes appear in a negative context. The male protagonist in the eighth novella has a penchant for "la diversité des viandes" (45). In another, the narrators refer to the higher sexuality of common people as opposed to noblemen, who are simply "gens bien nourrys" (XXIX, 196), whereas for the former, "leurs viandes ne sont si friandes, mais ilz ont meilleur appétit . . . et se nourrissent mieus de leurs pains que nous de restaurans" (197). When a man boasts vaguely of his conquests, he is asked: "De quelles viandes étiez vous nourry en la prison [of love], dont vous vous louez si for?" (XLIX, 273).[18] A rather degenerate female character, Yambique, who does not have high regard for her suitor, incorporates the word into a dynamic but somewhat gross expression: "Mais si vous oyez parler d'aler à la viande, vous pourrez bien pour le jour vous retirer" (XLII, 255). Among several other cases, and without going into specific details, a brief mention ought to be made of the rather short twenty-eighth tale, whose eroticism along the same linguistic lines is highly metaphoric.[19] Finally, in minor key, *viandes* takes on the meaning of a bitter lesson or tragic experiences in love; when the seigneur de Josselin tries to make up with his sister, "elle luy manda qu'il luy avoit donné un si mauvais diner, qu'elle ne vouloit point souper de telles viandes et qu'elle espéroit vivre en sorte, qu'il ne seroit point homicide du second mary" (XL, 237–38).[20]

The metaphoric transpositions of *nourriture* and its derivatives follow the same three lines as those of *viandes*: spiritual, erotic, and adverse sentiments. In the introduction to the fifth day, Oysille again has the task of preparing "un déjeuner spirituel . . . pour fortifier le cors et l'esprit" (242);

18. This forty-ninth novella develops on numerous occasions the erotic concept of the food metaphor, and right from the outset: "[il] leur feroit un conte d'une grand' Dame si infame . . . qui avoit assez à manger [mais] cerchoit sa friandise trop méchamment" (271).

19. The twenty-eighth novella belongs to the tradition of salacious fabliaux. A merchant from Bayonne arrives in town with one of the famous hams from that region. Immediately a double-entendre begins to pervade the tale as he seeks out young women: "La Damoyselle qui le creut, assembla deus ou troys des plus honnettes des ses voysines et les asseura de leur donner une viande nouvelle [ham] et dont jamais elles n'avoient taté . . ." (194); "Laissons là ces viandes fades et tatons de cet éguillon de vin" (195); ". . . s'en ala porter son present à la Damoyselle, qui avoit grande envye de sçavoir si les vivres de Guyenne étoient aussi bons que ceus de Paris" (195).

20. Cf. "Car vous avez veu assez de malades dégoutez, délaisser les bonnes et salutaires viandes pour manger les mauvaises et dommageables. Ainsi peut ettre que cette fille aymoit quelc'un aussi gentilhomme qu'elle, qui lui faisoit dépriser toute noblesse" (XLII, 252).

in a later instance a saintly wife "porta pour sa sauve garde, nourriture et consolation, un Nouveau Testament lequel elle lisoit . . ." (LXVII, 334). The conceptual antithesis but the thematic conjunction of spiritual food is the devotional fast: "[elle] jeusnoit non seullement les jeunes commandez de l'Eglise, mais plusieurs fois à sa dévotion" (XXXIII, 213); here, this particular devotional act loses any significance, since the heroine will soon have an incestuous relationship, resulting in pregnancy, with her brother priest. Of course, there are numerous occurrences of love taking away any will or need to eat or drink, but such a commonplace does not warrant any specific attention in this context.

Although the image of food and eating continues to have per se an explicit erotic meaning (in regard to a lecherous monk: "Il n'étoit pas friand, dit Saffredan, mais il étoit gourmand" [XXXI, 208]), at times it is only the vehicle for such a depiction. In other words, the exterior reflects the interior; an individual who has just reached physical maturity with the usual accompanying first sexual desires will appear as a well-fed person: "nature, qui est un maitre d'école bien secret, le trouvant trop nourry et plein d'oysiveté, luy appreind bien autre leçon que son Docteur ne faisoit" (XXX, 198).[21] From physical well-being, nourishment assumes the role of material security, with definite erotic undertones; a young monk is most delighted to transvest himself into becoming a husband because in addition to all the comforts of a house, he will also have "nourriture assurée" (LVI, 297).

21. In a typical medieval anticlerical manner, the lusty monk is seen fat, whereas the thin one, who should represent the one oriented toward a true spiritual life, only appears falsely so: "Et combien que sa règle portat de jamais ne manger chair, il s'en dispensa luy mesme, ce qu'il ne faisoit à nul autre, disant que sur luy étoit tout le fes de la Religion. Parquoy si bien se festoya, que d'un moyne for maigre, il en feit un bien gras" (154–55). Furthermore, hunger is equated with survival and the need for love: ". . . chose dont elle étoit affamée" (XV, 105); "Une femme fine sçaura vivre, où toutes les autres mourront de faim" (LIII, 291).

Even when not metaphorically erotic, the physiological notion of food still does not have an elevated meaning; it expresses bitterness and frustration in love: "Je suis tant nourry au torment, dit il [Saffredan] que je commence à me louer des maus dont les autres se plaindent" (L, 278).[22] Furthermore, the concept of eating occurs in a parasitic vein: "Si le gentilhomme n'eut voulu manger aus dépens d'autry, il n'eut bu aus siens un si vilain breuvage" (LII, 285). The need to feed one's body is in no way contested here, but excesses are, especially those at the expense of others; Marguerite tries to draw the thin line that separates egotism from love. As a matter of fact, the central image of this fifty-second novella is that of bread, the mainstay of food, but a corrupted bread, sugar-coated feces called *pain de sucre* with which the protagonist wants to fool others and buy his food.

The image of bread ranging from a perverted love of God to lust and obscenity remains essentially based on the idea of falsification. In the first category, a priest abuses the dogma of transubstantiation: "Et dit, quand on luy meit au devant qu'il avoit été si méchant de prendre le cors de notre Seigneur pour la faire jurer desus, qu'il n'étoit pas si hardy, et qu'il avoit pris un pain non sacré, ny bénit" (XXXIII, 214). Against this falsification is contrasted a model, an absolute, one God and one love, the true good bread; of course, the image has biblical origins, and whether or not the reader chooses to make this juxtaposition, the result remains the same: a considerable depreciation of a good substance both on a spiritual and concrete level.[23] A further corruption of the word hap-

---

22. Cf. also *La Comédie des quatre femmes* in which a jealous woman uses a similar image of bitterness caused by Jealousy: "L'amer morceau, que je mache à toute heure" (*Théâtre profane*, p. 99).

23. "Nous n'avons qu'un Sauveur, lequel en disant *Consumatum est* a montré qu'il ne laissoit point de lieu à un autre pour faire notre salut" (XXXIII, 215). In another instance, Marguerite paraphrases Genesis 3:19, in opposing religious hypocrisy: "Vous n'aurez plus le pain des pauvres enfans

pens on an erotic level: "Si est ce que suyvant la fragilité des hommes qui s'ennuyent de bon pain manger, fut amoureus d'une métaise qu'il avoit" (XXXVIII, 232); the distance between man's nature and an ideal condition cannot be narrowed.[24]

The final degeneration of the bread metaphor occurs in the fifty-second novella, as already noted; here the product no longer exists in its ordinary consistency, it is merely a vulgar imitation of it: "trouva derrière une maison un bel étron tout gelé, lequel il meit dedans un papier et l'envelopa si bien, qu'il sembloit un petit pain de sucre" (LII, 284). From the connotation of trickiness and eroded semblance that it has in the story, *pain de sucre* becomes the basis for a discussion of the role of obscenity and vulgar words in society and conversation; it comes to mean *paroles puantes*, that is, the falsification of the Word of God for Oysille and the hypocrisy of the language of love for Parlamente (286). The metaphoric journey may be a long and circuitous one, but the thematic nucleus emerges infallibly to reveal a tightly woven cohesion.

Specific edible items, such as preserves, drugs, and salad, assume a metaphoric function in the realm either of perfect

---

aquis par la sueur des pères" (XLIV, 258). Finally the image of bread in a biblical sense, meaning truth, can be found in one of her plays, *L'Inquisiteur*:

> THIERROT Les Dames de nostre maison
> C'est Unyon et Charitté
>
> CLÉROT L'on y menge toute saison
> Le pain de vye et veritté
> . . . .
> Allons soupper, la table est mise.
> [*Théâtre profane*, pp. 80–1]

24. See again novella XLIX for further examples of bread in an erotic sense: "Nous avons mangé de votre pain si longuement, nous serions bien ingratz si nous ne vous fesions service" (274); Mais encors faut il que je sache . . . si celuy qui vous tenoit prisonnier vous faisoit bien gangner votre pain" (273).

or of carnal love, or both. On a literal level, preserves appear as food offerings by a lady to a man, but subsequently this one-dimensional meaning vibrates in the reader's mind and leaves him wondering. In the twenty-fifth tale, a lawyer and his wife entertain a prince for a meal, and "ainsi que la Dame tenoit à genous les confitures devant le Prince" (178), she tells him to meet her afterwards in her bedroom; inevitably her offerings become a manifestation of her desires. In the following novella, a reverse situation takes place, since "confitures" stand for a refusal; after declaring to her would-be lover that his efforts will not be rewarded, "elle commanda qu'on apportat la collation de toutes sortes de confitures" (XXVI, 188), but he refuses, he is not hungry.

Similarly the image of the drug is a double-faced one, perfect love and an aphrodisiac; whereas those of salad and the garden imply vengeance and the pleasures of love. Dagoucin refers to perfect love as a "drogue précieuse" to be dispensed parsimoniously, that is, not to be made too evident to others (LIII, 291). On the other hand, in a strictly sexual context, this metaphor occupies a central place in a novella setting forth an apothecary who "aussi qu'il goutoit de différentes drogues, aussi faisoit il de différentes femmes, pour sçavoir mieus parler de toutes complexions" (LXVIII, 336). When female customers come to him, he gladly prescribes drugs that will change the *complexion* of their husbands into satisfying their wives again. His wife, however, reprimands him "si tres aprement de conseiller à autruy d'user de drogues qu'il ne vouloit prendre pour luy" (337). The drug becomes the equivalent of both promiscuity and healthy sexual satisfaction, depending on the dosage; obviously Marguerite advocates reason and moderation.

The image of the salad articulates further the theme of infidelity, if indeed it does not embody infidelity itself. This metaphor, summing up the meaning of the thirty-sixth story, is not suggested until the epilogue of the novella; to punish his wife, the husband "un beau jour du moys de may ala cueuillir en son jardin une salade de telles herbes, que sit tot que sa femmes en eut mangé, ne vécut que vingt quatre heures" (226–27). Then the narrators, true to one of their functions, fix and elaborate the metaphoric suggestion; Parlamente deplores women who have to "manger telles salades," and Saffredan comments on the husband's cruel madness when "il feit sa salade" (227).[25] The green salad of poisonous herbs constitutes an evident antidote to the victim of a love philter.

If food and eating belong to the metaphoric language of love, it follows that drinking does as well. Since it is a physiological need, figuratively speaking, drinking remains on the general level of physical love. However, it is used in a framework of hypocrisy and irony, or as a reaction to the former, except when it symbolizes caution and reason in seeking sexual satisfaction.[26] On the way to an assignation with his lady, a prince meets her husband on a narrow staircase; with a quick presence of mind, he declares: "J'ay bien voulu venir icy vous visiter privément, tant pour vous recommander mes affaires, que pour vous prier me donner à boire" (XXV, 178). As with fire, drinking has a purifying and revealing role; in one instance, a middle-class man enjoys a lowbrow affair with a peasant woman, and he comes to realize that his wife knows of it when his poor mistress "lui donna à boire dans une coupe d'argent" (XXVI, 233) given expressly to her by the wife. On a metaphoric plane, Marguerite prefers the expression *donner à boire* instead of the simple *boire*; this preference may be due to the resulting am-

25. Si toutes celles, dit Parlamente, qui ont aymé leurs valetz, étoient contraintes à manger telles salades, j'en connoi qui n'aymeroient pas tant leurs jardins, qu'elles font, mais en arracheroient toutes les herbes pour éviter celles qui rendent l'honneur à la lignée par la mor d'une fole mère" (227).

26. "Une femme ne doit donner à boire ou à manger à son mary, pour quelque occasion que ce soit, qu'elle ne sache tant par expérience, que par gens sçavans qu'il ne luy puisse nuyre" (LXVIII, 337).

bivalence in the ironic usage of *donner* meaning to give but implying to take away.

Significantly enough, wine and its deity Bacchus never have a positive connotation in the *Heptameron*; they stand for sheer carnal pleasures or as means to obtain them. Marguerite does not even attempt to exploit the duality in the concept of wine, a technique so dear to her, for wine also symbolizes inspiration and the new spirit of the Renaissance. Furthermore, wine takes up relatively little room as a metaphor in the novellas. Once in a while it occurs in relation to monks or wine stewards who remain slaves to lust or greed. Two monks who had seduced a bride by parading as her husband are soon caught "dedans les vignes. Et là furent traitez comme il leur appartenoit. Car apres les avoir bien battuz, leur couperent les bras et les jambes, et les laissérent dedans les vignes en la garde du dieu Bacchus et Vénus dont ilz étoient meilleurs disciples que de saint Françoys" (XLVIII, 271). In a similar vein, a wine steward lives up to his portrait ("serviteur de Bacchus [plutôt] que des prettres de Diane" [LXXI, 358]) when he tries to seduce the maid before the very eyes of his dying wife. Another wine steward, "valet du Diable," arranges a meeting between his sister-in-law and a prince in his vineyard (XLII, 250). The limited, even narrow use that Marguerite makes of the wine metaphor can certainly not be explained by a strong moral sense on her part. It remains rather a conjectural matter of sensibility, not sensitivity.[28]

The language of love returns to its more usual multidimensional realm with the various meanings that *faire bonne chère* and *contentement* assume in the novellas. Because of their

27. For a scatological use of "moust de Bacchus," in relation to monks, see novella XI, p. 81.

28. Again Hircan, in his own inimitable way, may give the cue: "Toutesfois ilz font semblant de n'aymer point les raizins quand ilz sont si haut, qu'ilz ne les peuvent cueuillir" (LIII, 291).

high frequency, these two metaphors form an important and integral part of the expression of sentiments ranging from perfect love to physical love, with intermediate points. In the former sense, "La vraye richesse consiste en contentement" (XIX, 127), and in the latter with Oysille speaking: "ce contentement [is experienced by] les charnelz qui trop envelopez de leur gresse ne connoiscent s'ilz ont ame ou non" (LXIII, 325). In between, *contentement* can also denote, in a context of genuine sentiments, satisfaction, happiness, ecstasy;[29] on a sexual level, the narrators bring forth the fluidity of the word: "Les femmes de bien, dit Longarine, n'ont besoin d'autre chose que de l'amour de leurs marys, qui seulz les peuvent contenter. Mais celles qui cherchent un contentement bestial, ne le trouveront jamais où l'honnetteté commande. Appelez vous contentement bestial, dit Géburon, si la femme veut avoir de son mary ce qui luy appertient?" (LXIV, 339). A further purposeful instability of *contentement* results from an ironic use of it; in such instances it means of course exactly the opposite of what it purports to express, and Marguerite vents in this manner her notion of a tragic cruel fate.[30] In fact, this oxymoronic use of *contentement*, spiritual versus carnal, negative versus positive, establishes the evasiveness and relativity of satisfaction and happiness in love.

By definition the expression *faire bonne chère* belongs to the realm of pleasure. In addition to its usual acceptation of having a good time, its obvious derivative occurs in a sexual context: "Elle . . . luy feit la meilleure chère qui luy fut pos-

29. Cf. XXI, 142; XXXVII, 230; L, 277.
30. "Le bon homme fut bien joyeus de croire que l'ame de sa femme étoit en Paradis, et luy dépesché d'un si méchant cors. Et avec ce contentement s'en retourna à Paris, où il se marya avec une belle honneste et june femme de bien . . ." (LX, 312), but unknown to him, his first wife who left him is really still alive, and the Church will make him take her back at the cost of his happiness.

sible" (XII, 101). Although because of their high frequency these two meanings predominate, they still do not require any critical amplification, for they are obvious, except that a most disparaging smile on Marguerite's part peers through; indeed, one discerns an indictment of pleasure somewhat à la Pascal, but an implied advocacy of naturalism in a Montaigne vein. Even when the expression offers a more particular meaning, it always implies criticism of an outward, nongenuine condition or action; here it means to be attentive, to satisfy whims or wishes: "Mais quelque bonne chère que luy feit son mary, la méchante amour qu'elle portoit au chanoyne luy faisoit tourner son repos en torment" (LXI, 317). One notable exception to the general negative connotation of the expression occurs not in the context of sentiments but in a creative spirit; the narrators revel in their storytelling: "le plaisir qu'ilz prenoient à la bonne chère qu'ilz faisoient" (242). In general both with *contentement* and *faire bonne chère*, Marguerite reverses their respective positive connotations and thus establishes the prevalence of an antimeaning, much of it with a certain mocking acrimony.

However, a category of *verba* strictly *erotica* leaves little room for ambivalence with an ideal counterpart; more important, it reveals some noteworthy inventiveness which dissipates any sense of vulgarity. The domain of religion provides a broad basis for such language. A monk promises a young lady complete absolution of her sins if she wears "ma corde sur votre chair toute nue. . . . If faut que les mienes propres [mains] desquelles vous devez avoir absolution, la vous ayent prémiérement cinte . . ." (XLI, 243). If any doubt ever existed about the specific meaning of "tying a cord," Marguerite has Oysille herself say to Nomerfide, the youngest and most frivolous female narrator: "Vous savez donc bien nouer" (V, 41). An upholsterer, using "des plus fines verges," enjoys "bailler les Innocents" (XLV, 261) to his

maid, following a folkloristic tradition,[31] and on other occasions he takes her outdoors to "faire le crucifyz sur la
neige" (262). The erotic notion of monks administering their
discipline, with the inevitable verbal play, receives further
development in subsequent novellas. In the very next one, as
a matter of fact, a mother entreats a monk to "teach her
daughter a lesson": "pleut à Dieu, mon Père, qu'elle eut un
peu taté des disciplines, que vous autres Religieus prenez."
After obeying the mother, he informs her "qu'il souviendra
à votre fille de ma discipline" (XLVI, 265). A wife soon forgets the sound of her husband's voice because she takes
greater pleasure in listening to the "chant du chantre avec
qui elle étoit" (LX, 311). Even when the metaphor becomes
suggestively graphic, it does not offend our sensibilities.[32] In
this particular religious context, Marguerite wants above all
to cast a doubtful light on the naive credulity of some individuals, perhaps too many, but at the same time these

31. The Day of the Innocents falls on December 28; cf. this text by Marot:

> Très chère soeur, si je savois où couche
> Vostre personne au jour des Innocens,
> De bon matin je yrois à vostre couche
> Veoir ce gent corps, que j'ayme entre cinq cens:
> Adonc ma main, veu l'ardeur que je sens,
> Ne se pourroit bonnement contenter
> Sans vous toucher, tenir, taster, tenter,
> Et, si quelcun survenoit d'aventure,
> Semblant ferois de vous innocenter.
> Seroit-ce pas honneste couverture?

Quoted in Marguerite de Navarre, *L'Heptaméron des Nouvelles*, eds. Le Roux
de Lincy and A. de Montaiglon, IV (Paris, 1880), p. 313.

32. A husband whose wife gave birth three weeks earlier asks a monk
when he can resume sexual relations with her and receives the following
answer: "Et ne fut que l'exemple de la Benoite Vierge Marie qui ne voulut
entrer au Temple jusques après les jours de sa Purgation" (XXIII, 163). The
innocuousness of obscenity in Marguerite de Navarre had been noted more
than a century ago by L. de Loménie, "La Littérature romanesque: La Reine
de Navarre et l'*Heptaméron* d'après de nouveaux documents," *Revue des
Deux Mondes*, 40 (1862), 679.

erotic metaphors reflect some creative imagination and continue to accentuate a degree of helplessness and weakness in men, the victims.

The realm of rural living and farming activities, reminiscent of Brueghel paintings, provides a source of erotic vocabulary. In the twenty-eighth tale, country dances take on a figurative meaning; the main protagonist "avec un vielle ou autre instrument apprenoit aus chambriéres de léans à danser les branles de Gascongne" (194). In the very next tale, the central image is that of the sieve that very soon is transposed to an erotic sense and thereby complements its male counterpart, the ham, in the shape of a wooden shoe, in the preceding novella.[33] A priest, caught with a parishioner's wife, is forced to hide in an attic, "et couvrit la trape par où il monta d'un van à vanner" (XXIX, 197). A stock situation, so common in the novella genre or in fabliaux, gains new life by means of a verbal juggling with *van* which rapidly manifests its erotic meaning.[34] *Bluter*, another verb for "sifting," appears in one of the last novellas, the sixty-eighth, in an erotic context.[35] However, here, it occurs in relation to an old man's intimacies with his chambermaids, and as one of the narrators eventually remarks, it implies an activity beyond his capacity: "il eut plus de plaisir de rire avec sa femme, que de s'aler tuer en l'aage où il étoit avec sa cham-

33. Cf. "luy montra le paté [de Jambon] qu'il avoit souz son manteau assez grand pour nourrir un camp" (XXVIII, 195).

34. The hidden priest "s'appuya par mégarde si lourdement sur le van, qu'homme et van trebuchèrent à bas aupres du bon homme [husband] qui dormoit . . . [et] luy dit: 'Mon compère, voylà votre van, et grand mercy'." The wife then says to her husband: "mon amy, c'est votre van que le Curé avoit emprunté, lequel il vous est venu rendre." The husband answers: "C'est bien rudement rendu ce qu'on emprunte" and finds wrong only "la rudesse dont il avoit usé en rendant son van" (197).

35. In his *Dictionnaire de la langue française du seizième siècle*, E. Huguet cites "bluter au sens libre" in Rabelais, but not in Marguerite where, according to him, it appears only in a literal sense (I [Paris, 1928], pp. 546–47). In Italian, "abburatare," to sift, also has an erotic meaning; see the *Vocabulario degli Accademici della Crusca*.

brière" (LXIX, 339). A sense of sterile activity emanates from this *bluter* which also means to idle the time away, and therefore a slashing irony devastates the husband's actions— most understandably so, since Hircan, the master naturalist, is the narrator of this tale.[36]

Sexual abstention and the loss of sexual capacity must have preoccupied Marguerite, as manifested by the meta- phoric language she forged to express them. Furthermore, it would not be mere conjecture to surmise an autobiographical note in this preoccupation. In this context, *work* denotes sexual activity and *rest* its opposite, whereas *wearing the harness* stands for tiredness caused by long or excessive de- mands. A husband abandons his wife "pour cercer son travail" (XIV, 102), and two lovers "travaillèrent la nuyt en peur et crainte que leur affaire fut révélé" (LIII, 290). An- other husband, whose wife may have become frigid, turns his attention toward his chambermaid;[37] because the tale is highly stylized, the narrators bring into focus its meaning: "Mais on dit que toutes choses se peuvent endurer si non l'ayse, et ne peut on connoitre le repos, si non quand on l'a perdu. Cette bonne femme, dit Oysille, qui rioit quand son mary étoit joyeus, avoit bien apris à trouver son repos par- tout. Je croi, dit Longarine, qu'elle aymoit mieus son repos que son mary veu qu'elle ne prenoit bien à cueur chose qu'il

36. There may even be here a suggestion of masturbation as opposed to "bluter" in an ordinary erotic sense, with overtones of excesses; at any rate, the nuances are plentiful and purposely difficult to delineate: "Un jour que la chambrière blutoit en la chambre de derrière, ayant son surcot sur sa teste à la mode du païs qui est fait comme un créneau, mais il couvre tout le cors et les épaules par derrière, son maitre la trouvant en cet abit la veut bien for presser . . . elle le pria de mettre son surcot en sa teste et de bluter en son absence afin que sa maitresse oÿt touiours le son du bluteau. . . . Venez voir votre mary auquel j'ai appris à bluter, pour me défaire de luy . . . [says the wife to him] Goujate! Combien veus tu par moys de ton labeur?" (338–39).

37. Again a euphemism, with an allusion to the Samson legend, expresses jocularly the husband's condition: "il étoit sujet à une grand' douleur au desouz de la racine des cheveus, tellement que les médicins luy conseillèrent de découcher d'avec sa femme" (LIV, 292).

feit. Elle prenoit bien à cueur, dit Parlamente, ce qui pouvoit nuyre à la conscience et santé de son mary" (LIV, 293–94).[38] *Repos*, then, represents a condition imposed, not chosen, and far from psychologically restful; in this instance, the inner contradiction of the word, despite the narrators' attempts to rationalize it, bursts with pathos.

With the image of the harness, Marguerite alternates between the knightly and the sexual level and thereby gives an insight into the nobility's frame of mind in regard to love. At first, wearing the harness implies physical fatigue due to endless fighting in wars, while robust monks or servants remain available, but a note of irony emerges from this burden to elicit compassion and favors from the ladies. Géburon claims that men of his standing are "tous cassez du harnoys" (V, 41), and Hircan echoes similar sentiments in defending a widow who prefers a servant to her noble lover: "Si vous sçaviez la différence qu'il y a d'un gentilhomme qui toute sa vie a porté le harnoys et suivy les guerres, au pris d'un valet bien nourry . . ." (XIX, 197). Then suddenly the image comes to mean the burden and frustration of perfect love and may have had the same implications in the preceding cases: " et aussi l'amour de qui le conte parle n'est pas de celle qui fait porter les harnoys" (XIX, 197).

Not until the second half of the *Heptameron* does the metaphor assume sexual overtones. In the fifty-fourth tale, it becomes the sign of the weight and boredom of conjugal physical love.[39] Shortly thereafter, it represents sexual prowess and potency, outside of marriage: "S'il étoit ainsi, répondit Symontaut, que les Dames fussent sans mercy, nous

38. In the seventieth novella, the duchess "lasse de trop de repos" (340), that is, not contented with her husband's love, seeks out the young nobleman.

39. "C'est pour ce que souvent notre valeur est éprouvée. Mais si se sentent bien noz épaules d'avoir longuement portée la cuyrasse. Si vous aviez été contraint, dit Ennasuite, de porter un an durant le harnoys et coucher sur la dure, vous auriez grand desir de recouvrer le lyt de votre bonne femme, et porter la cuyrasse dont maintenant vous vous plaindez" (293).

pourrions bien faire reposer nos chevaus, et laisser rouiller nos harnoys jusques à la première guerre, et ne faire que penser du ménage" (LVII, 300). The frequent thematic and tonal break between the first days and the last ones in the *Heptameron,* as will be subsequently shown, could indicate an evolution both in thought and in composition patterns. At any rate, the work-rest-harness metaphorical trilogy reveals Marguerite the sexual behavioralist, who talks frankly of transformations in love; this candor may not exclude a personal involvement.

Animal imagery forms one last, quite important category in the language of love. The least prevalent part of it revolves around hunting, with precious as well as carnal overtones. Then a reversed concept of the biblically based shepherd and lamb theme, with various derivatives, focuses on the monks to show up their abuses or perversions. Finally the bestiality of man in general, both in his desires and conduct, receives considerable attention; beasts generically and the horse family in particular provide the metaphorical backdrop for this condition.

The metaphor of hunting brings forth the notions of pursuit, trapping, and cuckoldry. For cuckoldry, horns of course express infidelity, and in stressing the size and weight of them, Marguerite means to indicate its destructive force and overwhelming burden on conjugal life: "quand voz marys vous donneront des cornes de cheuvreul, vous leur en rendez de celles de cerf . . . vous endurerez cornes aussi grandes qu'un chesne" (III, 32); "Car vos femmes sont si sages et vous ayment tant, que quand vous leur feriez des cornes aussi poisentes que celles d'un dain, encores voudroient elles persuader à tout le monde, que ce sont chapeaus de roses" (VIII, 48). This traditional metaphoric cuckoldry occurs only in the above two novellas; if one were trying to derive some morality from them, a double standard would emerge, since in the first one, set against a noble background, she advocates reciprocity, and in the second, with a middle-class setting, she recommends punishment.

The image of the snare either marks the downfall of the lover or the place where he declares his love and thereby frees himself of his incubus. A princely huntsman, while attending a hunt, begins instead to follow the king's sister; using a trap-door to gain access to her bedroom, below his, he is greeted by her scratches. The wounded "beast" afraid to show his mauled face in public is thus caught at his own game (IV, 33–37). In the twenty-fourth novella, "Apres avoir conduit la Royne jusques au lieu où étoient les toiles" (170), a knight euphemistically unveils his sentiments by exposing a mirror on his chest in which the queen is reflected.[40]

If the pursuit image has some precious Petrarchan resonances, it very soon comes down to a harsh and physical level. A gentleman "prouchassa si bien" a lady until "comme la biche navrée à mor, cuyde en changeant de lieu, changer le mal qu'elle porte avec soy" (XVI, 116, 117); before, she had been a wolf fleeing from a greyhound (116), a rather unhappy simile unless Marguerite intends to depreciate another instance of perfect love. This flight is mandatory because in life women must beware of men "comme le cer feroit de son chasseur s'il avoit entendement" (118). Géburon echoes the same sentiment out of necessity, not conviction, owing to his old age; he regrets the good "hunting" days of his youth, like Hugo in "Tristesse d'Olympio": "Mais pour ce que j'ai les dens si foibles que je ne puis plus macher de venaison, j'averti les pauvres biches de se garder des ve-

40. In a totally different context, the image of the snare is the central one in the seventeenth novella with a play on *hunt* and *chase away*. A mercenary nobleman, sent to assassinate the king (François I?) will use the hunt as a means to do so. The king, aware of the plot, reveals it himself to the would-be assassin whereupon he is forced to leave, as the king's advisors remark: "Vous avez envie de chasser le comte Guillaume, et vous voyez qu'il se chasse luy mesme" (170). This novella is narrated to praise the king's noble spirit and virtue.

neurs" (118). The metaphoric references to hunting are found in the first half of the *Heptameron*, with one exception in the second half.[41] This fact would indicate that Marguerite was evolving and abandoning a set of commonplace images in favor of others more to her own creative liking.

Among the various animal epithets monks receive, that of the wolf dominates. Because of this prevalence, the monks appear shrewd and aggressive, the abductors and eaters of lambs and ewes and therefore the false impersonators of the shepherd whose function the Church has bestowed upon them: "en lieu de faire office de Pasteur, il deveint loup" (XXII, 155); even the real shepherd, the one who lives by and carries out the true ecclesiastical precepts, must be vigilant, otherwise "il sera toujours trompé par les finesses du loup" (XLVI, 266). The mood of cruelty comes very close to the one exhibited in La Fontaine's fable: "Et la crainte qu'il avoit d'ettre surpris, et qu'on luy otat sa proye, lui faisoit emporter son aigneau, comme un loup sa breby, pour manger à son ayse" (XXXI, 208). In effect, in this guise the monks are transformed into beasts to be tracked down and disposed of.[42] This metaphorical anticlerical outlook has its roots in medieval bourgeois literature, which in turn could draw the wolf image from biblical sources,[43] but in Marguerite's days it had certainly become a *topos*.

When Marguerite compares monks to foxes or monkeys

41. "Car il n'y a veneur qui ne prenne plaisir à corner [sound the horn] sa prise, ny amoureus d'avoir la gloire de sa victoire" (XLIX, 275).

42. "Incontinent accoururent tous ses gens pour aler ayder leur maitre à amener le loup qu'il avoit pris" (XXXI, 207); a wife "va appeler son mary, et ceus de la justice, pour venir prendre les deus lous enragez, desquelz par la grace de Dieu, elle avoit échapé" (V, 39). Otherwise, if one is careless, the wolves come and steal, as a husband remarks whose wife ran off with a canon: "Luy qui vouloit recouvrer sa brebis perdue dont il avoit faite tres mauvaise garde" (LX, 311).

43. "Behold, I send you forth as sheep in the midst of wolves: be ye therefore wise as serpents and harmless as doves" (Matthew 10:16). Oysille paraphrases this warning: "Et s'il [God] commande d'ettre simples come colombes, il ne commande moins d'ettre prudens comme serpens" (LXV, 331).

to indicate slyness or physical and moral ugliness,[44] she can claim no more originality than in using the wolf; foxes and monkeys, however, receive very little attention. Only the renovation and the development of the metaphor matters, as in the metaphor that Marguerite develops of the pig, which has a central part in two novellas. In the thirty-fourth, two monks, a fat one and a thin one, overhear a butcher tell his wife that the next day he plans to kill his fat pig, referred to as *cordelier*; thereafter the purposeful confusion is complete to the point that the monks inadvertently seek refuge in the sty, and the fat one then "saillit à quatre piez hors du tect, criant tant qu'il pouvoit, miséricorde" (217). The total equation of monks and pigs indicates that neither can hear nor understand; by inference the monks misunderstand or pervert the Word of God. In the forty-fourth novella, a piglet is the concretion of perverted truth and abuse of God. When a Franciscan monk tells a lady the true nature of his order, hypocrisy and materialism, she no longer gives him his yearly alms, the piglet, but later the husband sends it to him anyway because nothing has really changed, the truth remains the same. Animal imagery in reference to monks always points out the supremacy in their minds of the love of the body over the love of God—and a false love toward their fellow man. Marguerite stands much more against violence and falsification of truth in order to achieve the pleasures of the flesh than against the validity and naturalness of these pleasures.

Men in general do not fare much better than monks; seen in this light Marguerite's anticlericalism in no way implies an anticatholicism but a verification of bestiality in all strata of society. Generically, for her, *beste* means deprived of reason, be it in the realm of common sense or desires of the flesh. What could be considered Marguerite's own version of

44. Cf. XXII, 127; XXVII, 193.

a Chain of Being is the basis for a declaration of relativism and another indication that she shies away from any absolute position: "Car puisque les espritz que l'on estime les plus subtilz et grans discoureurs, ont telle punition de devenir plus sotz que les bestes, il faut doncques conclure que ceus qui sont bas et de petite portée . . . seront remplys de la sapience des Anges" (LI, 283). She devotes a whole novella to this paradoxical concept of *beste*; after betraying his master, a man, accompanied by his wife, is abandoned on a deserted island inhabited only by wild animals, and the couple begin a Robinson Crusoe life. Symontaut, the wily narrator of this tale, tells us that their bodily life was bestial, but their spiritual life angelic (LXVII, 334). However, Parlamente soon downgrades this idyllic primordial setting and opposes to it the husband's indelible betrayal and the ensuing blind fidelity on the wife's part: "Je croi . . . qu'il y a des marys si bestes, que celles qui vivent avec eus ne doivent point trouver étrange de vivre avec leurs semblables" (335). The principal function of the Fauvist background of the island is to provide a metaphoric setting for the couple's "bestiality," the husband's moral corruption and the wife's mistaken love, however understandable.

The victims of a fatal uncontrollable passion, somewhat à la Phèdre, receive the epithet *bestial*. A wife who has left her husband for a priest because of an inexorable desire is referred to as "cette beste" (LXI, 319). "Bestiality" comes most notably to the fore in the seventieth novella, the Dame du Verger tale. From the very beginning of the tale the reader is informed that it will deal with the "insatiable cupidité des bestes" (339), in particular with the duchess, "une Dame belle et bien maryée, qui par faute de vivre de cette honnete amytié deveint plus charnelle que les pourceaus et plus cruelle que les lyons" (340). The animalistic metaphoric setting is thus clearly established and projected throughout the story, where it centers about the little dog, the intermediary so to speak, between the Dame du Verger and the young man loved by the rapacious duchess. When the duchess informs the Dame du Verger that she finally knows of the secret love between the two, the dog becomes the symbol of this love: "Il n'y a amour si secrette, qui ne soit sceue, ny petit chien si affété [groomed], ne si fait à la main, duquel l'on n'entende le japer" (350). No matter how well "groomed" a dog may be it can never be entirely trusted; a love no matter how perfect remains subject to human failings. The yapping of the spotless dog does not equal the "langage de bestes" (350) spoken by the duchess, but both expose a human weakness: the inherent inability on the young man's part to keep his love a secret from others, the only basis on which it can exist, and the duchess's implacable unnatural desire for the young man. Indeed, the duchess is compared to a Circe who reduces everyone about her to beast, even her husband, who upon hearing of her treachery becomes a wild boar as he rushes to kill her in a most ignominious fashion.[45] Bestiality reigns supreme; passion dominates love; man falls from an angelic potentiality into a blind night of instincts worthy of Racine.

If the equine family receives some metaphoric notice in the *Heptameron*, it is because of its erotic connotations originating in Greek mythology. Since the horse would appear to be a strong and beautiful animal, Marguerite prefers to attribute a figurative sense to stable and stable boys, both of which have a baser denotation. She does not hesitate, however, to give to a muleteer the crudest and most animalistic behavior, in keeping with the common opinion held of the

45. "La beauté de la Duchesse est elle si extrême, qu'elle vous ait trans-mué, comme faisoit celle de Circes . . ." (350); "Et tout ainsi qu'un sanglier étant navré d'un épieu, court d'impétuosité contre celuy qui a fait le coup, ainsi le Duc s'en ala cercher celle qui l'avoit navré jusques au fond de son ame" (354).

mule: "Et luy qui n'avoit amour que bestiale, et qui eut mieus entendu le langage des muletz, que ses honnettes raisons, se montra bien plus bestial que les bestes avec lesquelles il avoit été longtems" (II, 26). Animals transfer to men their mode of conduct. As a result, when a woman with a marked promiscuous drive goes to the stable "pour y mettre ordre" (XXVI, 183), the whole episode soon leaves the literal plane. A suitor, disguised as a stable boy, has no difficulty seducing her in the absence of the husband who had entreated her to care for "ses chevaus et son palefrenier" (183). If any doubt lingers concerning the erotic meaning of the equine metaphoric background, the narrator proceeds then to reveal the degenerate nature of this woman reduced to the sexual animality of the horse: "Ainsi vécut cette june Dame souz l'hypocrisie et habit de femme de bien, en telle volupté, que raison, conscience, ordre et mesure, n'avoient plus de lieu en elle" (184–85).

Hence, in love and in life Marguerite advocates reason, good conscience, order and moderation; these are the tenets of conduct she sets forth. They remain, however, ideals, even in the realm of daily earthly comportment, because the novellas depict the very opposite behavior actually endemic to man. As for the perfect love or friendship that she refers to frequently and attempts to exemplify in some stories and discussions, it seems fitter for saints than men and therefore doomed to failure. Thus Marguerite in the *Heptameron* seeks a *modus vivendi* based on natural physical love. The metaphoric language of love bears out this last premise: artifice, excess, and bestiality are implicitly opposed to naturalness, moderation, and reason.

3. THE LANGUAGE OF SHAM AND FAILURE

DECIPHERING the code and exploring the vast labyrinth of human relations—these remain Marguerite's primary task. Her endeavor, however, faces a major difficulty because of the discrepancy between man's intent and his actions. To depict this world in flux between seeming and being, the technique of the screen that separates truth from lies dominates; the screen can take the form of institutions, words, actions, places, or objects, and then the light / darkness notion further illustrates the true / false concept. In a world of appearances, truth disintegrates, words lose their original meanings; mistrust and feigning prevail. Since the search for an absolute would fail and result only in an awareness that a behavioral fluidity pervades society, falseness and falsification constitute both a shield and the only constant in the midst of an ungraspable universe in masquerade.

Religion offers a prime screen for engendering and concealing carnal desires. The church itself on several occasions serves as a meeting place for lovers (cf. XVI, 115; XLII, 246) or becomes the place where priests and monks initiate their conquest of women under the guise of administering sacerdotal functions. A prior "confessing" a nun "la mettoit *In Pace*, c'est à dire en chartre perpétuelle" (XXII, 160); during Lent, a woman receiving the ashes from a priest looks much more at his lovely hands than at what he gives her (XXXV, 220); a wife in order to leave her husband and join a canon abuses the last rites and goes through confession, extreme unction, and burial (LX and LXI). Losing the priest would be losing the faith; the cult of the flesh replaces the cult of God: "Car elle estimoit un enfer, perdre la vision de son Dieu" (LXI, 316). In the very last novella of the *Heptameron*, a monk's edifying language thinly veils his true intentions:

"commença le religieus à parler de la misère de la vie, et de la bienheureuté de la mor . . . il prenoit si grand plaisir, que parlant de la vie à venir, commença de l'embrasser, comme s'il eut eue envye de la porter entre ses bras au Paradis" (LXXII, 360). The religious façade is purposely quite transparent so that the barrier between the spiritual and the carnal hardly exists. The confusion—even the fusion—of the two makes for an ironic reversal of good and evil. Words take on a meaning the opposite of their usual acceptation.

In this mood of duplicity, Marguerite plays on the word *saint*, which she pictures either as a mask for the devil or as an abuse of truth in the realm of religion and love: "Voylà, mes Dames, comme les chesnes de saint Pierre sont converties par les mauvais ministres en celles de Sathan, et si fortes à rompre, que les sacremens, qui chacent les dyables des cors, sont à ceus cy les moyens de les faire plus longuement demeurer en leurs consciences" (LXI, 320); "nous couvrons notre Diable du plus bel Ange" (XII, 87).[1] Both clergy and layman parade as saints, and if priests and monks can take advantage of man's apparent gullibility, they only reflect their victims' own duplicity. A saint in love is an individual willing to macerate his body (cf. XXX) or one who operates under the guise of spiritual love (XIX). The real meaning of saint cannot be applied to man, only the false one can. This differentiation is not necessarily disparaging to man, because saintly behavior is humanly impossible; on the other hand, becoming a man equidistant between saint and devil remains quite possible and the authentic ideal to strive for.

A verbal feint or deceit expresses the dichotomy between the real and the false. A single word will not only have contrasting meanings but will also be fragmented into a variety of senses. In some instances, this process purposely blurs the

1. Cf. "Il y a des femmes si difficiles, dit Longarine, qu'il leur semble qu'elles doivent avoir des anges. Et voilà, dit Symontaut, pourquoy elles trouvent souvent des dyables" (LVI, 300).

truth. The verbal feint then becomes a screen between appearances and a fluid truth, either within a single novella or from one to another. In the eighteenth novella, a lady supposedly tests a man's love for her by having him lie in bed with her or her maid without allowing him any further advances. In such circumstances the key words of the tale, *patience, force, obéissance, fermeté, fidélité*, which describe the gentleman's endurance, lose their ordinary meanings because they are false substantives consciously misused; they form the verbal feint that scorns the man's comportment and sharpens the lady's cruelty.

The adjective *étonné* and the substantive *hardiesse* occur quite frequently in the *Heptameron*. On a thematic level they remain ambivalent because they are applied to both good and evil situations. The fragmentation of their meanings adds to this ambivalence and produces a verbal feint due to contrasts in sense, implied or explicit, and to litotes. Besides the evident "surprised" and "astounded," the word *étonné* takes on as well the sense of fright, real (VI, 42) or feigned (VIII, 46), loss of reason (VII, 44), sadness or shock (XII, 86), grief (XII, 90). As a substantive, it conveys a loss of one's self-control or one's senses: "Et pour la grande effusion de sang, tomba tout mort aus piez de s'amye, qui demeura hors de soymesme par étonnement" (L, 277); upon seeing her son-in-law in the garb of the priest that he really is, a woman "fut toute surprise d'étonnement" (LVI, 298). Most of the time *hardiesse* contains a negative connotation; in these cases, it expresses an inverted courage, a cunning premeditation (cf. X and XVI), and even a perversion, the incestuous relationship between a priest and his sister (XXXIII, 215). Or within the same novella, the cunning *hardiesse* of the king's would-be murderer (XVII, 119) is opposed to the king's true *hardiesse* (121), which incorporates all his virtues.

For Marguerite, words constitute a weak barrier between the true and the false. Since words are spoken by individuals, they cannot be trusted any more than the persons themselves. To express this verbal failure, she splits a word into all its possible components that bring forth its impurity, or she reverts to its pristine acceptation. Here the juggling with *fine*, the adjective, the substantive, and the adverb, accentuates nuances ranging from hypocrisy to slyness and astuteness—but in the guise of a positive quality: "Croyez, dit Hircan, qu'une femme fine sçaura vivre, où toutes autres mourront de faim. Aussi, dit Longarine, quand leur finesse est connue, c'est bien la mor. Mais la vie, dit Symontaut. Car elles n'estiment à petite gloire, d'ettre réputées plus fines que leurs compagnes. Et ce nom là de fines qu'elles ont apris à leur dépens, fait plus hardyment venir les serviteurs à leur obéissance, que la beauté. Car un des plus grans plaisirs qui soit entre elles, est de conduire leur amytié finement" (LIII, 291). In the thirty-ninth novella, the tale itself covers slightly more than one page, the word *esprit* used for "ghost," "wit," "soul," "devil," occurs eight times. Here too the presentation of the various contrasting facets of a single word raises the question of credibility, the nature of a specter in this particular instance.

In the forty-fourth story a paradox delineates the dichotomy between the false *fondement* of religion and the true one. Once more the frequent repetition of the key word within a relatively short space focuses on a notion of falseness, a religious foundation based upon "la folye des femmes" (259).[2] Only the discussions bring out the real foundation, the Gospel—but well interpreted, not abused. By coincidence

2. "Les Cordeliers doncq', dit Hircan, ne devroient jamais prescher pour faire sages les femmes, veu que leur folye leur sert tant. Ilz ne les preschent pas, dit Parlamente, d'ettre sages, mais bien de le cuyder ettre. Car celles qui sont du tout mondaines et foles, ne donnent pas grandes aumonnes. Mais celles qui pour fréquenter leur convent, et porter leurs Paternotres marquées de testes de mor, et leurs cornettes plus basses que les autres, cuydent ettre les plus sages, sont celles que lon peut dire les plus foles. Car elles constituent leur salut en la confiance qu'elles ont en la sainteté des iniques, qui pour un petit d'apparence finte, s'estiment demys dieus" (259).

or design, there is a word used in its pristine meaning—
impeccable, "sinless"; however, sinlessness does not exist
among men, who only parade as *impeccable*. The word therefore actually indicates the opposite of what it means. Self-
flagellation or masochism to repent of past sins or to test
one's will does not make one sinless; the answer is elsewhere:
"c'est bien l'extrémité de folie de se vouloir rendre de soymesme impeccable et cercher si for les occasions de pécher.
. . . Parquoy se faut recommander à Dieu" (XXX, 202). In a
world of appearances, the evanescence of words transmits
the duplicity of man's actions and thoughts.

Materialism falsifies values; it is a deceptive screen for
base and sterile sentiments, or even parades as an osten-
tatious adornment. The immediate result of such a vision is
a blurring, even an inversion, of the terms *rich* and *poor*; the
materially rich are spiritually poor, and vice versa. Furthermore, avarice and prodigality become one, because both distort the value of money at the expense of spiritual needs, love,
and religion. In a woman, avarice means a very parsimonious
distribution of her favors (XIII, 97); in a man, avarice operates on a literal level, for the man loves, not the woman,
but her material wealth (XXI, 151); or a father loves his
money so much that he neglects his daughter's well-being
and overrides her feelings (XXI, 140). When a maiden refuses
a prince's monetary advances, her "honnette pauvreté" becomes her real wealth (XLII, 250); in this novella a "thésaur-
argent" theme forms the basic metaphoric language. Buying God's love will fail even more surely than buying the love
of a woman: "les plus grans usuriers [font] les plus belles
et triumphantes chapelles . . . voulans appaiser Dieu pour dys
mille ducatz, du larcin de cent mil, comme si Dieu ne sçavoit
conter. . . . Dieu [réprouve] grans batimens, dorure, fardz et
pintures" (LV, 295–96). In this fifty-fifth novella, first, the
avarice of the dying husband, then that of the crafty wife in
the story, and that of the monks in the discussion are con-

trasted to one another with no attempt to judge which may be the worst. Avarice therefore represents a denatured love; still more revealing, it constitutes a façade behind which man wants to appear virtuous, magnanimous, and even religious.[3]

Precious stones and jewelry, especially rings, are typical items of adornment. In virtue of being decorative, they automatically convey a notion of falseness in Marguerite's aesthetics; they reflect a negative condition, the very opposite of their intrinsic beauty. Such a viewpoint runs contrary to the prevalent Renaissance concept of decorative beauty. In Castiglione's *Cortegiano* and in Rabelais's Abbey of Thélème, elaborate jewelry and clothes on individuals are correlated with the perfection of their spirit; exterior beauty corresponds to interior beauty. But Marguerite does not picture a utopia in the *Heptameron*; instead she depicts life as it is: a world of false appearances and false hopes. Therefore a diamond ring supposed to be a "pierre de fermeté" (XIII, 95) becomes nothing more than an object to "se parer aus dépens d'autres" (XIII, 94). Or any notion of adornment disappears altogether when a diamond ring simply stands for venal love (XV, 113). The idea of double falseness belongs to monks who are referred to as doublet, "false diamond" (XLI, 245).

Precious stones represent form rather than substance, a bitter and artificial substitute for real love: "un Milhor de grand' maison lequel avoit attaché sur son saye un petit gant comme pour femme, à crochetz d'aur, et sur les pointures des doigtz, y avoit force dyamans, rubys, émeraudes et perles, tant que ce gant étoit estimé un bien grand argent" (LVII, 301). In fact the narrators mock this unfortunate English nobleman, who exhibits a rather fatuous smugness. The one exception to this metaphoric use of precious stones as artifice

3. For other similar treatments of avarice, see novellas LII and LVI. Furthermore the whole nineteenth tale, the rather well-known one of Poline, is based on the rich / poor inversion.

and falseness concerns the pearl, Marguerite's own name-sake. A nun, Sister Marie Heroet, who successfully resists the ferocious advances of a prior, is compared to a "perle d'honneur et de virginité" (XXII, 161). Indeed, Marguerite in person intervenes at the end of this tale to punish the aggressive monk, as if the clerical setting were a transposition of an autobiographical event.

The image of the ring can mean perfection and eternity or, in the context of love, fidelity before or after marriage. However, from Marguerite's point of view, it has the opposite significance; it is the object of deception and disappointment that does not fulfill its stated purpose. To prove his success, a man shows to his friend the ring he has taken from this friend's wife while they were in bed (VIII). In the famous story of Rolandine, she and her lover, who is of noble but bastard lineage, pledge to each other an eternal spiritual love: "se donnèrent chacun un anneau en nom de maryage, et se baisèrent en l'église devant Dieu, qu'ils preindrent pour témoin de leur promesse" (XXI, 151). But faced with the waning likelihood that their love will ever come to fruition, the lover breaks the bond and finds a different satisfaction, first with a German lady and then with others. Or again, two lovers, to pledge eternal fidelity, break a ring in two and each takes one half; when the man returns his half, it is to break the relation because his sincerity and sentiments have been tried excessively. Hence the reunion of the two halves of the ring has the opposite effect of the one originally intended, the end of a love that could never prosper.

In very few instances does nature appear in a trustworthy role; for the most part, Marguerite presents it when dealing with moral questions, as a beautiful exterior concealing an evil interior. In such a context, the beauty of a tree or plant is irrelevant; only the nature of the root matters, the hidden part: "Car ne dissimulans point noz fruys, connoisçons facilement notre racine. Mais vous qui ne les ausez mettre dehors, et qui faites tant de beaus oeuvres apparens à grand péne connoiscez vous cette racine d'orgueil qui croit souz si belle couverture" (XXXIV, 219).[4] Man may choose to till the soil, but he cannot be assured of the quality of the product; the interior beauty answers to God's will, not man's. Although toward the beginning of the *Heptameron* man is advised to love woman as an intermediary to the love of God in order to gain an interior beauty derived only from God, in accordance with the Platonic or courtly-love doctrine, the same metaphor family of planting and harvesting in one of the last novellas centers on the woman either as subjected to the will of God or as a helpmate to man, depending on the debaters' viewpoint:

> Ne voyez vous pas bien, dit Longarine, que la terre non cultivée, quand elle porte beaucoup d'herbes et arbres, combien qu'ilz soient inutiles donne espérance qu'elle apportera bon fruyt, quand elle sera défrichée et amandée. Aussi le cueur de l'homme qui n'a sentiment d'amour aus choses visibles, ne viendra jamais à l'amour de Dieu par la semence de sa parole. Car la terre de son cueur est stérile, froide et damnée. [XIX, 134].
>
> Car l'un [man] et l'autre [woman] par son courir et son vouloir ne fait que planter et Dieu donne accroissement [says Oysille]. Si vous avez bien veue l'Ecriture, dit Saffredan, saint Paul dit qu'Appollo a planté et qu'il a arrosé [I Cor. 3:6]. Mais il ne parle point que les femmes ayent mises les mains à l'ouvrage de Dieu. Vous voudriez suyvre, dit Parlamente, l'opinion des mauvais hommes, qui prénent un passage de l'Ecriture pour eus,

4. Cf. "Mais la racine de l'orgueil que le péché extérieur doit guérir croisçoit touiours dedans son cueur . . ." (XXX, 200). One exception to this usage is in regard to monks whose deeds are mostly negative, whereas man's can be falsely good: "Mais de ceus là [good monks] ne sont pas tant les rues pavées, que marchées de leurs contraires, et au fruyt connoit on le bon arbre" (XLIV, 259); this last quote may be inspired from Luke 6:44, but not necessarily so.

et laissent celuy qui leur est contraire. Si vous avez leu saint Paul jusques au bout, vous trouverez qu'il se recommande aus Dames, qui ont beaucoup labouré avec luy en l'Evangile. [Philippians 4:3; LXVII, 335]

The imagery of earth cultivation thus not only deals with hidden or distorted truth but can also be used to reveal an increasing stress on evangelism at the end of the *Heptameron*, as opposed to courtly or Platonic arguments toward the beginning.[5]

Nature plays only a minor role in the novellas. In this regard, Marguerite seems closer to Rabelais than to the Pléiade poets, even though she is herself a poetess as well.[6] As a rule, the beauty of nature remains deceptive, even in the worn out commonplaces; love "dura selon la coutume, comme la beauté des fleurs des chams" (XIV, 102). Only the image of the field or meadow pictures the truth, total or relative; yet on occasion an ironic strain eliminates the absoluteness. A nobleman whose love has been tested by a supposedly virtuous lady finds out the harsh truth when he discovers her with the stable boy in a "garenne . . . lieu tant beau et plaisant qu'il n'étoit possible de plus beau" (XX, 136). The milord of the fifty-seventh tale declares his love to his lady "dedans un pré" (301) and is rejected by her in the same place. In both instances the beauty of the meadow is destroyed by the brutal facts that issue from it. Therefore, the beauty of the meadow still acts as a truthful but deceptive veil.

In the same vein, the meadow that pervades all of the *Heptameron* is the one where the narrators spend their days

5. A table of biblical quotations in the critical edition we use (p. 335) indicates indeed an increasing number of allusions to the New Testament beginning with the fourth and fifth days.

6. In one pastoral poem, "L'Histoire des Satyres et nymphes de Dyane," nature has a frozen decorative role, but not at all authentically functional; cf. *Les Marguerites de la Marguerite des princesses*, ed. F. Frank, III (Paris, 1873), pp. 167–200.

telling stories. It figures as a source of both entertainment and delusion for them and for the reader, because while the novellas constitute a pastime, they reveal a varied and pessimistic view of the human condition that contrasts with the beauty of the surroundings (see chapter 6). Following the model of the *Decameron* and other framework tales, the initial description occurs in the Prologue: "ce beau pré, le long de la rivière du Gave, où les arbres sont si feuilluz que le soleil n'y sçauroit percer l'ombre, n'y échaufer la frécheur" (18). Then it is referred to as the "siége naturel de l'herbe verde" (80), and almost at the very end as the "chambre des contes sur le bureau de l'herbe verde" (LXXI, 357). If the mistrust and the scarcity of nature reflect the falsity of the world of appearances, they do not contradict in any way Marguerite's naturalism in the sense that she advocates measure and reason.[7]

Marguerite ardently believes in naturalness and honesty toward oneself; therefore she presents situations and actions dominated by self-interest and hypocrisy to stress the opposite. In this belief, she foreshadows La Rochefoucauld; she even coins maxims that he could have written: "Et ne pensez pas que ceus qui poursuyvent les Dames prénent tant de péne pour l'amour d'elles. Car c'est seulement pour l'amour d'eus et de leur plaisir" (XIV, 103); "il ne faut point donner tant de louenge à une seule vertu, qu'il la faille servir de manteau à couvrir un si grand vice" (XXXVI, 228–29). An identical state of flux marks both authors in regard to the relativity of joy and sorrow: "Vous sçavez, mes Dames, ainsi qu'-extréme joye est occupée par pleurs, ainsi extréme ennuy prend fin par quelque joye" (XV, 105; cf. the forty-ninth

7. Yves Delègue in his article on the prologues of the *Decameron* and the *Heptameron*, sees Marguerite's short description of the field in her prologue as an indication of her anti-Boccaccio attitude (p. 34), a dubious assertion. Marguerite and Boccaccio seek the same ends, sometimes through different means.

maxim: "On n'est jamais si heureux ni si malheureux qu'on s'imagine").[8] On one level, the confrontation with La Rochefoucauld indicates a common view of society, and on another, it imparts to Marguerite the characteristics of a *moraliste* who observes much more than she criticizes.

The protagonists in the novellas move about in a world of screens that shield their true thoughts and intentions from others. These shields can be composed of other individuals, objects, or feigned physiological conditions. In the tenth story, Amadour marries so that he can remain near Floride; then he feigns love for another woman, Poline, to gain Floride's affection. Friendships are formed between two men so that one may get access to the other's lady (XIV). A woman sends a young maiden to bed with her lover to test the nature of his sentiments; her ruse borders on the diabolical (XVIII). A prince uses a friend's schemes to attempt the conquest of a young woman of lower social status, although he himself remains steadfast toward the ultimate goal but doubts the devious means (XLII). Earlier in the same forty-second novella, the nature of the prince's real intentions became correlated with a mud puddle into which he purposely falls to attract the girl's attention and sympathy: "Et apres avoir fait maintes courses et sans qu'elle pouvoit bien voir, se laissa tomber de son cheval dedans une grande fange, si molement, qu'il ne se feit point mal, combien qu'il se plaindit assez" (247). The mud is both the essential screen of the story and the metaphor that summarizes it. For screen or scheme, Marguerite herself prefers the word *invention* which in this context denotes false or hypocritical action; it occurs in a novella

8. Among others, two more maxims à la Rochefoucauld are worth quoting: "Il n'y a nulle de nous, dit Parlamente, qui ne confesse que tous les péchez extérieurs ne soient les fruys de l'infidélité intérieure, laquelle plus est couverte de vertus et de miracles, plus est dangereuse à arracher" (XXXIV, 219); "Et voyans les Dames n'avoir en leur cueur cette vertu de vraye amour, et que ce nom d'hypocrisie étoit tant odieux entre les hommes, luy donnèrent le surnom d'honneur" (XLII, 252).

where a prior, endeavoring to seduce a nun, has the mother superior replaced, frames the nun into dishonorable deeds, and hires a young monk to seduce her and discredit her reputation (cf. XXI). In the gradation of screens, this type fuses with malice; most, however, do not exhibit such acrimonious perseverance.

Reading a book provides an opportunity for close proximity between two individuals as well as a cover for signs of affection, well-intentioned or not. One of the literary archetypes of this sort of scene takes place in the *Divine Comedy*, the famous episode of Paolo and Francesca (*Inferno*, canto 5), but Marguerite also has behind her the whole tradition of courtly love. As a matter of fact the book as a screen inserts itself clearly in the courtly tradition toward the beginning of the *Heptameron*, and toward the end it could almost be taken as a pastiche of that tradition; in all cases, however, feigning to read the book is somehow related to wanting to see the other party, literally or figuratively. A lover "feit semblant de prendre grand plaisir à lire un livre des chevaliers de la Table Ronde qui étoit en la chambre du Prince. Et quand chacun s'en aloit diner, prioit un valet de chambre le vouloir laisser parachever de lire, et l'enfermer dedans la chambre, et qu'il le garderoit bien" (XXI, 144).[9] In the suggested pastiche, the book appears as a pastime which in turn leads to another pastime, the search for the pleasures of love, all within the deceptive framework of seeing and looking. Reading a book becomes a screen because of the irony underlying the actions:

> et souvent que son mary et elle [wife] étoient couchez, prenoit chacun d'eus quelque livre de passetems pour lire en son lyt. Et leur chambriéres tenoient la chandelle:

9. See also novella XV: "Or un soir apres souper qu'il faisoit bien obscur, se déroba ladite Dame, sans appeler nulle compagnie, entra en la chambre des Dames, où étoit celuy qu'elle aymoit mieus que soymesme, près duquel elle s'asseit pour deviser, appuyée sur une table, findant lire en un livre" (107).

c'est à sçavoir la june au seigneur, et l'autre à la Damoyselle. Ce gentilhomme voyant sa chambriére plus june
et plus belle que sa femme, prenoit si grand plaisir à la
regarder, qu'il interrompoit sa lecture pour l'entretenir.
Ce que sa femme voyoit tresbien, et trouvoit bon que
ses serviteurs et servantes feissent passer le tems à son
mary, pensant qu'il n'eut amytié à autre qu'à elle. [LIV,
292]

Feigned sickness offers a rather foolproof screen, which
has again the purpose of concealing the protagonist's real
sentiments or thoughts. A mild form is the feigned migraine
headache, or a paleness due to fasting, as Rolandine, for example, gives the impression of experiencing while she tries
to arrange meetings with her lover (XXI, 141, 142). Marguerite does not exaggerate or falsify; she simply chooses a
characteristic of female psychology, peculiar to no single
stratum of society, that supports her own viewpoint. Even
a well-meaning husband, calling his wife's ingenuity to his
aid, is perfectly correct in adopting this sort of scheme; as
a matter of fact it is a way of life:

j'ai toujours oÿ dire que le sage a communément une
maladie ou un voyage en sa manche pour s'en ayder à
nécessité. Parquoy j'ai delibéré de findre quatre ou cinq
jours devant, ettre bien for malade, à quoy votre contenance me pourra bien servir. Voylà dit sa femme, une
bonne et sainte hypocrisie à quoy je ne faudrai vous
servir de la plus triste mine dont je me pourrai aviser.
[LXIII, 324]

Even if this situation smacks a bit of the scene between the
draper and his wife in the *Farce de Maître Pathelin*, the screen
will serve a good end; the husband's feint will save the king's
honor and four young ladies from the sovereign's lust. In

most cases, however, women pretend to be ill in order to deceive their husbands and leave them in favor of other men (cf. LX, 311, and LXI, 317).

As the husband explains in the above quotation, journeys constitute a major screen. Usually, in a positive context, a trip has an educational purpose; it will provide the traveler with experiences that will shape his judgment and make him aware of the variety of cultures and opinions while at the same time it tests his intellect and moral fortitude. Instead Marguerite stresses travel as a means of tricking or deceiving someone else; wives take advantage of their husbands' absence on an inspection of their lands.[10] The void then created by journeys comes forth. Partners can act freely while the husband or wife is away, often not of his own volition but obliged by the plotters. In other cases a trip becomes a subterfuge which has little to do with the avowed aim. In a novella toward the beginning, a captain, following a courtly tradition, starts out on a pilgrimage to Jerusalem. The honest purpose of such a journey should be the discovery of self and God; instead it is a mere sham to hide his sentiments momentarily from the lady he loves (cf. XIII). More explicitly, the journey as self-discovery has the very opposite meaning in the sixty-first and sixty-second novellas, where it is transformed into self-destruction. Finally, the subterfuge of the journey lets a protagonist leave his home for a long trip but return the next day to be with his sweetheart (cf. XLIX). The spiritual journey of life is briefly alluded to in the Prologue (p. 15), but its distorted counterpart in the novellas becomes the word *chemin*, the falsified road to love of God and man.[11]

What marks the world of appearances and screens is the lack of freedom which man experiences because a general

10. Cf. novellas III, 29; XXXI, 205; XXXII, 210; XXXV, 221; XLII, 250; XLIX, 272.
11. Cf. novellas XIX, 132; XXII, 161; XXIII, 163.

mistrust and a lack of reason limit or warp his actions. The obvious metaphor to describe this condition is that of the prison. We are prisoners of what we say because it fixes us in the eyes of others and because the variability of words deforms the truth. We are prisoners of what others say of us since their opinions, be they real or false, freeze our personality in their eyes and in the eyes of others. From the darkness of these prisons man seeks to emerge into the light of truth, unattainable with human means, but reachable through God. Holding to the prison metaphor, Marguerite summed up her thought in a rather prolix poem of more than five thousand verses, *Les Prisons*, divided into three books.[12] The first book deals with the vanity of love on earth, the second with the vanity of ambition and worldly life, and the third advocates a fusion of meaningful learning, accompanied by experience, and faith in order to escape from the prisons of life. The novellas of the *Heptameron* fit precisely the formula set forth in this third book. And if man in these tales falls a good deal short of perfection, Marguerite provides the answer in a very Pascalian vein by opposing *Rien* (man) to *Tout* (God) toward the end of her poem: "Car ce grand Tout fait de Rien son chef d'œuvre" (p. 296). Marguerite stresses how relative is the potentiality of man within his extensive means and limits, because if he is pitted against an absolute, he fails.

In the *Heptameron*, the metaphor of the prison as such occurs in a minor key; its correlative of tying and breaking bonds and chains is somewhat more frequent. Perhaps an attempt to avoid adopting a much-abused commonplace would explain this scarcity. One of the narrators, Nomerfide, speaks of the elimination of the traditional "prison du corps" when there is love of God; and if "la prison n'est jamais étroite où la pensée se peut promener à son ayse" (XL, 239),

12. *Les Dernières poésies de Marguerite de Navarre*, ed. A. Lefranc (Paris, 1896), pp. 121–297.

the assumption remains that such freedom exists in a man only when he has seen the light of God. Therefore, given man's opposite propensity, freedom is rather restricted—indeed, distorted. When Marguerite decides to develop more fully the image of the prison, she does so in an ironic vein as if to poke fun at the original concept. In the forty-ninth tale, the irony emerges quite clearly through the repetition of the image, at least eight times, and through its inverted meaning; here the prison is actually a source of intense pleasure—as well as deception. A lady extremely free with her favors receives her suitors in her boudoir: "Et apres eus veindrent deus ou troys autres qui eurent par à la douce prison" (272). A further paradox underlines the author's laconic smile when the successful suitors "se ventent de leur prison" (275). Upon discovering the vacuous nature of their conquest, they decide to confront the libidinous lady, each wearing a chain around his neck (274). Their apparent bondage marks their new-found liberty from a seemingly possessive lady; the willful discrepancy between fact and action, intent and evidence, continues.

Marguerite attaches particular importance to the concept of bonds or ties, which she expresses with the word *lien* or its derivatives, and to the inevitable counterpart, *rompre.* These words are applied to love relations, believed to be perfect, and to marriage. Under these latter circumstances, being tied, restricted in movement, constitutes an ideal condition that is the object of desire. But the very opposite looms large in the stories, since perfect love fails and marriage remains precarious. Oysille is most accurate so far as theory goes and remains very consistent in her belief until the end: "Et plus l'amour est honneste et vertueuse, et plus le lyen en est difficile à rompre" (LXX, 354), but Saffredan, the male narrator diametrically opposed to her who observes closely instead of blandly theorizing, puts marriage in the penultimate story into a relativistic light: "Car l'on sçait que le lyen de maryage ne peut durer, si non autant que la vie, et puis apres on est délyé" (LXXI, 359). One rather short story is based on an effort not to "rompre l'amytié," an expression repeated four times within little more than two pages; then the discussion echoes with "rompre les doigz" (XLVII, 269), which connotes an involvement in a useless activity and thus warns us to choose relationships carefully. Again Marguerite shows an affinity for seizing upon a word and molding it to her needs into an unusual acceptation.[13] Ultimately *lien* and *rompre* become almost interchangeable; behind one looms the other. If the protagonists in the novellas may be deceived, Marguerite and the reader are not.

The relation between a story itself and the discussion that follows it becomes an integral part of the game of concealing and unveiling; in a technique of point and counterpoint key words or images occurring in the tale are picked up by the narrators and given a different and revealing meaning for the interpretation of the novella. In this way the narrators give their reading of the story to us. The technique already became quite evident in the analysis of such images as fire and food, or such expressions as *contentement*; without hesitation the narrators strip the mask off the word. In the seventeenth novella the key words are *vray* and *nayve*; in the narrators' mouths they become *hardi* and *deliberé*, to praise the king's virtue (121). A monk's *visites* to his lady parishioner come into clearer focus when the narrators call them *fréquentations* of a most dubious nature and *hantises* (XXII, 162).

On a syntactical level, the point-and-counterpoint tech-

13. Cf. "Car si Amour et bonne volonté fondée sur la crainte de Dieu, est le vray et seur lyen de maryage, elle étoit si bien lyée que fer, foeu ne eaue, ne pouvoient rompre son lyen, sinon la mort" (XXI, 51). For further examples, among others, see novellas XXII, 168; XXIII, 174; XXXV, 224; LX, 313; LXIII, 324; LXIV, 329. We do not insist on the frequent thematic usage of *lien, alliance,* one of its natural derivatives, and on clandestine marriages because E. Telle in his book has so aptly treated it, especially in relation to the literature of the time (see pp. 299–354). What interests us here is its double-faced value, heretofore unnoticed.

nique turns up when a part of speech through an extremely frequent usage becomes the leitmotif of a tale. In the eighteenth novella, both in the story itself and in the discussion, the word *si* occurs incessantly meaning either "if" or "so," and "so much." The juxtaposition of the two meanings unveils the narrator's (Hircan's) scorn and mockery toward the behavior of the two protagonists: the woman's sadism and the man's love and fidelity under these circumstances. In fact, Hircan stands aside smirking while the other narrators attempt to decide which of the two may be at fault; the woman for her extreme cruelty or the man for foolishly giving in to her demands. The "if," as a result, represents her cruel requests (e.g., that he should sleep with her maid without touching her) and the "so much" the heavy suffering he endures, but which he deserves as well according to some of the commentators. The two false faces of *si* dissolve before the two real faces of measure and wisdom.

There is a variant of the point-and-counterpoint motif that could be called the technique of metaphorical symmetry. The narrator-commentators seize upon a central theme or image of the story and develop it in the course of their discussion, but under a sharper or different light. In a novella which plays upon the rich / poor theme, both in material possessions and in love, a significant simile in the discussion pulls the veil from the shallowness of materialism and earthly love: "Mais quand elle [âme, "soul"] les a cerchées et expérimentées, n'y trouvant point celuy qu'elle ayme, elle passe outre, ainsi que l'enfant selon sa petitesse ayme les poupines, et autres petites choses que son œil peut voir les plus belles, et estime richesse d'assembler de petites pierres, mais croisçant ayme les poupines vives, et amasse les biens nécessaires pour la vie humaine" (XIX, 134).

If the image of fire occupies a fundamental role in a story, the commentators do not fail to bring it back in the appraisal of the tale. Here it is a monk's fire of concupiscence whose destructive power remains literal as well, since it breaks down the harmony of a household: "Et ainsi que le fœu peu à peu s'allume tellement qu'il vient à embraser toute la maison, ce pauvre frater commença à bruler par telle concupiescence" (XXIII, 164). The commentators turn the image against the monks first, and afterwards against themselves: "On les devroit bruler tout vifz [says Oysille]. Vous feriez bien mieus de les honorer, que de les bruler, dit Saffredan, et de les flater, que de les injurier. Car ce sont ceus qui ont puissance de bruler et deshonorer les autres" (168). Each of the contrasting opinions is as frightful as the other, although they represent extreme viewpoints—moderated in the latter case by Saffredan's transparent smirk. If any ambivalence exists thematically, none prevails on the aesthetic level; the commentators use the dominant image of the tale to unmask their own varied attitudes toward monks. In this technique of metaphor symmetry, the image in the tale has a creative value because it reflects inventiveness, whereas in the discussion it is a mere vehicle for the expression of a thematic or moral viewpoint.

Even when the most sincere intentions prevail, the dilemma between speaking and concealing the truth persists. Eyes and words form the usual language of love, but no one trusts it. Well-meaning individuals refrain from using it because they fear to expose their inner selves; and when they do pour out their sentiments, they are indeed deceived and victims of their own words. Dishonest persons either adopt it as a screen or refuse it altogether, aware of its inefficacy; Yambique, one of the more perfidious female protagonists of the *Heptameron*, does not want to reveal her unnatural passion for a man, "ne se voulant soulager commes les autres qui ayment par le regard et la parole" (XLIII, 254). Furthermore any satisfaction in hearing the long-awaited words of love does not last because of the ensuing disappointment (cf. L, 277). As a result, one never knows what to believe and what not to believe "pour ce que le vray et le faus n'ont qu'un mesme langage" (LVIII, 306). This uncertainty of language creates an abyss between what words say and what they mean.

Ordinary language fails, for it leads to disaster. Suffice it to mention one exemplary instance, the seventieth novella. Here a love is destroyed because a young man has spoken the name of his beloved; the real culprit is *langue,* meaning both tongue and language: "O ma langue punye sois tu . . . je vous embrasse morte, malcontente de moy, de mon cueur et de ma langue. . . . Hélas, et qui est cause de cecy? . . . Votre langue et la miéne" (352, 353). Faced with the inadequacy of everyday language, some writers attempt to formulate a new one of their own. In fact, in the sixteenth century, neologisms based on classical languages and dialects provided a vital force for a language otherwise constantly in flux. French novella writers of the period especially dipped deep into dialects to rejuvenate the linguistic material at their disposal.

Only one such extensive passage of dialectal usage exists in the *Heptameron,* and it poses a knotty problem because it does not occur in all editions. In seeking to portray a saddlemaker who worships Bacchus, Marguerite laments the insufficiency of ordinary language and even of dialect, which she will nevertheless proceed to use; "Mais pour bien le représenter, faudroit parler gras comme luy, et encores seroit ce plus qui pourroit prendre <pindre> son visage et sa contenance" (LXXI, 358).[14] There is, of course a sprinkling of

14. The rather lengthy dialectal dialogue spoken by the saddlemaker occurs in the edition we use, the one that follows de Thou, whereas the previous editors followed Gruget (cf. the Leroux de Lincy edition and the one by M. François in the Classiques Garnier). Yves Le Hir makes a very good case for the authenticity of the version of the tale with the dialect and for his choice of the de Thou MS (cf. p. XI), a conviction we also share. However, it will never be possible to establish categorically, with the presently existing MSS, if Gruget eliminated the dialect to conform with the image of a refined queen, or if de Thou added it to give some color to the novella. At any rate, a sample of the dialogue may still be useful to the reader interested in capturing

neologisms and dialectal words in the novellas, but certainly not in any such amount as to constitute a new mode of expression. Some would maintain that Marguerite did not have sufficient creative verve to formulate a new language, but from her own viewpoint, she would probably regard such means of expression as just another artifice that she preferred not to use, and most certainly not for social or prudish reasons. Instead she chose a simple language which made its limits all the more evident, while still containing numerous possibilities for metaphor.

The obvious answer to the limits of a language is silence. But Marguerite, although extremely open-minded, is not a *révoltée*; she does not seek to overturn; she simply depicts as she sees and understands with the existing means, especially from the formal point of view. Thematically, however, she does advocate silence because perfect or ideal love can go on only when the two individuals involved are discreet about their relationship. This prerequisite condition she calls a good dissimulation. Given the nature of man, though, he leans more often toward a bad dissimulation, one that screens unvirtuous intentions. The tragedy lies in the fact that the difference between the two is frequently indiscernible, and the enemy of both is *bruit,* which may uncover or falsify true thoughts and intentions. In her unflagging effort to expose the prevalent falseness of society, Marguerite formulates a cluster of words that through their high frequency testify to

---

this special flavor gained by its use: "M'amye, ze me meuilz, et suy pis que tliépassé de voil ainsi moulir ta maiteliesse, ze ne zai que faille, ne que dille, si non que ze me liecommande à toy, et te plie de plendle le soin de ma maison et de mes enfans. Tien lies cliez que zay à mon coté, et donne odle au ménaze. Cal ze n'y sauloi plus entendle. [Je me meur et suy pire que le trépassé, de voir ainsi mourir ta maitresse. Je ne sçai que faire ne que dire, si non je me recommande à toy et te prie de prendre le soin de ma maison et de mes enfans. Tien les clez que j'ai à mon coté et donne ordre au ménage. Car je n'y sçauroye plus entendre.]" (358). The dialect, it should be added, makes up a half of the very tale, itself only about a page long.

the predominance of the theme: *bruit-dissimulation-couver-ture-manteau* or *robe*.

Bruit means reputation, the opinion we have of others or the judgment others make of us. As Sartre was to point out so pungently four centuries later in his *Huis Clos,* one cannot escape from the vise his fellow men have created about him. The meshwork of opinions and judgments, varied and often contradictory, make a knowledge of the individual all the more elusive. The individual himself lives under the fear of being misunderstood—or discovered—or he never quite lives up to an apparent good reputation. Admiral Bonnivet, one of the better-known personages of the *Heptameron* who fig- ures as a protagonist in two novellas (IV and XIV) is ad- mired "pour le bruyt que chacun luy donnoit d'ettre l'un des plus adroitz et hardys aus armes qui fut point de son tems" (XIV, 99). Transferred to his aggressiveness in amo- rous adventures, this *bruyt* takes on a totally different mean- ing. Yambique, that notorious female in the novellas, "avoit le bruyt d'ettre ennemye mortelle de toute amour" (XLIII, 254); this reputation, a false one, was acquired by concealing very ingeniously her true nature. Much less ambivalence emerges when *bruyt* means rumor: "ceus qui avoient semé ce bruyt avoient méchamment menty" (XLVII, 267). Mar- guerite purposely remains near the literal meaning of *bruyt,* which in this particular case acquires a muted and dubious reverberation worse than sin.[15] If she wants to convey a no- tion of uncovered news, she foregoes *bruyt* and replaces it with a periphrasis: "faire sonner le tabouring de ce qu'elles avoient accordé" (VIII, 49).

Bruyt then is just a projection of the fact or substance, and only blurred echoes reach us. Marguerite thereby gives further sustenance to her depiction of a world of appearances

15. "Car le scandale [i.e. bruyt] est souvent pire que le péché [truth]" (XXV, 180).

where man lives in an environment of hearsay that sheds its metaphoric mask at times and becomes an implacable substitute for fortune or God: "Mais à la fin la Renommée . . . ne peut rien celer" (LX, 312).[16] The notion of true or false does not depend on the intrinsic validity of a man's actions interpreted by himself, but on how others interpret them. Again four centuries later, Pirandello made these tenets a basis of his theater, as in *Sei personaggi in cerca d'autore* or in *Enrico IV*.

One of the main objectives in life is to avoid "making noise," that is, having rumors spread or being discovered. Or again, one ought to be extremely careful about speaking. Silence may be golden in matters of love, but, according to Marguerite (cf. VIII, 49; IX, 51), it stands as an ideal of courtly love difficult to attain. In fact, when silence does succeed, it is when it conceals a sin or abuses a religious doctrine (XLI, 245). Otherwise the fear of making noise governs actions and thoughts. Some characters take precautions that soon leave the plane of trivial daily activity and acquire a metaphoric significance; an individual takes his shoes off going to or leaving a lover's abode. The famous admiral Bonnivet has some felt slippers specially made to go see his lady "de peur de faire bruyt" (XIV, 100). If any doubt ever existed concerning the metaphoric value of this act, much later in the *Heptameron* Marguerite crystallizes its figurative meaning: "Toutesfois où elle [virtue] defaudroit, ne luy sembloit hors de raison s'ayder de l'hypocrisie, comme nous faisons de pantoufles, pour faire oublyer notre petitesse" (LIII, 286).[17]

On a literal level, not making noise means to conceal. In

16. The various usages of *bruyt* as outlined above can be ascertained in numerous novellas; see for example XIII, 89; XIV, 101; XV, 111; XXI, 141, 151–52; XXII, 154; XXV, 177; XXVI, 188; 8; XXVII, 192; XXXIII, 213; XLI, 243; XLII, 250; XLVI, 264; LI, 281.

17. For instances of characters who take off shoes in similar circumstances, see XV, 108; XVIII, 124; LIX, 308.

fact, the universe of the *Heptameron* is one of constant dissimulation due to mistrust. One form or another of *dissimuler* or *couvrir* permeates most novellas; therefore, the ultimate goal is an attempt to arrive at the facts or to veil another person's intentions. In keeping with her dichotomous outlook, Marguerite will even adopt a good dissimulation to bare someone's real or dishonest intentions: "Et elle connoisçant la méchante volonté du sécretaire, ayma mieus par une dissimulation déclarer son vice, que par un soudin refus le couvrir, et feit semblant de trouver bons ses propos" (XXVII, 192). If this preponderance of dissimulation reflects a view of a world riddled with falseness and deception, the stories themselves and the accompanying discussions become the agents that expose the human comedy and try to unravel the truth behind a veil, the only element visible to man's eye.

This veil assumes a further visual quality when the word *color* expresses it metaphorically: "je la [truth] dirai si purement, qu'il n'y aura nulle couleur pour la déguiser" (LXIII, 324). In keeping with her view of a topsy-turvy world, Marguerite does not consider color a beautiful or beautifying substance; instead she pictures it as a matter that defiles a pure white surface, the truth. This attitude explains the rather high frequency of the expression "sous couleur de" in the novellas: "Car j'en ai assez veu, qui souz couleur de parler de Dieu, commençoient une amytié dont à la fin se vouloient retirer, et ne pouvoient, pour ce que l'honnette couverture les tenoit en sujétion," says Parlamente (XXV, 224).[18] Marguerite's affinity for this expression constitutes one more indication of the world of appearances that she observes about her. It does not mean that she thinks beauty does not exist on earth—on the contrary, it is omnipresent—but man usurps it and misuses it to his own selfish and vitiated ends.

18. Cf. XXI, 144; XXIII, 167; XXV, 176; XXXII, 215; XLV, 262; XLVI, 265; LVIII, 304.

The same kind of abuse holds for the concept of the dance. As a rule the dance should provide pleasure; during the Renaissance it also stands for freedom of movement and beauty of the body. Instead, in the *Heptameron*, dance figures as a screen or deception, a meeting place for lovers or an activity to veil one's real preoccupations.[19] After a husband learns of his wife's infidelity, he forces her and her lover to continue going to dances and parties in order to avoid arousing the suspicion of others until he decides to chase away the lover in the middle of a dance, with a curt and ominous "va-t-en" (XXXVI, 226). The duchess, in the seventieth tale, goes dancing after revealing in public the Dame du Verger's secret love; here the *divertissement* reflects a state of mind of vengeful satisfaction but feigned serenity (354). A bridegroom enjoys dancing so much that a monk profits from the opportunity to take his place in bed with the bride on the wedding night; the bridegroom's excess becomes a screen for the monk (XLVIII, 270). It would be hazardous to conclude, however, that Marguerite takes a stand against a worldly life and dancing; she simply exposes how man does not content himself with dancing as a wholesome enjoyment, but again perverts it to satisfy vicious aims.

In a more concrete vein, characters cover up their imperfections, both literally and figuratively, with dresses, coats, and capes: "leurs robes sont si longues, et si bien tissues de dissimulation, que l'on ne peut connoitre ce qui est de souz" (XXVI, 191). Since their chief concern is to conceal their inner self, they cover fundamental vice with apparent virtue, in very much the way that La Rochefoucauld observes in the people about him. Yambique was doubly accused "d'avoir couvert sa malice du manteau d'honneur et de gloire, et se faire devant Dieu et les hommes autre qu'elle n'étoit. Mais luy qui ne donne point sa gloire à autry, en découvrant ce

19. For examples of this kind of meeting place, see XXV, 177; XXVI, 181; XXVIII, 194.

manteau, luy en a donné double infamie" (XLIII, 257).[20] One goes through life in constant fear of being exposed, of being found naked; we expect it to happen to others, but not to us: "Jamais femme ne fut plus étonnée que moy, quand je me trouvai toute nue" (LXII, 322). Only those who have received God's grace have nothing to hide and remain in a constant pure nakedness, but in their minimal number, they do not of course constitute the norm. In an earlier instance, Hircan had suggested a more plausible and yet quite improbable means for achieving a state of purity and good conscience: man should confess his frailness.[21] But obviously most do not. However, Marguerite herself has the last word in this matter, for the act of writing the novellas presents man in his utmost unpleasant bareness. Therefore she could have just as readily given to her collection of short stories the Pirandellian title of *Naked Masks*.

As a matter of fact, some characters in the *Heptameron* literally wear masks or costumes in order to veil their real intent or condition. As a rule, the mask conceals the lasciviousness or hedonism of an individual; Marguerite has in mind here the carnival tradition. In the two novellas that feature him, Admiral Bonnivet wears a mask as he pursues his female prey (XIV, 99, 101; XVI, 115). The depraved Yambique never allows her lover to see her face (XLIII, 254). A husband hides his face and borrows the family confessor's habit to discover his wife's real love (XXXV, 221–22);[22] a literal disguise bares a figurative mask. Concealing one's face, then, with a mask or any other object means to be devoured by carnal appetites; these protagonists do not want to expose

20. For a few more of the very frequent instances of the *couverture* theme with a clothing metaphor, see XXX, 200; XXXV, 224; XLI, 244, 245; LIII, 289, 290; LVI, 298; LVIII, 305.
21. "Mais quand à la chasteté de cueur, je croi qu'elle et moy sommes enfans d'Adam et Eve. Parquoy en bien nous mirant, n'aurons besoin couvrir notre nudité de feuilles, mais plus tot confesser notre fragilité" (XXVI, 191).
22. Cf. also XXXI, 206; LVI, 298.

their loss of reason and measure. The naked face would become a metaphor of honesty. However, disguise as a means of arriving at the truth occurs only in a minor key.

Since man covers up his weaknesses and base appetites, others attempt to *see* them. Consequently the notion of seeing occupies an important place in the novellas. Within the short stories, the characters want to see, to find out the truth, because it affects their happiness and daily living. And Marguerite narrates the tales so that we the readers can see, can observe and judge, the behavior of others, and therefore of ourselves. On another level the idea of sight has a topology of its own; the eye is the initiator of love between man and woman and between man and God. At the same time, God himself is the omnipresent eye that sees and judges all. Clear sight, then, has a close correlation with awareness, truth, and beauty, and it follows that a metaphorical interplay of light and darkness can reverse or juggle with this concept.

In the first half of the *Heptameron*, the theme of seeing occurs in novellas that follow a medieval tradition. It is expressed by means of rather self-evident metaphors that recall earlier tales or fabliaux. In order to allow her lover to escape, a wife shields with her hand the remaining eye of her one-eyed husband, who then cannot see, but knows because of the *bruyt* (VI). Physical sight is never foolproof; this is one point of the story. Yet hearing contains a marked ambivalence; a *bruyt* may be false or not. Marguerite stresses the paradox of seeing while blind. *Voir* constitutes the thematic basis of the thirty-second novella, where some form of the word occurs at least fifteen times. A woman is forced by her husband to drink from her lover's cranium, in which the eye sockets have been filled with silver. The lover never saw; she now sees, she expiates her sin. Finally the husband himself sees, realizes, that the cruel punishment has lasted long enough, and they begin a new life together to continue the lineage. At the end the visual theme takes on a pictorial di-

mension when the husband, as a further sign of reconciliation, has her portrait painted in order to immortalize her
newly acquired beauty, a counterpart to what Marguerite
herself does through the creation of the story.

Marguerite counterbalances the seeing of the characters in
the novellas with that of the audience in the stories, the com-
mentator-narrators, and outside the stories, us the readers.
In the forty-second novella, a prince casting his eye on a
seemingly ordinary servant girl provides the spark for the
action. An interplay between seeing, looking, and hiding follows; through various subterfuges the prince seeks out the
girl, but she avoids him. Although attracted to him, the girl
does not wish to entertain the prince's advances because she
suspects dishonorable intentions: "Je ne suis point si sote,
Monseigneur, ne si aveuglée, que je ne voie bien la beauté
et ne connoisce les graces que Dieu a mises en vous" (248).
She thinks she sees through him. But does she? Here lies the
whole point of the story, as the commentators point out.
Each of them has a different opinion on the matter; some
even feel that she missed the chance of a lifetime and sacri-
ficed herself to a secret love for him.[23] In this earthly realm,
the impossibility or failure of seeing remains a dominant
certainty.

Even the self-deluding omniscient narrator of the novella
cannot perceive beyond his own field of vision. On numerous
occasions a tale is introduced by some form of *voir*. Again the
forty-second novella can serve as a case in point: "Je feroy tor
à la vertu que j'ai veue cachée sous un si pauvre manteau"
(245). However, for the most part the narrator addresses
himself directly to his audience, the other commentator-

23. "Toutesfois, dit Dagoucin, on dit que l'amour la plus secrette est la
plus louable. Ouy, dit Symontaut, aus yeus de ceus qui en pourroient mal
juger, mais claire et connue pour le moins aus deus personnes à qui elle
touche. Je l'enten ainsi, dit Dagoucin. Encores vaudroit elle mieus ignorée
d'un coté, qu'entendue d'un tiers. Et je croi que cette femme l'aymoit plus for,
d'autant qu'elle ne le déclaroit point" (253).

narrators, either at the outset or at the end of the story or both: "Mais vous verrez, mes Dames, que sa prudence ne son hypocrisie ne l'a pas garantie que son secret n'ait été révélé. . . . Par cecy, mes Dames, pouvez vous voir, comme celle qui avoit préféré la gloire du monde à sa conscience, a perdu l'une et l'autre" (XLIII, 254, 257). Marguerite repeatedly affirms that only one infallible Seer exists, God; yet she examines human sight and judgment, in spite of all their limitations and failures, because if a man refuses to accept the real Light in all its splendor, he must rely on his own means of achieving practical solutions, even if they are not the best.

One way characters in the *Heptameron* seek out earthly light is by looking out windows.[24] As a rule, windows are an extension of eyes and become at times the eyes of the mind. Windows allow an escape from oneself into an outside world. They afford new experiences; they make visible things not seen previously. Or again, they reveal life as a prison in a no-exit situation, with man unable to leave his immediate environment.[25] In one of her plays, *Trop, Prou, Peu, Moins,* Marguerite indicates one such meaning associated with pleasures:

> PEU. Nous sommes ja pleins de plaisirs,
> Et confessons qu'il n'est rien, qu'estre.
> TROP. Estre quoy?
> MOINS. A une fenestre,
> Regardant le beau temps venir,
> Vivant du joyeux souvenir
> De nos cornes tant amoureuses.
> [*Théâtre profane,* 190]

24. Yves Le Hir, our editor of the *Heptameron,* is the first to allude to the recurrence of the window metaphor, but he does not develop it (cf. pp. xxvii–xxix).

25. Brueghel's poignant "Two Monkeys" provides a striking pictorial example of this kind of interpretation.

The window is a point in time and space of illusory expectation, for happiness does not exist in the present but in a static and distant past or in an unattainable future. From this window, only deception greets the viewer.

In the novellas, the window stands for a means of communication, a catalyst for desire, an escape from a devious peril, an opening to a dubious and ugly fact. All these figurative circumstances relate closely to lust or disappointment in love. Only in one case does communication occur on an ordinary literal level, and at the very beginning; a maid upon finding her mistress dying from wounds inflicted by a sexual attacker, shouts out the window for help (II, 26). The window is a direct meeting place between two lovers (XXI, LXX) or an indirect one through letters read there (XIII, 90). One husband spies on his wife through a window (XV, 106), and another asks neighbors where the fire is, not realizing that the real fire is in the process of figuratively burning down his own house (XXVI, 187). A woman looking out to ascertain the weather sees her neighbor with another woman "faire le crucefyz sur la neige" (XLV, 262).[26] Elsewhere the window becomes the metaphor of tricks and lies; three women plot to expose a man's love which they have themselves contrived for him: "Et quand il aura passé les galeries et voudra monter le degré, je vous prye vous mettre à la fenettre, pour m'ayder toutes deux à cryer: Au larron" (LVIII, 304). Fearing death and not realizing that they are being confused with pigs, two monks escape through a window because the door is locked but are later caught (XXXIV, 217). In a subsequent story, owing to a premeditated move by his enemies, who wish to expose and catch him coming out of his mistress's quarters,

26. The action of this forty-fifth novella moves in a totally visual aesthetic realm. The protagonist is a tapestry-worker who knows how to "donner couleur à toute tapisserie" (262), to falsify and deceive. The core of the story appears as a sexual tableau; the tapestry-worker and his mate are seen not only "faire le crucefyz sur la neige" but then throwing snowballs at each other, a pre- and post-sexual play.

a nobleman is forced to flee through a window and leave his cape behind. Here the assailants quote a proverb which illuminates the metaphoric meaning: "Qui ne peut passer par la porte, saille par la fenettre" (LIII, 289). The sardonic undertone of the aphorism brings out the temporary relief gained by escaping through a window, the ephemeral nature of pleasures.

Finally the window provides the vista upon the object of one's desire. The coveted person, an innocent victim, is seen in the light, while the preying individual, remaining hidden in the dark behind the window, casts long and rapacious looks and savors his plan of attack: "regardant sur une terrace, [Yambique] vid promener celuy qu'elle aymoit tant et apres l'avoir regardé si longuement, que le jour qui se couchoit n'emportoit avec soy la veue" (XLIII, 254); "Quand le soir fut venu et que les danses comencèrent, le Cordelier par une fenettre regarda longtems la maryée" (LXVIII, 270). In essence then, Marguerite proposes that the window actually impairs the real view; she considers it just another screen, a subterfuge, the very antithesis of truth. Once again she has taken the usually accepted metaphoric associations of an object and reversed them to underline distorted wordly values; the window leads only to darkness. In this sense, she has kept the meaning of the window as a seeming escape from one dark prison into another, à la Pascal.

Since windows do not permit escape or provide solutions, the answer may lie in introspection. Mirrors can give the opportunity for this because by looking at ourselves in them, either through our own choice or through coercion, we see and learn something of ourselves. During the Renaissance, the mirror for the most part reflects faithfully the image projected on it, and beauty and goodness are synonymous. Whereas later in the sixteenth century and in the seventeenth century, the mirror, symbol of inconstancy and change, projects only an illusion based on a concept of a double-faced nature.[27] On the few occasions that Marguerite uses the image of the mirror it is indeed in this sense. The mirror will at first bear witness to a woman's beauty: "quand elle se verra grande et telle que son mirouer luy mons-trera . . ." (XV, 104), but eventually her actions will bring out an interior ugliness. Here, therefore, the mirror turns out to be a posteriori a deceitful object.

In a novella whose central image is a mirror (XXIV), a beautiful queen looks at herself and does not like what she sees. Marguerite thus destroys any apparent harmony be-tween object and person and completely undermines the usual function of the object. A nobleman finally reveals his long-standing love to his lady by means of shiny chest armor, used as a mirror, in which she should recognize herself as the person loved: "et feit faire un grand mirouër d'acier en façon de halecret, et le metant devant son esthommach, le couvrit tresbien d'un manteau de frise noire qui étoit tout brodé de cannetille [lace], et couvert d'autres enrichissements rares et singuliers" (169). Black, symbolizing "mélencolye" (cf. XV, 105), at once gives a clear notion of the tortured nature of this relation. But the uncovering of the mirror falls far short of its intended effect: "mais que vous ai je montré décendant de cheval? Rien, dit la Royne, si non un mirouër devant votre estomach" (170). Hence the mirror does not reveal the truth as planned. To the queen, the real truth will develop from a long testing period of the nobleman, who after several years will tire of his plight and abandon his effort, at which time the queen, realizing her mistake, is ready to accept him. But

27. "Loin d'être fidèle, le miroir baroque devient donc le symbole de l'inconstance, du changement. Et non seulement son image est synonyme d'illusion, elle l'est aussi de tromperie; c'est l'apparence d'un objet qu'elle nous donne, non son être véritable. La beauté de la femme ne nous garantit pas de sa bonté; au contraire, l'équivoque et la contradiction triomphent dans une nature conçue désormais comme essentiellement double." C. Rizza, "L'Image du miroir chez quelques poètes italiens et français de l'âge baroque," *Cahiers du Centre International de Synthèse du Baroque*, 3 (1969), 57.

she has waited too long. The darkness of the black coat and the false brightness of the image in the mirror fuse into one opaque light.

The dialectic of light / darkness and its correlate sight / blindness forms a most important metaphoric part of Marguerite's aesthetics. It opposes ideal love to lust, dissimulation to discovery, the earthly realm to the divine one, and human judgment to divine judgment, and it occurs as a very successful narrative technique. Evidently in this highly frequent and common body of metaphors, the courtly love, biblical, and Platonic traditions converge on Marguerite.[28] Its prominence could easily contribute to substantiating an evangelical or Platonic Marguerite. But such an evaluation may narrow her intentions, for ultimately she means to point out contradictions and relativism in man. Accordingly, either the line of demarcation between light and darkness soon becomes quite blurred, or each concept loses its usual acceptation and results in an intentional inversion.

Although the meaning of the concept of light / darkness may at first appear quite clear, eventually it is undermined in order to stress human fallibility and diversity of opinions and to oppose them to the one omniscient Light. In the case of love, the net result is a pastiche of a commonplace vocabulary: "Amour . . . les rendit tous deus si remplis de sa claire lumière" (XVIII, 122) and "alluma de la clairté dedans, qui faisoit que la beauté de cette fille pouvoit ettre veue clairement" (124). Since the sardonic Hircan narrates this tale, its spoofing of the abusive testing of love surfaces rapidly; here this woman, filled with light, demands that her "servant" in order to prove the sincerity of his sentiments sleep with her and then with another young woman, but without touching either one. Even if human sight momentarily has infallible judging powers, the commentators do not hesitate to chal-

28. For the Platonic tradition, see E. Garin, *Medioevo e Rinascimento. Studi e ricerche* (Bari, 1961).

lenge it; in one novella, it may well be Louise of Savoy who intercedes for a woman who has lived in sin with a monk: "Car le regard de ma Dame la Régente étoit de telle vertu, qu'il n'y avoit si femme de bien, qui ne craindit se trouver devant ses yeus indigne de sa veue" (LXI, 320). The pure light emanating from the regent queen contrasts with the behavior of the blinded woman who travels at night to see the canon. However, one of the commentators, Symontaut, doubts the efficacy of Louise's healing intervention; he claims that the woman left the eighty-year-old clergyman because of his age, and being only in her forties, she preferred returning to her husband. Nomerfide, another participant, declares that the woman did well to hide her sin and not confess it, since she is responsible only to God, who forgives all. Nomerfide thereby questions the role of the queen, to whom the woman confessed.

What compounds the tragic inversion of light and darkness is that even when an individual has the reasoning capacity to distinguish one from the other, he chooses not to do so. Because of their nature, women simply prefer dissimulation to honor and virtue although "elles connoissent la différence des ténèbres et de la lumière, et que leur vray honneur git à montrer la pudicité du cueur, qui ne doit vivre que d'amour et non point s'honorer du vice de dissimulation" (XLII, 253). Yet the abyss between facts and a desired perfection remains wider than ever. Marguerite simply ascertains this condition and hopes that man will take a few steps away from the twilight of life, even if temptation never leaves the scene: "Ce Dyable de mydy est le plus dangereus de tous. Car il se sçait si bien transfigurer en Ange de lumière" (XLVI, 265). The solution, implied here by Parlamente, lies in staying in a constant state of awareness and suspicion in order not to fall into danger. This condition may avoid beneficial or detrimental involvements, but at the same time it leaves the individual in a freedom-of-choice situation. Furthermore it points to the tension between the fixity of the light / darkness duality in the tale and its fragmentation by the varying participants' comments.

When this light / darkness dichotomy leaves the symbolic plane and reaches a level of total metaphoric integration with the narrative fabric, its meaning does not waiver, but is clearly delineated. In the fifty-fourth novella, the shadow / light concept dominates the action. A husband and wife who like to read in their separate beds align them in a straight line opposite each other so that they can see each other if they look out from behind the bed curtains, while their respective maids hold out a candle so that the couple can see the print and the opposite partner—if need be. But soon the stage is set in a manner that makes shadowy reflections more revealing than the light: "Le coté de la cheminée qui tournoit devant son lyt étoit d'une muraille blanche, où réverbéroit la clairté de la chandelle, et contre ladite muraille se voyoit fort bien le portrait du visage de son mary et celuy de sa chambrière; s'ilz s'éloignoient, s'ilz s'approchoient, ou s'ilz rioient, elle en avoit aussi bonne connoiscence que si elle les eut veuz" (292). At first the wife accepts the substitution of these shadowy reflections for light, indubitable facts; "mais quand elle vid que les umbres retournoient souvent à cette réunion, elle eut peur que la vérité fut couverte de souz. Par quoy elle se preind tout haut à rire, en sorte que les umbres eurent peur de son rys et se séparèrent" (293). And when the fellow asks his wife why she laughed, she answers: "Mon amy je suy si sote, que je ri de mon umbre . . . si est ce qu'il laissa cette face umbrageuse [the maid]" (293).

Laughter here means awareness and truth, and at the same time a certain permissiveness on the wife's part. The shadows stand for the husband's and maid's illicit activities and specifically in the maid's case for a usurpation of the wife's prerogatives. Yet the wife is not entirely blameless; the light she basks in certainly lacks purity. Her abstinence from sexual activity with her husband may find a happy substitute in reading, but he modifies his reading at the first opportunity. One of the commentators, Ennasuite, in fact points out this ambivalence when she states that, had it been her maid, she would have gotten out of her bed and put out the candle held by the maid on the maid's nose (293). In other words, the candle's light has no more value than the shadows it produces; it prevents husband and wife from engaging in an activity that would preserve their marriage. Although a crisp bitter laugh has momentarily solved the problem, nothing essential has been done to rectify the situation. Shadow or darkness brings human behavior into sharper focus than would a wavering light that encourages passivity and inaction. This paradox does not surprise, for on earth the two merge as they are cast against the omniscient Light.

Conscious of the metaphoric prevalence of darkness enveloping man's condition, Marguerite creates a cellular universe that allows no light into it. Characters seek out above all dressing-room closets, but attics and narrow winding staircases will serve as well as places to meet in or to wait for and reach the partner. In these enclosed locales, the protagonists abandon reason and moderation and usually give in to their base desires; when in the attic or the staircase, they are already prey to concupiscence. Marguerite likes to use the image of the door, or the trap door, as the object that separates reason from lustful passion.

If the Renaissance dressing room has the same function as the nineteenth-century boudoir, the connotation finds its basis in reality, for the *garderobe* did serve in the same way. Yet its frequency in the *Heptameron* attests to its symbolic meaning and to its value as an important "sign." In the very first novella, an ambush takes place in a *garderobe* (21). In the second one, a servant breaks down a door separating his room from that of the mistress of the house, in order to attack her (25). Hence the stage is set for the numerous successive occurrences of these two central metaphors.[29] Of course, there is room for variations in their usage, but without any significant change in their meaning; only the form of the object changes, not its function.

When this cellular universe takes its shape from nature, it contrasts a deceptive interior beauty with truly beautiful, but abused, surroundings. Marguerite does not mean to express an antinature feeling; on the contrary, she thus exposes the falsification and corruption of what she precisely believes ought not to be defiled. Such is the case of a garden house used as a meeting place: "Alez en dedans notre jardin, et m'attendez en un cabinet qui est au bout de l'alée" (XXVI, 184). In another instance she chooses a warren, to stress the animality of the protagonists, not to express scorn for the place; here a religious screen heightens her derogatory attitude toward a noble lady and her stable boy found lying there by her suitor: "On luy dit qu'elle ne faisoit que venir de Veppres, et étoit entrée en sa garenne [in her park] pour parachever son service" (XX, 136).

Characters in the novellas wish to escape from the eyes of others, and at the same time they find themselves prisoners in the night of their intelligence. Even if they place themselves, intentionally or not, in higher rooms to wait for or to prey on women, much less light enters an attic or a room under a mansarde roof. As a matter of fact, Marguerite does not mind developing the paradox—the less light or darkness there is, the higher the places may be—and then picturing them as pitfalls. A monk follows a woman to an attic only to be thrown back down by the husband (XLVI, 264). In a more explicit vein, when surprised by the husband, a monk escapes to an attic, closes the trapdoor, but reopens it when he no longer hears noise and falls out. The trapdoor provides the

29. In addition, cf. novellas VII, VIII, XI, XII, XV, XXV, XXX, XXXVI, XLI, XLIII, XLIX, LIX, for the *garderobe* and *cabinet* imagery. For another example of the *ais*, or here *guichet*, see novella XV.

real ugly light and not an escape route.[30] As for the *galetas* (a room under a mansarde roof), it too becomes a prison into which men are tricked by women; Marguerite even coins a metaphoric expression: "mais incontinent luy dit qu'il ne faloit que monter au galetas" (XXVII, 192).[31] Then the woman as captor helps to underline the concept of a trapped man as she snares him in a cage: "car quand elle en tenoit un en cage, elle pratiquoit l'autre, pour n'ettre jamais sans pas-setems" (XLIX, 274). In the same animalistic vein, a monk seeking refuge flees into a pigsty; when he comes out of the "tect de pourceaus" (XXXIV, 217), he is transformed into this very creature as he walks out of the pigpen on all fours and thus epitomizes the total transformation resulting from his escape into darkness, no matter how temporary it may be.

Logically the imagery of a cellular world would stand in direct contrast to that of the window; instead, in the *Heptameron* they complement each other and are reduced to the common denominator of darkness. Marguerite cultivates this paradox and others in order to stress her conviction of a world of appearances dominated by a web of inextricable motivations behind human drives. The metaphor of the staircase provides a further opportunity to develop an acceptation opposite to the one it usually has. Ascending a dark stair does not eventually lead to light—on the contrary; it may seem so, literally and on the surface, but not so, figuratively and in fact. Therefore stairs can only take an individual down, no matter what direction he himself may choose: "quand elle veint décendre le premier degré de son honneteté, se trouva soudinnement portée jusques au dernier" (XXX, 199). How-

30. In an earlier tale, the admiral Bonnivet had used a trapdoor to gain access to a lady's bedroom situated below his (IV, 34). He too comes out of this adventure his face all scratched by the resisting lady; furthermore Marguerite emphasizes in this novella the light-darkness imagery.

31. Cf. also "et luy dit que pour cette occasion elle s'en aloit en sa chambre qui étoit en un galetas où elle sçavoit bien qu'il n'y avoit personne" (LVIII, 304), but she has prearranged to call for help when he gets there.

ever, this singular connotation of stairs derives from comments and interpretations of the novellas; within the story itself a certain cynicism prevails. Admiral Bonnivet observes others go up to the lady and return unsuccessfully from the place where he succeeded; they think the stairs lead to pleasure (XIV, 102). A mother sends a monk to cure her daughter of sloth, unaware of what the cure may be; this mother proves to be foolish whereas another woman, a judge's wife, had kicked the same monk down the stairs when he attempted to follow her up to the attic: "si elle [mother] eut été aussi sage que la jugesse, elle luy eut plustot fait décendre le degré que monter" (XLVI, 265). The tales show both sides of the coin, success and failure in using the staircase, and the comments in turn reverse the commonly accepted connotations of the word, thus producing a double chiasmic effect that reinforces a concept of flux.

Again, the image of the door offers apparent contrasting meanings, especially through the juxtaposition of its occurrences at the beginning and at the end of the *Heptameron*. In the first novellas, it has been noted, the *ais* acts as a barrier between a mask of reason and bestiality when the protagonist breaks it down to abandon himself to the pleasures of the flesh. Now in the very last stories, the metaphor of the *huys* occurs twice; it is the object behind which or through which one learns the truth, but a truth that eventually boomerangs, since it brings about disaster. So it happens to an apothecary who will receive some of the medicine that he prescribes to others after his wife discovers that he gives advice to other wives on their sex life and fails to act on it with his own mate until she serves him the drug he gave out freely: "Un jour étant l'apoticaire en sa boutique, et sa femme cachée derrière l'huys écoutant ce qu'il disoit, veint une femme de la ville, commère dudit apoticaire, frapée de mesme maladie que l'autre [his own wife]" (LXVIII, 336). The wife, however, gives him an excessive overdose that produces the opposite result of the one desired and actually a return to the point of departure. In the seventieth tale, "le gentilhomme feit entrer le Duc au jardin par le petit huys, le priant demeurer derrière un gros noyer duquel il pourroit voir s'il disoit vray, ou non" (347-48). There the duke learns that the young nobleman's love is the Dame du Verger. The "huys" opened into a truth that causes the complete disintegration of an ordered universe about the duke: the death of those he loves—his wife and the nobleman—and of the Dame du Verger. Therefore, the metaphoric door, whether it leads man from a sensible to an irrational world, or for a moment opens upon hope and then relentlessly ends in tragedy, remains the same dark cul-de-sac.

If Marguerite sees chiefly darkness about her, it is because she considers man ugly, as she is able to observe him; she equates darkness with this moral ugliness.[32] Her observations do not necessarily express a hopeless pessimism. They reveal instead the discrepancy between reality and the ideal. The obvious solution lies in superposing the theory of faith and the practice of life, a near impossibility for the vast majority of men. What Marguerite advocates is that man drop his mask; in so doing he will either force on himself a correction in his behavior, or his fellow men, now aware of his true aims, can act and react accordingly. In the *Heptameron*, Marguerite does not wish to flee the earthly realm in favor of a spiritual one in a rarefied atmosphere; she is firmly planted in the here and now and does not reject it. On the contrary, she accepts it and is involved in it, yet not before it has cast off its stifling mantle of abuse and falsification.

32. Cf. novella XXVII for an evident exposition of this concept; there a corrupt male secretary is pictured as a savage, a cannibal and a magot.

4. AMBIGUITY OR THE SPLINTERING OF TRUTH

"Puis notre bouquet sera plus beau, tant plus il sera remply de différentes choses" (XLVIII, 271). There can be no doubt of the wide variety of novellas offered in the *Heptameron* on the sociological, ethical, and behavioral levels. In this vein, Marguerite emulates Boccaccio and prefigures Balzac; all three create their own version of the human comedy and demonstrate that on the whole it has not greatly changed; the set evolves, but not the actors on stage. The question remains, however, as to the meaning and purpose of this variety.

In the past some felt that the variety involved contradictions disrupting the unity of the work as a whole or creating an enigma of the novellas.[1] An incompatibility between religion and ethics may help to explain away some conflicts among the commentators or between the boldness of the novellas and the idyllic and scriptural setting of the *Heptameron*.[2] Recently Jourda has seen the participants as a constant and unifying force: "Récits variés et qui, pourtant, témoignent d'une unité: ces deux caractères sont assurés par la diversité et la permanence des devisants, comme par la permanence et les santés de leur caractère."[3] Finally an

1. "Il est assez difficile de décider si cet ouvrage, dans son ensemble, est moral ou immoral. L'austérité et la légèreté, la délicatesse sentimentale ou pathétique et la gaillardise plus ou moins grivoise, parfois même un peu grossière, l'esprit d'ironie et l'accent d'une piété sincère s'y mélangent à doses presque égales et en font une des compositions les plus bizarres de notre littérature." L. de Loménie, "La Littérature romanesque . . . ," p. 683. Cf. P. Toldo, "Rileggendo il novelliere della Regina di Navarra," *Rivista d'Italia*, 26 (July 15, 1923), 380–405, who points out apparent discrepancies as major flaws, but his article still has some value if seen in light of our argument, for uniformity was never Marguerite's intent.

2. Cf. L. Febvre, *Autour de l'Heptaméron*, p. 282.

3. P. Jourda, "*L'Heptaméron*: Livre préclassique," p. 134. Because of this permanence, Marguerite formulates a "moral pratique et concrète" (p. 136).

American critic, Jules Gelernt, took a long step forward along this critical line of thought, but without pronouncing the essential word: "[The *Heptameron*] is a discussion which illuminates without claiming to reach absolutely final conclusions . . . the path leading through reality to an ideal remains to be discovered by every man through the trial-error process of living . . . the *Heptameron* finds in the midst of its inconclusiveness and contradictions tentative resting points from which the human scene may be surveyed with sympathetic understanding."[4]

The key word is *ambiguity*. At last a French critic, Henri Coulet, utters it and considers it a fundamental basis for the thought and form of the *Heptameron*:

> Elle [ambiguity] ne résulte pas seulement des opinions divergentes qui se font entendre dans le débat (opinions toutes également modernes, il faut le noter; sur la condamnation du passé tous les personnages sont bien d'accord); elle tient aussi au ton sur lequel elles sont prononcées, et parfois à l'humour du récit lui-même. . . . Cette ambiguïté explique la forme de l'ouvrage. Si Marguerite s'y était complu, ou si elle avait fait confiance à la vie pour dépasser et résoudre tous les problèmes, elle se serait contentée du récit, mais une telle conception du roman est impossible avant le XIXe siècle ou quelques précurseurs de génie au XVIIIe siècle. Si elle avait voulu développer des idées, s'exercer au discours et à la dialectique, elle eût fait comme beaucoup de conteurs de son temps, elle eût noyé l'anecdote dans le dialogue. Mais elle en est au stade de l'interrogation et de l'espé-

---

Jourda's position, here, rightfully emphasizes Marguerite's earthiness instead of her spirituality. Furthermore he no longer considers it, and correctly so, chiefly under a psychological light, as he had done in his monumental thesis thirty years previously. For a similar point of view on the *Heptameron*, cf. J. Ferrier, *Forerunners of the French Novel: An Essay on the Development of the Novella in the late Middle Ages* (London, 1954), pp. 89–91.

4. J. Gelernt, *World of Many Loves . . .*, p. 166.

rance: ses convictions sont plus des actes de foi que des idées démontrées, elle les confronte avec l'expérience, d'une part, avec les convictions de ses compagnons, d'autre part; l'expérience, c'est-à-dire le récit, suscite le heurt des convictions; le heurt des convictions renvoie à une nouvelle expérience.[5]

Ambiguity results naturally from a confrontation among a variety of experiences or among opinions based on formal knowledge; it can lead to some form of skepticism or positive questioning. Seen in this light, Marguerite figures as a typical prose writer of her century and takes her place between Rabelais and Montaigne. Concerning Rabelais, the notion of ambiguity, dialectical knowledge, is just beginning to elicit critical attention,[6] although in retrospect it appears quite evident throughout his books and especially in the *Third Book*. Indeed, the *Third Book* is dedicated to Marguerite not merely because Rabelais on the surface treats in it a topic dear to her, marriage, but perhaps above all because he demonstrates the impossibility of attaining absolute truth or knowledge just as she does in the *Heptameron*.[7] Rabelais then pays homage to the queen's viewpoint. Concerning Montaigne's position, the ambiguity and relativism of his thought is such a critical truism that it does not warrant here any explanation. The important fact, however, is that Montaigne no longer occupies the unique position which may have been attributed to him previously. Rabelais and Marguerite take

5. H. Coulet, *Le Roman jusqu'à la révolution* (Paris, 1967), pp. 126, 128.
6. Cf. F. Gray, "Ambiguity and Point of View in the Prologue to *Gargantua*," *Romanic Review*, 56 (1965), 12–21; both J. Paris (*Rabelais au futur* [Paris, 1970]) and M. Beaujour (*Le Jeu de Rabelais* [Paris, 1969]) base a good deal of their study on the concept of ambiguity.
7. The *Third Book* (1546) obviously was published before the *Heptameron* (1558), but the dedication would indicate that Rabelais was quite familiar with Marguerite's works, some still in manuscript form, such as the novellas.

their places in what becomes a major trait of the century that weakens the Romantic concept of boundless optimism during the Renaissance.[8]

Ambiguity depends to some degree on a consciously created uncertainty of belief in the reader. The technique of toying with the reader's credibility forms an integral part of the traditional popular *conteur*, and in the *Heptameron* it has two totally different functions as well. Continuous protestations of veracity delineate the question of the relationship between fiction and reality, as will be seen in our last chapter. And then, testing the reader's credibility envelops the novella in a sheath of doubt: "Je croy, mes dames, que vous n'estes pas si sottes de croyre en toutes les nouvelles que l'on vous vient compter, quelque apparence qu'elles puissent avoir de saincteté, si la preuve n'y est si grande qu'elle ne puisse estre remise en doubte" (XXXIII, 213). Precisely the

---

8. Musset, a notable exception who knew well the *Heptameron* as is proven by his *Lorenzaccio* (based on novella XII), already perceived this new view of Marguerite:

> Je veux voir moins loin, mais plus clair;
> Je me console de Werther
> Avec la reine de Navarre.
> Et pourquoi pas? Croyez-vous donc,
> Quand on n'a qu'une page en tête,
> Qu'il en faille chercher si long,
> Et que tant parler soit honnête?
> Qui des deux est stérilité,
> Ou l'antique sobriété
> Qui n'écrit que ce qu'elle pense,
> Ou la moderne intempérance
> Qui croit penser dès qu'elle écrit?
>
> . . . .
>
> Cette belle âme si hardie,
> Qui pleura tant après Pavie,
> Et dans la fleur de ses beaux jours,
> Quitta la France et les amours
> Pour aller consoler son frère
> Au fond des prisons de Madrid,
> Croyez-vous qu'elle n'eût pu faire

conflict in the commentators' opinions, in Marguerite's experiences, brings forth another tale, and yet another, each contradicting the preceding one and illuminating it at the same time. And so Panurge in the *Third Book* propels himself from one consultation to another, seeking an absolute solution to his dilemma that he cannot ever hope to attain. The *Essais* fall into an identical category; each takes a step toward a position that merely becomes the springboard toward another different one. Gide must have had this in mind when he wrote "Oasis. La prochaine est toujours la plus belle."[9] These works by Marguerite, Rabelais, and Montaigne were never by their very nature designed to be finished. Therefore it really does not matter if the *Heptameron* remains at seventy-two novellas; even if it had reached a hundred, there would have been more examples, but still the same suspended result with a greater diversity of opinions and experiences and no final judgment.

The search for a constant produces ambiguity because it

Un roman comme Scudéry?
Elle aima mieux mettre en lumière
Une larme qui lui fut chère,
Un bon mot dont elle avait ri.
Et ceux qui lisaient son doux livre
Pouvaient passer pour connaisseurs . . .

cited in C. Garosci, *Margherita di Navarra* (Turin, 1908), pp. 146–47. In this relatively early study on Marguerite, the author discerns a beginning of ambiguity but does not quite know what to make of it:

Qui Margherita ci rivela un'altra delle sue spiccate facoltà; quella di saper proporsi, intorno ad un argomento, tutte le opinioni e di mostrare di fronte ad esse una strana indecisione. . . . Certo Margherita spinge il piacere di comprendere fino ai limiti estremi, fino al punto in cui esso diventa un ostacolo al giudizio, alla scelta; ella entra naturalmente nell'opinione altrui e si mette dal punto di vista del suo interlocutore ora sedotta dallo spirito arguto dello scetticismo, ora dall'austerità della Riforma, ora dagli splendori immortali dell' amore filosofico, ora dagli aspetti mutevoli, dai pittoreschi contrasti della passione umana (pp. 167–68).

9. A. Gide, *Les Nourritures terrestres*, in *Romans, récits, soties et œuvres lyriques* (Paris: Bibliothèque de la Pléiade, 1964), p. 235.

creates an acute realization of the insufficiency of human judgment. The modernity of this concept, starting with its all-pervading presence in the three major prose writers of the sixteenth century, manifests itself later in Diderot and then in this century with Proust, Pirandello, and Sartre. The image of scales and weight figures as one of the more obvious means to express the opposite of absoluteness, and Marguerite uses it in the discussion of an important story, that of Rolandine (XXI), where she imparts to Parlamente, one of her most explicit spokesmen, a very significant statement of relativistic judgment: "Car il n'y a fes si poisant que l'amour de deus personnes bien unies, ne puisse doucement supporter. Mais quand l'un faut à son devoir, et laisse toute la charge sur l'autre, la poisanteur est insuportable. Vous deveriez doncq, dit Géburon, avoir pitié de nous, qui portons l'amour entiére, sans que vous y dégnez mettre le bout du doigt, pour la soulager. Ha Géburon, dit Parlamente, souvent sont différens les fardeaus de l'homme et de la femme" (153). The particular dimension that Marguerite gives to this image is that each person must carry his own burden and decide for himself, even at the risk of being misunderstood by others.

The one dominant is absolute suspension of judgment; the commentators find themselves unable to concur because the purpose of the novellas is not to settle matters but to decipher them: "Or laissons ce propos, dit Symontaut. Car pour faire conclusion du cueur de l'homme et de la femme, le meilleur des deus n'en vaut rien. . . . La compagnie se teint à la conclusion de Symontaut, pour n'ettre plus au desavantage de l'une que de l'autre partie" (XXI, 153, and XXII, 154); or again, "Les propos précédens meirent la compagnie en telle contradiction d'opinions, que pour en avoir résolution, fut à la fin contrainte renvoyer cette dispute aus Théologiens" (XXVI, 180). Whether one wishes it or not, choice implies an arbitrariness: "Vous prendrez l'exemple qui vous plaira le mieus" (XXVI, 180). Yet choosing involves an inescapable judgment that could very well affect opinions others have of us; only an omniscient God can perceive the true motivations behind our actions. Living on earth, we must protect ourselves from each other—hence the masks and other subterfuges.[10] The commentators find a momentary solution to their impasse by moving to another novella. They do not try to resolve the issue at hand, because there is no irrevocable solution; only another enriching experience prevails for the moment, and it will color a constantly changing conviction that dissolves in contact with others: "Mais laissons ces propoz d'impossibilité, et regardons à qui Symontaut donnera sa voys" (XIV, 103).[11]

Ultimately the answer lies within oneself; this Delphic oracle comes toward the end of the *Heptameron*, and Oysille, the spiritual leader of the narrators, expresses this Pauline notion: "Par quoy ne faut juger que soy mesme" (LXV, 331). Panurge reaches an identical conclusion at the end of the *Third Book*, although he refuses to accept it. Montaigne, on the other hand, sets up self-awareness and self-knowledge as the very premise of his *Essais* and proposes himself as a model for others. The deficiency of human reason and judgment, whether real or contrived, still constitutes one of man's major assets and gives humanism its strongest foundation.

In face of the disintegration wrought on the novella by the commentators, it would appear that the tale has an inviolable fixity of meaning in contrast to the fluid discussions following it. But the fact remains that through various means such as a discrepancy between the avowed purpose of the story, stated at the beginning, and the end of the action, the use of antithesis and flaws in the characters that explain their

10. Cf. "Dieu qui juge le cueur, dit Longarine, en donnera sa sentence, mais c'est beaucoup que les hommes ne nous puissent accuser" (XXVI, 191).

11. This notion of suspension of judgment at the end of novellas does not occur on an isolated basis; on the contrary, it is quite pervasive; cf. XVI, 115; XX, 137; XXIII, 162; XXXI, 208; XXXVI, 225; XLV, 263.

vices or doom a relationship to failure, Marguerite creates ambiguity in her novellas. In about a fourth of them an unnatural element gives the impression that any analysis of a character's behavior will be futile if it does not take into account this flaw, and yet it is merely mentioned at the outset and rarely reappears in the course of the discussion. Thus Marguerite lays a trap that for the most part goes unnoticed. One is a wide age gap between the wife and husband; when twenty or thirty years separate them, infidelity does not surprise: "cette femme voyant que son mary étoit viel, preint en amour un june clerc nommé Nicolas" (XXXVI, 225).[12] For instance, in the notoriously famous story of Lorenzaccio, it is overlooked that this character's lasciviousness results in great part from his wife's very tender age which does not allow sexual relations yet. A sterile marriage, one without children, also leads the wife to seek solace with a younger partner (cf. XXV, XXVI).

A difference in social or class status prevents the happy fruition of love. In these frequent circumstances the couple suffers from the rigidity of a code imposed upon them by society and from which they cannot escape, no matter how well-meaning and pure their love may be, or how beneficial its success might be to both of them. It could be argued that Marguerite simply abides by a social code that she herself believes in and also follows a courtly love tradition; but given her relativistic frame of mind and her adherence as well to reason and nature, such an interpretation no longer has any validity.[13] In these novellas she stresses too much the tragedy

12. For additional examples of age flaws see XIII, XV, XXVI, XXIX, LXV, LXII.

13. Cf. Gelernt, "love is a perfectly appropriate foundation for marriage, provided that the match does not violate important tenets of social propriety" (163); in other words no social breach should occur. But on the contrary, Marguerite underlines the tragedy resulting from these rigid and senseless codes; in this vein, she follows the naturalistic trend set by Boccaccio. For examples of social breach see IX, XL, XLII.

in the protagonists' lives brought about by their indecisions and feints, so that the social discrepancy becomes essentially another agent to be blamed for this condition, and Marguerite derides it. Fused with this social flaw is an avarice on the part of either parents or guardians of the young person in love who is not allowed to marry because the other party is not rich enough or because a greedy father refuses a dowry to his daughter. In the final analysis Marguerite depicts an individual emprisoned by society's unnatural restrictions and by man's own vices so that in one respect any following discussions attempting to explain the protagonist's actions are futile and are undermined by a basic flaw making the outcome inevitable. Marguerite then keeps the interpretative foundations of her novellas purposely quite fluid, and in creating unnatural barriers between her characters' freedom of action and their search for happiness she establishes an insuperable condition that could be termed an "espace tragique."

Any literary text lends itself to varying and contradictory interpretations by the reader, but when the author narrates or structures her tale in order to consciously shroud it into a questioning veil, then this ambiguity can be considered an integral part of her thought and aesthetics. In some cases, the narrator states a given purpose for telling the story, then another one after narrating it, while the novella itself stresses still a different one. For example, the twenty-third tale claims to "dire quelque chose en l'honneur de sainte religion" (162), but actually it portrays the depravity of a monk who sleeps with his host's wife. The moral is that we have to be careful not to have our faith "divertie du droit chemin" and to beware of the "Ange Sathan [qui] se transforme en Ange de lumière à fin que l'œuil extérieur aveuglé par apparence de sainteté et dévotion, ne s'arrette à ce qu'il doit fuyr" (163). This moral, stated before the tale begins, applies not only to the monk but to the wife as well, because she gives in to him and because she loses her faith, abandoning all reason, by committing suicide. The aim of the novella, expressed after the narration, bears only a slight relationship to its previously avowed purpose: "Je croi, mes Dames, qu'apres avoir entendu cette histoire tresvéritable, il n'y aura aucune de vous qui ne pense deus fois à loger telz Pélerins en sa maison, et sçaurez qu'il n'y a venin plus dangereus que celuy qui est plus dissimulé" (168). Pointing out apparent contradictions may be an idle task here, for Marguerite toys consciously with shifts of emphasis in her tales, and not to confuse the reader. On the contrary she develops some varying interpretive avenues suggested by the story in order to avoid any absolute meaning which would conflict with the very essence of the *Heptameron*; every human act or thought has a multidimensional purpose and effect, perhaps contradictory on the surface, but basically complementary.

The discrepancy between the avowed purpose of a story and its meaning has the hallmark of a narrative technique typical of the novella genre and its medieval development. Again Boccaccio provides an excellent prototype; in addition to the framework setting that already creates several viewpoints, he also gives a very short synopsis as a title to each tale that cannot but slant the action along a certain interpretive line. Gruget, one of the *Heptameron*'s first editors, must have had this model in mind when he added a title synopsis to each novella, but in doing so he interpreted the story to accord with his own viewpoints and thereby sought to fix its meaning sometimes in a manner contrary to Marguerite's thinking. In fact, he attempted to purify the novellas and their significance in order to portray a Queen of Navarre cast in a divine image. But Marguerite tended toward a dialectical presentation; therefore she eliminated the Boccaccio type of synopsis in favor of evaluations by the narrator-commentators at the end of each tale which fragments the narration even more. The fragmentation reflects a weighty

preoccupation that makes the universe appear to the be-
holder more complex than it must have seemed to Boccaccio,
although it may not necessarily be so. To Marguerite, the rise
of Protestantism and the appeal of Platonism give insights
into the place of man in the universe that defy any simpli-
fied or monolithic solution.

The twenty-fifth tale offers a further instance of a broad-
ening scope of the narrative as a result of one avowed purpose stated at the beginning and another stated at the end
of the story. After Oysille's belief that it is too easy to speak
badly of women, Longarine will tell of "les inventions d'un
jeune prince par lesquelles il trompa ceus qui ont accoutumé
tromper tout le monde" (177); this prince, assumed to be
François I and quite correctly so, lives under the aegis of
Cupid who compels his subjects "d'user mensonge, hypocrisie et fiction" (177), although the king "passa en vertu
tous les autres de son tems" (176). Apparent contradictions
immediately come to the surface; no matter how virtuous one
may be, he is seldom strong enough not to fall prey to Cupid's
arrows. He may rationalize his actions by taking pleasure
in seducing the wife of a lawyer who himself has tricked
many defendants in his professional life, or by using a monastery to gain secret access to the woman's quarters and
thereby do unto the monks what they frequently do unto
others, yet the real underlying reason, stated at the end of the
novella itself, remains quite different: "Et puis qu'Amour
sçait tromper les trompeurs, nous autres simples et igno-
rantes le devons bien craindre" (180).

The avowed purpose of this twenty-fifth novella may be
to demonstrate that lawyers and monks who so often deceive
others can in turn be deceived themselves, a typical fabliau
concept; yet it is heavily counterpointed to the omnipotence
of Cupid, which overshadows more innocuous deceptions, as
the discussion following the tale emphasizes. The commentators focus on the merits of *plaisir* and its relation to con-

fession and repentance. They oppose one's own morality to God's, and the creation of one's own god (Venus, Cupid) to the One that really exists. It follows implicitly that the prince's relative valor in tricking those whom literary tradition has always attacked is being questioned, notwithstanding his probable kinship to Marguerite. After all his craftiness in seducing the lawyer's wife and his feigning piety and receiving confession when he repeatedly crosses the monastery to gain secret access to her house do not quite befit a king. The abyss between man as he is and ought to be brings about a sense of relativism and its inevitable result: ambiguity. Nearly every one wears the irreducible three-cornered hat of deception, pleasure, and the need of religion, and in a daily situation Marguerite shows the difficulty man encounters in choosing one over the other —not in an ideal framework which would really not serve a valuable didactic purpose.

The fixity of a dominant meaning continues to be fractured when an apparent disconnection surfaces between the pre- and post-story purpose on the one hand and the discussion on the other hand. The thirtieth tale, for instance, is described as "piteuse et étrange" (198); "piteuse" because it elicits the reader's pity and compassion, and "étrange" because it deals with an incestuous relationship between mother and son. Here Marguerite points again to the helplessness and weakness of man, for no one is "impeccable" (202); even following Nature, always a cardinal rule, can have its definite dangers, and even if it has sinful results one cannot resist, as Racine's Phèdre knew so well. Marguerite makes this precept quite obvious: "Car elle pensoit que l'occasion faisoit le péché et ne sçavoit pas que le péché forge l'occasion" (202). Then in the commentaries following the novella itself, the emphasis shifts to an analysis of masochism; on the surface, the discussion of this subject would appear to have little connection with the theme of incest prevalent in the tale.

Marguerite aims, however, at exposing two sides of the anti-Nature coin, masochism and incest; giving in to certain ugly pleasures of the flesh, although they cannot be avoided, is just as unnatural as restraining them beyond measure or reason. Both are extremes and equally "piteux et étranges." Therefore, the discussion when apparently divorced from the theme of the story actually reinforces it or reveals another facet of it.

Because of the complexity and inherent contradictions of any given notion, Marguerite endeavors to explain actions and reactions. To this end she makes a most abundant use of explicative conjunctions such as *tant que, autant que, plus que, si bien que, moins que, tel que*; and very often she will also begin sentences with *car*. The frequency of such conjunctions, especially in the longer novella dominated by a dialectical concept of love, may cause a somewhat clumsy and emphatic syntax, but at the same time it bears witness to the need Marguerite feels to argue logically and multifariously. In turn these explicative conjunctions affect the composition of a tale: "La narration semble ne pas se composer toujours d'une série de faits mais plutôt d'un perpétuel va-et-vient entre deux pôles: d'un côté, le détail descriptif, l'exaltation d'une qualité ou l'exagération d'une quantité; de l'autre, l'effet, les répercussions, qui constituent l'action proprement dite."[14] This oscillating movement brings out the discrepancy between a vain, empty, condition and the causes that overwhelm it or make it ironically meaningless and irresoluble:

> Et combien que quelques uns la demandassent en mary-age, ils n'avoient néantmoins autre réponse d'elle si non, puis qu'elle avoit tant demeuré sans ettre maryée, qu'elle ne le vouloit ettre. [XXI, 142]
> Car ainsi que l'amour se diminuoit du coté de luy,

14. A. Lorian, "Intensité et conséquence dans l'*Heptaméron* de Marguerite de Navarre," *Neuphilologische Mitteilungen*, 63 (1963), 118.

ainsi augmentoit du sien, et demeura, malgré qu'il en eut, l'amour entiére et perfette. Car l'amytié qui failloit du coté de luy, tourna en elle. [XXI, 152][15]

Explanation then leads to irresolution: a sign of consciousness and pain; what Montaigne calls his "scar."[16]

Since attempts at explanation fail, the downward movement of the story itself will provide an additional means of producing ambiguity; therefore it becomes rather difficult to seize upon a stable point of reference that would fix a meaning for the tale. Doubtless deception and treachery constitute the theme of the thirteenth novella, but a question remains as to which of the protagonists is the most guilty, especially since the degree of the vices intensifies in the course of the narrative. Under the guise of planning a pilgrimage to Jerusalem with a lady and her husband, a captain deceives the woman into believing that he loves her purely; then unsuccessful in his bid, he leaves her. At this point she returns the ring she had received from him to his wife, telling her laughingly that he really loved her [his wife], hence a second deception. While he was away at war and on a crusade as well, we learn ipso facto that the officer second in command betrayed him and left him on a deserted island to be massacred by savages. Then this officer, after his return, succeeds in explaining away his treachery and receives acclaim from the king for his victories. Treachery triumphs, from an innocuous beginning to a costly end. Little consolation results from Oysille's assertion that only God can judge (98) who was the wickedest because we the readers have been purposely put at a loss by Marguerite to make a choice,

15. These two examples from the same novella are only a mere sample of their high frequency. The above article by Lorian gives numerous examples of the use of explicative conjunctions but does not quite see them in the light that we wish to stress here.

16. "Je ne veux donc pas oublier encor cette cicatrice, bien mal propre à produire en public: c'est l'irrésolution." "De la præsumption," Œuvres complètes, ed. M. Rat. Bibliothèque de la Pléiade (Paris, 1965), p. 637.

all the more so because the bloodiest treachery and deception, on the officer's part, does not necessarily coincide with the worst moral wrong.

The discrepancy between the two purposes of the tale stated before and after the narrative illuminates the downward movement of a novella which in turn has a direct effect on its fluid meaning. At the beginning of the fifteenth story Longarine claims that she tells it in order to prove "qu'il y en [women] a d'aussi bon cueur, d'aussi bon esprit, et aussi plénes de finesse" (104). But then at the end she asserts that "j'ai voulu montrer . . . que souvent les femmes de grand cueur sont plus tot vincues de l'ire et de vengence . . . de désespoir" (114). Longarine's view of her own novella has indeed evolved from hope and praise to pessimism. The turn that the narrative took may have changed her mind, as if she herself had been unable to control it. Unloved by her husband, the female protagonist of this tale turns toward a "parfaict amy." The downward spiral has already started, and it accelerates as she tests his love. He remains faithful partly because of her wealth; finally she casts him off for others. What caused her downfall will always remain problematic; the downfall can only be ascertained, not judged, for the outcome rests on a concatenation of events, not just a single one. Longarine's position at the start of the novella may be seen under an ironic light, and then some contradictions disappear; however, this viewpoint does not alter the protagonist's degeneration. Furthermore if the lady's behavior had stayed on an irreproachable level, the answer would be easier, but Marguerite does not wish to be simplistic; literature tends toward uncertainty and flexibility, rhetoric toward fixed positions.

Mutability and antithesis become then the order of the day; one leads to the other. Since sentiments are in a state of flux and stress, aims remain quite unclear. The tension between opposites comes to the fore; a step in one direction does not take the protagonist forward but actually brings him back a step in the other direction. As a result, indecision dominates, and attempts at movements of the mind produce immobility. Antithetical concepts in Marguerite may have a direct point of contact with the medieval *débat*, but they differ from this literary ancestor in that they do not constitute a mere rhetorical game between two opposites; instead they demonstrate the difficulty of choosing one over another. Argumentative principles yield to the edification of judgment and the development of reason.

In expressing antithetical notions, Marguerite fuses form and content; syntax reflects a conflicting meaning. The *bruit/dissimulation* antithesis illustrates such a fusion:

> De sorte qu'elle ne fut non seulement consolée, mais contente de l'absence do son mary. Et avant les troys semainnes qu'il [husband] devoit retourner, fut si amoureuse du Roy, qu'elle étoit aussi ennuyée du retour de son mary, qu'elle avoit été de son alée. . . . Ma Dame la vengeance est douce de celuy qui en lieu de tuer l'ennemy, donne vie à son perfet amy. Il me semble qu'il est tems, que la vérité vous ote la sote Amour que vous portez à celuy qui ne vous ayme point et l'amour juste et raisonnable chace hors de vous la crainte qui jamais ne doit demeurer en un cœur grand et vertueus. [III, 29, 30]

Antinomies stress ambivalence and indecision: "Or fut Nicolas bien marry de laisser sa Dame; et non moins joyeus d'avoir la vie sauve" (XXXVI, 226); "et ne veuil pas nyer, mes Dames, que la patience du gentilhomme de Pampelune et du Président de Grenoble n'ait été grande, mais la vengeance n'en a été moindre" (XXXVII, 228); "Car les plus asseurez étoient desespérez et les desespérez en prenoient assurance" (LVIII, 304). The object is not to produce agreement or harmony since it really does not exist; even the participants sometimes cannot agree on the choice of the next narrator (cf. LXXI, 357). The use of antitheses, and similar techniques, does not play at all the role of a stylistic artifice or of a mere rhetorical figure but integrates explicitly the notion of ambiguity on Marguerite's part.[17]

Marguerite ascribes to her characters an antithesis of concepts when she wishes to depict an interior conflict of a Cornelian nature between two senses of duty. Although she pits one side of the argument against the other, this would-be simplicity soon disappears as the characters' inner tension grows in complexity when set against a stated purpose of the novella, pregnant with chiasmic effects. In the Lorenzaccio story, the anonymous duke's friend upon hearing that his master has cast lustful eyes upon his sister finds himself in a quandary: "D'un coté luy venoit au devant l'obligation qu'il avoit à son maitre, les biens et les honneurs qu'il avoit receus de luy; de l'autre coté, l'honneur de sa maison, l'honnetteté et chasteté de sa sœur, qu'il sçavoit bien ne se devoir jamais consentir à telle méchanceté . . ." (XII, 83). By resolving his dilemma with the duke's assassination, he does not exactly absolve himself; in fact, the nature of this act and its goriness immediately put into question who may be the real villain, the promiscuous duke or his extremely vengeful friend-servant.

In one way, the whole tale also raises the question of breaking friendship bonds; here, of course, both parties abuse their trust toward each other.[18] As a result, the purpose

17. Evidently we do not quite agree with Jourda's assessment of this stylistic trait: "elle sait user de l'antithèse dans le développement même de ses nouvelles: il y a là un effet de style un peu précieux que nous n'apprécions plus guère aujourd'hui, mais qui était alors fort à la mode" (*Marguerite d'Angoulême*, II, p. 968).

18. As a matter of fact, the basic antithetical metaphor in one novella is the "unir-rompre amytié" theme, cf. XLVII. These verbs, with an emphasis on *rompre*, recur as a leitmotiv throughout the tale and the discussion and become integrated therefore with the notion of mistrust promulgated by the story.

of the novella stated at the beginning takes on quite a fluid meaning: "comment Amour aveuglit les plus grans et honnettes cueurs, et comme une méchanceté est difficile à vincre par quelque bénéfice ou bien que ce soit" (82). *Amour* here means deformed passion, a loss of reason, and it applies both to the duke and his friend-assassin. At first, *méchanceté* would seem to relate only to the assassin, but actually it refers to the duke as well. And when the debaters in the course of the discussion wonder aloud if a woman's virtue or love is worth a murder, any attempt at synthesis or choice on our part fails under the weight of a helpless judgment.

Protagonists who find themselves in a situation where they are forced to make a choice never make the right one; otherwise the tragic sense surrounding man's condition along a Pauline line would cease to exist, as would all irony heightening this basic human incapacity. In the seventieth novella, the two male protagonists, the young nobleman and the duke, find themselves torn between two courses: "Le Duc d'un coté aymoit sa femme, et se sentoit fort injurié, d'autre coté portoit bien bonne affection à son serviteur" (343); "Or choisissez de deus choses l'une, de me dire celle que vous aymez plus que toutes, ou de vous aler banny de toutes les terres où j'ai autorité. . . . Ainsi pressé de deus cotés . . . Car d'un coté il voyoit qu'en disant la vérité il perdoit s'amye . . . Aussi en ne la confessant il étoit banny du païs" (346). Marguerite likes to place her characters in these *situations limites*, but they come out of them shattered and deprived of moderation and reason. Here, just as in the twelfth tale, a murder offers an imperfect solution; upon finding out the truth, the duke slits his wife's throat. Although this novella can be viewed under the lens of a no-exit situation, none of the four protagonists, including the Dame du Verger, has any real choice; the fundamental point is that a breach of trust constitutes the lowest form of human behavior and in a way explains, and perhaps even excuses, the murder. In such cases,

Dante quite possibly looms around the corner, for betrayers occupy the very last circle in Hell.

A dominating antithesis in the *Heptameron* is the wise-fool oxymoron, a Renaissance *topos* that Erasmus' *Praise of Folly* epitomizes and Montaigne's *Essais* later continue. Of course, Marguerite also acts as another link in the chain that could start with Plato's *Symposium* and proceed to Saint Paul.[19] Although this spiritual parentage ought not to be denied, in this vein Marguerite is above all a daughter of her age. Her own contemporary, Rabelais bears witness to this fact. In his dizain dedicating the *Third Book* to her, he beseeches her "Esprit abstraict, ravy et ecstatic" to come down and partake of the "faictz joyeux de bon Pantagruel." This dedication does not necessarily attest to the queen's spiritualism and mysticism, as some have claimed.[20] On the contrary, in offering his book to her, Rabelais testifies to their kinship and certainly not to the differences which this spiritualism and mysticism would imply.

Indeed, following the Platonic rule of expressing serious thoughts through irony,[21] he admonishes her to take a position that she has already taken; and he knows it, for he has taken the same position in his own work. After numerous peregrinations in consulting all forms of human, natural, and supernatural knowledge, Panurge arrives before Triboulet the Fool, who advises him to continue his quest toward perfection, toward knowledge; the search may end up an empty one and a failure, but in the process Panurge has grown in stature. Naturally Rabelais did not see the publication of the *Heptameron*; he must have read some of the tales in manuscript form, widely circulated at the time. Furthermore, Rabelais's knowledge of the queen is not just an abstract one of

19. Cf. I Corinthians, 3:18–20; 4:10; and II, 11:23.

20. Cf. A. Lefranc's comments to this poem in his critical edition of the *Third Book* (Paris, 1931), p. 2.

21. Cf. E. Wing, *Pagan Mysteries in the Renaissance* (New York, 1968), p. 236.

the kind that might have been gained through the reading of her works. His position at her brother's court in the 1540s must have put him in frequent personal contact with her; thus he was able to read her mind at first hand. Finally, dedicating a book, or any other kind of creative work, to a person usually indicates either an affinity of spirit or is meant to praise. Both Marguerite in the *Heptameron* and Rabelais in the *Third Book* start on an intellectual journey to explore amenable avenues to achieve happiness through exposure to human experience and realization of the relativistic nature and value of these explorations. Herein lies the essential meaning of this dedication, as well as the reconciliation of the paradoxical concept of the wise fool.

Because the notion of *fou-sage* implies a judgment, it is quite fitting that it should occur in the discussion following a tale, where the narrator-debaters examine the merits of the story. This particular presence further exemplifies the relativistic basis of the discussions. In one discussion the wise-fool dichotomy leads to a purposeful confusion of vice and virtue, while advocating freedom of action and truth toward oneself: "Je vous dirai, dit Nomerfide, je voi que les folz, si on ne les tue, vivent plus longuement que les sages, et n'y trouvent qu'une raison: c'est qu'ilz ne dissimulent leurs passions. S'ilz sont courroucez, ilz frapent, s'ilz sont joyeus, ilz rient. Et ceus qui cuydent ettre sages dissimulent tant leurs imperfections, qu'ilz en ont tout leurs cueurs empoisonnez" (XXXIII, 215). In stressing the interchangeability of the two concepts, Marguerite may not hesitate to paraphrase Saint Paul: "Et qui se cuyde sage est fol devant Dieu" (XXXVIII, 234; I Cor. 3:18), but any theological or dogmatic basis of this statement has a much broader scope: it relates to the wide spectrum of human behavior just as the apostle himself meant it.

Since what and how to know forms the underlying basis of the discussions following each novella, the ambivalent *fou-*

sage concept inevitably becomes an integral part of them. We listen to what we want to hear and shut ourselves out of what we would reject. In other words, we interpret as we see fit; hence the brittleness and insufficiency of words in expressing thoughts. Laughter may momentarily shield us from this fundamental epistemology, but at the same time it reinforces our consciousness of the dilemma. Stoicism and skepticism may offer a solution; Diogenes' scorn of knowledge may be preferable to Plato's vanity of attempting to attain it, but not necessarily so. This viable debate is triggered by a story that depicts two monks, who, upon hearing the farmer who is their host say he is going to kill his two pigs, think they are the intended victims:

> Et qu'est ce à dire, dit Nomerfide, que nous sommes plus enclins à rire d'une folie, que d'une chose sagement faite? Pour ce, dit Hircan, qu'elle nous est plus agréable, d'autant qu'elle est plus semblable à notre nature, qui de soy n'est jamais sage. Et chacun prend plaisir à son semblable, les folz aus folies, et les sages à la prudence. Je croi, dit Symontaut, qu'il n'y a ne sages ne folz qui se sceussent garder de rire de cette histoire. Il y en a, dit Géburon, qui sont tant adonnez à l'amour de sapience, que pour choses qu'ils sceussent oÿr, on ne les sçauroit faire rire. Car ilz ont une joye en leur cueur, et un contentement si modéré, que nul accident ne les peut muer . . . et mesmes Diogénes foula aus piez le lyt de Platon, par ce qu'il étoit trop curieux à son gré pour montrer qu'il déprisoit, et vouloit mettre sous les piez la vaine gloire du dit Platon, en disant: Je foule l'orgueil de Platon. Mais vous ne dites pas tout, dit Saffredan. Car Platon soudinnement luy répondit, que vrayement il le fouloit, mais avec une plus grand' présumption, d'autant que Dyogénes usoit d'un tel mépris de netteté, par une certaine gloire et arrogance. [XXXIV, 218]

The vanity of self-knowledge focuses on a religious level. Marguerite does not merely score deceitful and hypocritical monks, but above all the women, "fausses dévotes," who believe themselves wise when fulfilling their religious duties by giving large contributions, going to church, and wearing crucifixes; actually they are the epitome of folly.[22] As a matter of fact, in such circumstances *sage* does not have an intrinsic or absolute function; it simply exists as a variant of *fol* which acquires thereby a dominant if not absolute role. Is it a wise wife who will mock her unfaithful husband by deceiving him with another man (cf. LXIX, 338)? Love of God or man seen in this light may very well lead one of the narrators, Ennasuite, to think that "tous les amours du monde soient fondées sur les folies" (XIX, 126). If any doubt is cast on the meaning of *sage*, none prevails for *fol*. The actions of a young lady who poses in bed with a man at the urging of his own lady are described as "folie" (XVIII, 124). So is the prior's carnal love for Sister Heroet (XXII, 159), and a mother's incestuous love for her son (XXX, 202), if she thought she was a saint, helplessly driven to it; and so are masochists who likewise think they are saints. However, the absoluteness of *folie* remains quite precarious since it reflects the opinion of one or more voices in a discussion, but very rarely a unanimous viewpoint.

At all times *fou* merges into *sage*, and vice versa, in order to produce a very fluid and relativistic concept. The twenty-sixth novella provides a notable prototype of such a fusion. The presentation of the tale sets forth immediately the dichotomy and at the same time breaks down the duality:

22. "Les Cordeliers doncq, dit Hircan, ne devroient jamais prescher pour faire sages les femmes, veu que leur folye leur sert tant. Ilz ne les preschent pas, dit Parlamente, d'ettre sages, mais bien de le cuyder ettre. Car celles qui sont du tout mondaines et foles, ne donnent pas grandes aumonnes. Mais celles qui pour fréquenter leur convent, et porter leurs Paternotres marquées de testes de mor, et leurs cornettes plus basses que les autres, cuydent ettre les plus sages, sont celles que lon peut dire les plus foles. Car elles constituent leur salut en la confience qu'elles ont en la sainteté des iniques" (XLIV, 259).

"J'ai en main l'histoire d'un sage et d'une fole. Vous prendrez l'exemple qui vous plaira le mieus et connoitrez qu'autant qu'Amour fait faire en un cueur méchant, de méchancetez, en un cueur honnette fait faire choses dignes de louange. Car Amour de soy est bon mais la malice du sujet luy fait prendre souvent un mauvais surnom de fol, léger ou vilain. . . . Amour ne change point le cueur, mais le montre tel qu'il est, fol aus folz, et sage aus sages" (180–81). Here the gentleman d'Avannes goes from an anonymous lady, living near Pampeluna, who did not resist her natural inclinations and loved him passionately, to the Lady of Pampeluna who refuses to uncover her love and to follow her real desires. In the story itself, the wise woman would seemingly be the latter one; even the sly narrator, Saffredan, momentarily takes this point of view (cf. 190). But the discussion following the tale definitely shifts the blame to the Lady of Pampeluna. One of the debaters, Géburon, paraphrasing Saint Matthew (6: 28), crystallizes the majority opinion: "Quiconque regarde par concupiscence est jà adultère en son cueur" (191). As for the anonymous lady, she at least followed her natural instincts, somewhat unrestrained to be sure; at least she did not conceal herself behind pretenses. Both *sage* and *fole* can apply to either woman; these terms therefore become interchangeable. It all depends on which mirror one looks at.

Whether or not they focus on the interchangeability of terms, the discussions following each novella still substantiate quite clearly the ambiguity pervading the *Heptameron*. Since each debater-narrator in the course of these discussions interprets the novella according to his own beliefs and viewpoint, its meaning can never be clearly defined; it may be absolute if one takes a given debater's opinion, but divergent, contrasting, and fluid, if a composite picture of these viewpoints is drawn. Indeed, the discussions form the essential originality of the *Heptameron* over the imitated framework of the *Decameron*. These conversations bring Marguerite's work into closer alignment with Castiglione's *Courtier*, for they reflect the dialectic strain of Platonism and the communicating code among the noble class.[23] And by introducing this conversational element with its resulting disparateness, Marguerite leaves no doubt about the disintegrating effect of this device upon a clear cohesive meaning of the tale.

Furthermore the discussion imparts a certain dynamism to the whole complex of this new brand of novella, composed of a tale and judging conversations, since it is neatly separated from the relatively static story. Then too, these discussions by the narrators create a contrasting reality in relation to the tale itself (see chapter 6). Their argumentative nature reflects Marguerite's strong affinity for the debate on ethical issues, as in her theater. The discussions also form a counterpart to the dialogues and the long monologues in the stories, for which Marguerite shows a strong liking because all these means of communication allow her to bring together and to focus on diverging viewpoints. Finally this affinity for argumentation reveals the variability of logic and reason, for each debater in propounding his opinion offers his own approach to a particular question or action and his own reasoning on it. The importance of the word *reason* has even warranted recently an extensive study on its numerous meanings clustering about (1) explanation-argument-proof, (2) law on which man must regulate his conduct, and (3) just measure, moderation.[24] The multidimensional qualities of this word bear out once again the pressure Marguerite feels to explore all facets of a concept, which in turn destroy its arbitrariness.

The discussions following each novella reflect Mar-

---

23. Cf. Garosci, p. 133 and Loménie, p. 686; the former stresses the affinities with Castiglione while the latter focuses on the social behavioral value of these conversations.

24. H. Vernay, esp. pp. 179–81.

guerite's view of a fragmented and dialectical universe. Yet in the *Heptameron* she gradually eases into the symposium concept of these post-tale conversations. As a matter of fact, one has to wait until the twelfth novella, dealing with the murder of Lorenzaccio, to find the first fully developed debate. At the start, it elicits contrasting views as to whether the murder was warranted:

> Cette histoire fut bien écoutée de toute la compagnie, mais elle y engendra diverses opinions. Car les uns soutenoient que le gentilhomme avoit fait son devoir de sauver sa vie et l'honneur de sa sœur, ensemble d'avoir délivré sa patrie d'un tel tyran. Les autres disoient que non, mais que c'étoit trop grande ingratitude de mettre à mor celuy qui luy avoit fait tant de bien et d'honneur. Les dames disoient qu'il estoit bon frere et vertueus citoyen; les hommes au contraire qu'il étoit traitre et méchant serviteur. Et faisoit bon oyr les raisons alleguées des deus costez. [86]

Since this issue cannot be resolved, the discussion shifts to the question of whether a lady, the proverbial abstract "belle Dame sans mercy," should cause a man's death by not responding to him, not even with a verbal acknowledgment, when she may feel positively toward him. Because of the impossibility of assessing an individual's basic motivations, the debaters cannot arrive at an agreement, and the long argument remains suspended.[25] The story itself almost acts as a catalyst for a discussion moving across strata of nar-

25. In tracing the sources of these discussions, R. Lebègue suggests the "dialogue naturel" of Boccaccio's characters, the medieval farce, medieval religious and profane theater, and the lively conversations at the court, but he fails to mention the Platonic dialogue which would also be the basis of these debates, especially in view of the subject matter of the *Heptameron* love and the human behavioral code, which relates directly to the *Symposium* "Réalisme et apprêt dans la langue des personnages de l'*Heptaméron*," *Actes du Colloque de Strasbourg: La littérature narrative d'imagination* (Paris 1961), p. 83.

rative, from a failure to judge a crucial point in the tale, to a critical attitude toward a deviated concept of perfect love caused by a human flaw, and to insights in the private lives of debaters, such as Géburon (87).

If ideologically the discussions diffuse instead of synthesize notions, linguistically they tend to fix the metaphoric meaning of words or to point up their oxymoronic nature. The story itself of the thirtieth novella, depicting a husband who seeks solace with a lower-class woman, juggles with the concept of health and cold, *guérir* and *morfondu*. Then the debaters in the course of their conversations seize upon these notions and proceed to transform them into fundamental metaphors of the narrative: "Il me semble, dit Symontaut, qu'il avoit plus d'occasion de retourner à sa femme, quand il avoit froid à sa métairie, que quand il y étoit si bien traité"; and then the novella ends with a paraphrase from Luke 5:31 and I Corinthians, 1:27–30: "Ceus, dit Géburon, qui par eus mesmes se peuvent ayder, n'ont point besoin d'ayde. Car celuy qui a dit qu'il étoit venu pour les malades, et non point pour les sains, est venu par la loy de miséricorde secourir à noz infirmitez, rompant les arrestz de la rigueur de sa justice. Et qui se cuyde sage, est fol devant Dieu" (233–34). It remains quite difficult to decide who is healthy and who is not, or who fares better, the man in the cold or the man in the warm; in fact, the wise-fool paradox accentuates this uncertainty of judgment.

It would be incorrect to assume that every debate on a given tale remains unresolved. Some (though few) arrive at a synthesis within that specific debate, and yet even among these a wavering aura weakens their strength. Indeed it is quite fitting that the discussion on a story marking the end of a day, here the fourth, should come to rest on a synthesizing notion. The story in question deals with a man who kills his sister's lover so that she will not marry him, because he disapproves of him as a brother-in-law. The discussion centers on the hideousness of the crime as well as on the foolishness of the maiden, who, never recovering from this missed opportunity, does not ever marry. It also pits the pros and cons of arranged marriages against the dangers and delights of marriages based on love that often result in jealousy and anger. And it criticizes social discrepancies between two lovers as a barrier to their marriage. A sizable portion of the discussion, especially toward the beginning, brings out the merits and agonies of life's inevitable and incessant sufferings. Finally Parlamente is given the opportunity by Marguerite to have the last word and to conclude that marriage, if adhered to according to its reputed vows, can provide the only modus vivendi to overcome man's weaknesses and misery:

> Il me semble . . . que l'un et l'autre est louable, mais qu'il faut que les personnes se soumettent à la volonté de Dieu, ne regardans ny à la gloire, ny à l'avarice, ny à la volupté, mais par une amour vertueuse et d'un consentement desirent vivre en l'état de maryage comme Dieu et nature l'ordonnent. Et combien qu'il n'y ait état sans tribulation, si ai je veu ceus la vivre sans repentence. Et nous ne sommes pas si malheureus en cette compagnie, que nul des maryez ne soit de ce nombre la. Hircan, Geburon, Symontaut et Saffredan jurérent qu'ilz s'étoient mariez en pareille intention, et que jamais ne s'en étoient repentys. Mais quoy qu'il en fut de la vérité, celles à qui il touchoit en furent si contentes, que ne pouvans oÿr un meilleur propos à leur gré, se levérent pour en aler rendre graces à Dieu. . . . [XL, 240–41]

Some couples—a few—succeed in marriage if they are able to close their eyes to each other's faults and make the best of the ups and downs of life; these individuals find a measure of happiness if they continue to be drawn to each other. However, this practical reality becomes almost an ideal because of the relatively small number of couples that fall in the category. A small number of tales substantiate this accommodation in marriage; the vast majority do not, for man cannot easily shed himself of *gloire, avarice,* and *volupté.* Hence the relatively ideal conception of marriage is cast against the ugly realities of life in the tales themselves, which are supposed to be one mirror of society. The debaters themselves then become another mirror of society, thus creating an interplay between two levels of fiction, but their condition in marriage only reinforces the condition observed in the stories they relate.

The debaters may seem on the surface to enjoy a degree of happiness in marriage, "Mais quoy qu'il en fut de la vérité. . . ." As far as the debaters are concerned, Marguerite the omniscient narrator intervenes to dispel Parlamente's thesis and to maintain that self-delusion plays an important part in achieving happiness in marriage; the facts do not bear out appearances. Parlamente's attempt at synthesis therefore fails because neither the bulk of the tales nor the private lives of the debators support her argument, all the less since she supposes a certain perfection in man. Marguerite's universe, therefore, remains quite fragmented and diversified; peeling off one mask only leads to another and adds to the uncertainty of truth. At the end of the day in this instance, even the usually infallible solace of "aler rendre graces à Dieu" is tinted with irony—and with a good dose of bitterness.

Yet, in spite of inevitable failure, attempts at synthesis must be made to seek knowledge about oneself and the world about us. The symposia at the end of the novellas provide a means to arrive at a composite and ever-changing synthesis. Marguerite prefers thesis and antithesis to absolute synthesis because according to her own observations human behavior comprises a succession of conflicting examples that make uniformity and cohesion impossible. In the narration of the tales themselves, Marguerite institutes the technique of long declarations which actually sometimes become full-fledged discourses, through which two protagonists confront each other from conflicting points of view. Or the thesis-antithesis pattern may result from an opposition between a single declaration in a story that acts as the pivot of the action, and the arguments in the ensuing symposium that destroy its focal position and its momentary synthesizing effect. Because a declaration of this sort is an attempt at synthesis, it represents within the protagonist a convergence of interior dialogues which are then externalized, and formalizes a state of mind or a particular opinion at a given time.

Although in the past these declarations have been interpreted as offering another method for detailed psychological analysis of the characters that indulge in them, their excessive rhetoric could not be entirely reconciled with this stated purpose.[26] This is certainly one valid interpretation of the discourses, for in them the protagonists not only state their sentiments but grope for motivations behind them. Yet the emotive rhetoric of these long tirades puzzles. Viewing them as preclassical, in the Cornelian or Racinian traditions, or as preromantic, in an Hernani vein, does not help to understand their meaning. Or again, to attribute their frequency to Marguerite's feminine lyricism remains unsatisfactory, although perhaps quite valid. In the final analysis, this abusive rhetoric, although elegant, repeatedly brings out a lack of sincerity or a complete helplessness on the part of the one who speaks, so that the shallowness of words and the difficulty of arriving at truth stand out more than ever. Then the clash among the long discourses within a story and between a pivotal discourse and the discussion at the end of a tale reinforces the notion of an ambivalent truth pervading the novellas.

The more developed tales contain the interplay of these declarations, whereas the shorter stories may have only one

26. Cf. Jourda, *Marguerite d'Angoulême*, II, 973–74.

or at the most two discourse-declarations. Since the tenth and seventieth novellas are the best developed, they provide the more notable examples of this interplay, while declarations in them also provide interpretative guideposts. Looking first at the seventieth novella may prove to be useful because, being one of the last ones, it reflects the ultimate in Marguerite's affinity for the discourse form. In this tale, the first declaration occurs in an indirect way; by means of an allusive dialogue the duchess informs the young gentleman of her passion toward him (341, 342, 343). Allusion and indirectness then express true sentiments instead of frankness. In the first real discourse, the duchess needs almost a whole page to tell her husband, falsely, that the young man he has nurtured for years is now trying to seduce his wife (p. 343). This first full-fledged declaration in the story is thus a vehicle for lies and deception, meant to gain for the duchess her revenge against the man who has refused her advances. The pivotal part of the story consists of a dialogue between the duke and the young man in the course of which the latter agrees to divulge the identity of the lady he loves, i.e., to tell the truth, an act that will bring his own downfall as well as that of the famous Dame du Verger (346–47).

Both truth and lies bring about the death of all but the duke. The lengthy laments before their deaths, first by the Dame du Verger and then by her "amy," although deploring the breach of secrecy in their relationship based on a courtly love concept, reveal above all their helplessness and their victimization due to these lies and truths. And it is actually difficult to distinguish which is the main causal agent of this tragic outcome: the expression of a dubious truth, the duchess's declaration of her somewhat unnatural passion; the same duchess's false confession to her husband; or the gentleman's confiding to the duke his protector the ultimate truth that will boomerang. The two ensuing laments form a counterpart and an inevitable result of the preceding declarations.

Both the Dame du Verger, punctuating her despairing tirade with overabundant "O" and "Helas," and the young nobleman, cursing extensively his ignorance of the world's wickedness, really fail to discern the truth of the matter;[27] she seizes upon her lover's verbal betrayal of her, and he simply puts all the blame upon himself.

Each of these laments expresses genuine inner sentiments, but when projected on the three previous forms of declaration, none any longer conveys an absolute or believable truth. Furthermore, seen in this light, the overinflated rhetoric of these two despairing discourses contributes to a certain loss of their credibility; in other words, a discrepancy exists between what the two protagonists say and what Marguerite means. Therefore the interaction among the five declarations has a disintegrating effect upon the truth and

27. "O malheureuse, quelle parole est ce que j'ai oÿe? quel arrest de ma mor ai je entendu? Quelle sentence de ma fin ai je receuë? O le plus aymé qui oncques fut, est ce la récompense de ma chaste, honnette et vertueuse amour? O mon cueur, avez vous faite une si perilleuse election de choisir pour le plus loyal, le plus infidèle, pour le plus véritable, le plus fint, pour le plus secret, le plus médisant? Hélas est il possible qu'une chose cachée aus yeus de tous les humains, ait été révélée à ma Dame la Duchesse? Hélas mon petit chien tant bien appris, le seul moyen de ma longue et vertueuse amytié, ce n'a pas été de vous qui m'avez décelée, mais celuy qui a la voys plus éclatante que le chien abboyant, et le cueur plus ingrat que nulle beste. C'est luy, qui contre son serment et sa promesse a découverte l'heureuse vie que nous avons longuement mené, sans tenir tor à personne" (351); "O mon Dieu, pour quoy me créates vous homme ayant l'amour si légère et le cueur si ignorant? Pour quoy ne me créates vous le petit chien qui a fidèlement servi sa maitresse? Hélas, mon petit amy, la joye que me donnoit votre japer, est tournée en tristesse mortelle, puis que par moy, autre que nous deus a oÿe votre voys. Si est ce, m'amye, que l'amour de la Duchesse ny de femme vivante ne m'a fait varier, combien que plusieurs fois la méchante m'en ait requis et prié. Mais ignorance m'a vincu pensant à jamais asseurer notre amytié. Toutesfois, pour cette ignorance je ne laisse d'ettre coulpable. Car j'ai révélé le secret de m'amye, j'ai faucé ma promesse, qui est la seule cause dont je la voi morte devant mes yeus . . ." (352–53).

Although rhetoric and redundance may abound in these declarations, they are not carelessly assembled. J. Frappier has shown how rhythmic patterns exist in them that can actually be structured into rhymed verses ("La Chastelaine de Vergi, Marguerite de Navarre et Bandello," pp. 139–41).

upon a clear meaning for the seventieth tale. An additional benefit of considering the various declarations as guideposts or signs of action and meaning is that this novella then transforms itself into a five-act tragedy.

In the tenth novella the two protagonists' declarations serve to unmask each other; often one mask is used against another, that is, the stated intentions differ vastly from unstated ones. These speeches then form the essential elements of a fencing or sparring match; they do not lead, however, to a light-hearted *marivaudage*, but to a Stendhalian exploration of motives dominated by self-interest or social restraint. A truthful relationship between Amadour and Floride never existed; actually the story moves from the area of an apparent truth to that of a totally falsified one, but ambiguity sets in when the reader or the debaters try to decide who or what is to blame for the tragic outcome: Amadour, Floride, external forces, or the inner-core frailness or preordained corruption in those two protagonists. Already the very first exchange of speeches casts a cunning Amadour against an incredulous Floride:

Ma Dame, je ne vous ai encores voulu dire la tresgrande affection que je vous porte, pour deus raisons. L'une, que j'attendoie par long service vous en donner l'expérience; l'autre, que je doutoie que penseriez une grande outre-cuydance à moy, qui suis simple gentilhomme, de m'addresser en lieu qui ne m'appartient regarder. Et encores que je fusse Prince comme vous, la loyauté de votre cueur ne permetroit qu'autre que celuy qui en a pris la possession . . . Mais, ma Dame, tout ainsi que la nécessité en une forte guerre contraind faire degast du propre bien et ruyner le blé en herbe, à fin que l'ennemy n'en puisse faire son profit, ainsi pren-je le hazard d'avancer le fruyt qu'avec le tems j'espéroie cueuillir à fin que les ennemys de vous et moy ne puissent faire leur profit de votre dommage. . . .

Puis que ainsi est, Amadour, que ne demandez de moy que ce qu'en avez, pourquoy est ce que vous me faites une si longue harangue? J'ai si grand' peur que souz voz honnestes propoz, il y ait de la malice cachée pour decevoir l'ignorance jointe à ma junesse, que je suis en grande perplexité de vous répondre. Car de refuser l'honnete amytié que vous m'offrez, je feroye le contraire de ce que j'ai fait, qui me suis plus fiée en vous, qu'en tous les hommes du monde. . . . Je ne sçache chose qui me doive empécher de vous faire réponse selon votre desir, si non une crainte que j'ai en mon cueur, fondée sur le peu d'occasion que vous avez de me tenir telz propos. [X, 61–62]

These declarations therefore blur the line between truth and lie, for neither protagonist operates on a sure footing. And as the tale (actually a novelette in length) progresses, Amadour's mask melts and Floride's gains depth because of her acquired sophistication and bitterness. The confrontations between the two, resulting from a succession of these speeches, instead of clarifying their relationship make its difficulty more distinct to both of them. At each meeting a chance for truth brings about another veil, until Amadour finally declares his lustful desires (74); this naked fact makes a sham out of his previous statements and explains Floride's protective jockeying. Yet for the many years that this offensive-defensive game persisted, Floride was under the illusion that conversation and attention alone would satisfy him; until at the end in utter despair he seeks out death on the battlefield. The declarations then delineate the downward curve of the action and focus on a psychological fencing that destroys any attempt of sincerity on the characters' part. However, if their lengthy speeches obscure truth and judgment, they do provide for the novella a framework that holds a key to its elusive meaning.

When only one or two declarations occur in a novella, they automatically become the focal point of the narrative and often the axis around which the action revolves. Due to its very length, a declaration acquires a central and overwhelming position in a relatively short tale. It supposedly reflects a state of mind or of the emotions, truthful or not, and thereby acquires a lyrical quality, but it can also be a vehicle for self-justification or for blame toward others.[28] At all times it is a rhetorical dramatization of facts and sentiments already established or stated previously; therefore its logical redundance cries out. And even if such a speech reflects sincerity, the verbose inflation that truth undergoes undermines the credibility of the sentiments expressed. Thus what some consider a narrative defect assumes the status of a conscious effort on Marguerite's part to reveal falseness of purpose or ambiguity.[29] The rhetoric of the long declarations outweighs the actual meaning and intent of the stated feeling, because elegant speech producing an unnatural and contrived tone does not necessarily convey a sense of genuineness. Accordingly, the artifice of the declarations does not constitute a defect but fits once again into Marguerite's aesthetics of exposing false appearances and disguised or impenetrable truth.

Pitting a lengthy declaration against the debate at the end of the tale creates a further disintegration of any hoped-for synthesis or near absolute. By its very nature a rhetorical exposition of sentiments represents a position reached at that moment and not necessarily indicative of the speaker's sincerity or social status. Given this framework, there will be a loss of cohesive meaning in every novella that contains such

28. Novellas XV, XIX, XXII, XXIV, XL, XLII, XLVII, LIII, LXIII contain one or two declarations as central elements in the narrative pattern and attest to this frequency.

29. One of the most recent such opinions in a rather fairly long accepted line of criticism can be found in R. Lebègue, "Réalisme et apprêt dans la langue des personnages de l'Heptaméron," p. 80.

a pivotal declaration. The forty-second tale offers a typical example. Here a prince makes advances to a servant girl who naturally mistrusts him, and in a two-page oration which reveals a deliberate discrepancy between her elegant speech and her status, she admonishes him for not respecting her honor:

Non, Monseigneur, non. Ce que vous cerchez ne se peut faire. Car combien que je ne soi qu'un ver de terre, au pris de vous, j'ai mon honneur si cher, que j'aymeroie mieus mourir, que l'avoir diminué, pour quelque plaisir qui soit en ce monde. Et la crainte que j'ai que ceus qui vous ont veu venir céans se doutent de la vérité, me donne la peur et le tremblement que j'ai. Et puisqu'il vous plait me faire cet honneur de parler à moy, vous me pardonnerez aussi si je vous répon comme mon honneur le me commande. Je ne suis point si sote, Monseigneur, ne si aveuglée, que je ne voie bien la beauté et ne con-noisce les graces que Dieu a mises en vous, et que je n'estime la plus heureuse du monde celle qui possédera le cors et l'amour d'un tel Prince. Mais de quoy me sert cela, veu que ce n'est pour moy, ny pour femme de ma sorte, et que seulement le desir seroit à moy perfette folye. [XL, 248–49]

At first this harangue wards off the prince; ultimately it con-tributes to transforming his love into a sincere one toward her, but she still rejects him.

The debate at the end revolves around the question of honor, both the servant girl's and the prince's. And the over-whelming blame falls on Françoise the servant because what she considers honor may very well be hypocrisy and mortifi-cation, a blind refusal to accept true love when both parties love each other. The real hero of the tale turns out to be the prince, according to Longarine, the debater who has the last word: "Car qui peut faire mal et ne le fait point, cettuy la est bien heureus" (253). To the extent that it is possible, he has reached a degree of happiness by exhibiting an inner goodness and self-honesty that Françoise is not capable of, for she remains in darkness and in an ambiguous, even false context. Therefore her flowery declamation to him becomes in retrospect empty words and a mutilation of ideals. When cast against the disintegrating effects of the debate, the redundancy and inflated rhetoric in defense of her honor acquire a purpose: to better illustrate her mistaken or fluid position. The more a character attempts to substantiate a viewpoint or state of mind, the more he or she will reveal, in the eyes of the debaters and of Marguerite, flaws and uncertainties in motivation and attitude toward human conduct.

Marguerite's propensity for these dominating rhetorical patterns in tales appears in the form of long epistle-poems in four other novellas. These occurrences are nothing but a variation on the declaration-discourse technique and serve an identical purpose; they are found for the most part toward the beginning of the *Heptameron* with only one toward the end.[30] Prolixity and artifice mark these versified letters that contain the commoner clichés of love poetry and emulate the bombast of the Grands Rhétoriqueurs. It is all too easy to criticize the poor quality of this poetry, just as it may be tempting to blame the presence of these effusive and pretentious poems on Marguerite's carelessness in composing her novellas. Yet such immediate reactions deceive, for she must have been aware of the potential defects of these poem-epistles. Some may also criticize Balzac's long descriptive introductions before placing his characters into action or his affinity for letters that are accused of interrupting the flow of the narrative but in fact represent a portrait technique.

In the *Heptameron*, the poem-letter pierces through the veil of lies; in the very first example it unmasks its sender. Here the poem, just about four pages long, occupies almost

30. See novellas XIII, XIX, XXIV, LXIV.

half of the novella; it reveals a knight's love for his lady, a carnal love under a guise of purity. The accompanying diamond, featured in the *envoi*, pretends to symbolize this purity, but at the same time it implies a coldness:

> O diamant, di, un amant m'envoie[31]
> Qui entreprend cette douteuse voie,
> Pour mériter par ses oeuvres et faitz
> D'ettre du reng des vertueus perfetz,
> A fin qu'un jour il puisse avoir sa place
> Au désiré lieu de ta bonne grace.
>
> [XIII, 94]

Because of its rhetorical prolixity, this poem echoes Jean Lemaire de Belges's *Epistre à l'Amant Vert*, but it lacks the latter's rhythm, fecund imagery, and sincere lyricism, though both use an artifice for a mouthpiece to express sentiments to a lady: a diamond and a parrot. Marguerite gives to her poem-letter an inflated and contrived look in order to stress the falsity of the knight's love; a mood of affectation then permeates the whole novella, so that when the lady cruelly and laughingly avenges herself upon the knight's wife, no sense of tragedy emerges. One understands but without condoning.

Marguerite condemns excessive *parler*, which is the exact opposite of truth. Hence when the debate at the end of the novella focuses on the lady's reaction and conduct and pictures them in a positive light, but without attacking the knight's intentions that caused this cruelty, the poetic epistle's emptiness stands out all the more; the longer it is, the emptier it looms. Structurally it has a pivotal position since

31. As part of a parody of love poetry, and the abuses of Petrarchism, Rabelais uses a similar play on words when Pantagruel receives a note, cast in a ring, from a Parisian lady he has abandoned: "Dy amant faulx, pourquoy me as tu laissée?" (*Pantagruel*, ch. XXIV). Interestingly enough, this pun is not as frequent as one may think. Cf. my *Rabelais et l'Italie* (Florence, 1969), p. 94.

it stands between the narration of the knight's advances and the lady's reaction to them; thus it points both to his hypocrisy and to her learning the truth. A long-winded, false verbal edifice becomes ironically a conveyor of the truth; however, if it exposes the knight, it unleashes the lady's calculated cruelty which is certainly not any more laudable than his calculated steps toward seducing her. Not only then is the poem-letter a dubious expression of sentiments, but it causes perplexing results that defy judgment.

Marguerite presents polarized situations based on irreconcilable viewpoints. The tale itself may lack such a polarization, but the ensuing debate is sure to introduce it, since each debater has his own irreducible logic. Faced with a universe of opposites, contradictions, and paradoxes, Marguerite does not helplessly abandon herself to the maelstrom about her; on the contrary, she observes and weighs and tries to understand, but not necessarily to judge. This process may occur implicitly in the presentation of the story, but it surfaces in the debate following the tale.

Thanks to its dialogue form the genre of the theater allows her further to picture contrasting characters who actually impersonate ethical or religious concepts. Her plays are a precise counterpart to the debates in the novellas, for she seeks to reproduce the conflicts in life, not an invisible harmony. In *Le Mallade* (1535?), an early play, she casts a Sick Man, worldliness; a Wife, superstition; a Doctor, wisdom; and a Chambermaid, ecstasy or faith. No attempt will be made to cure the wife, a hopeless case. But the chambermaid, counseled by the physician who is just as rapacious as he is sagacious, will heal the husband, without even any bloodletting. At this stage, black can turn into white; faith and reason may cure a spiritual illness, but only a moderate one. In a later play, however, the *Comédie de Mont-de-Marsan* (1548) written a year before her death, Marguerite recasts the same four characters; here La Sage stands up to La Ravie on an equal footing, and neither La Mondainne nor La Supersticieuse give in to their two rivals. Marguerite has lost the limited optimism she once had.

On the specific subject of love, two plays offer a microcosm of the *Heptameron*. The *Comédie des quatre femmes* (1542), two maidens and two married women, actually has a cast of ten since it also features an elderly couple, the wisdom of age, and four men who confess past unhappy loves; it could very well be that these ten characters mirror the ten debater-narrators of tales in the *Heptameron*. The first wife incarnates resentment and bitterness; she continues to love her husband, who is actually unworthy of her love. The second one impersonates jealousy; her husband loves elsewhere.[32] The first maiden flaunts her indifference toward love—because she has never experienced it. The second one, recalling Louise Labé's *Débat de Folie et d'Amour*, praises the beneficial effects of love.[33] The elderly counseling couple cautions each of these protagonists against the weakness of her position, but to no avail; they do not and cannot change. When the four men appear toward the end of the play, their role will be again to oppose the women's attitudes and experiences; they will invite the ladies to dance, and Marguerite will not fail to pun on *danser-tenser*, "to quarrel."

The *Comédie du parfait amant* (1549), written the year of Marguerite's death, echoes the *Comédie des quatre femmes*

32. See *Théâtre profane*, p. 107:

> Il ayme ailleurs: voilà ma mort, ma guerre
> Je brusle, et ards: je me morfonds, je sue.
> En fièvre suis: mais mon seul Medecin [mari]
> Qui me pourroit du tout guarir, me tue.

33. See again *Théâtre profane*, pp. 110, 111:

> Sans Amour, un homme   Qui tient donc Amour
> Est tout ainsi, comme   Pour prison, et tour,
> Une froide Idole.   Il ha tresgrand tort.
> Sans Amour, la Femme   Amour je soustiens,
> Est fascheuse, infame,   Cause de tous biens
> Mal plaisante, et folle . . .   Jusques à la mort.

and in addition demonstrates that to the very last Marguerite faced, without solving it, the dialectics of an ideal set against the conflicting varieties of life. She condenses this failing search in just 186 verses, which in essence becomes a prototype of a debate at the end of a novella in the *Heptameron*. A timeless old woman is in search of crowning a "parfait amant." First she finds a faithful wife who remained so only until her husband had to be away for three months. A second wife has remained faithful because there have not been any temptations yet; the husband has always stayed home. In the third case, a wife has remained faithful in spite of her husband's absence for six months, but if she ever learned of his betraying her, she would repay him in kind. Finally the old woman finds a perfect couple; however neither man or woman wants to accept the crown and thinks the other deserves it, thus exhibiting a positive lack of vanity and of *philautie*, love of self. In this last play Marguerite wrote, a kind of testament, it could be argued that she does not lose hope since an ideal is realized. But it is realized in a dream more than in reality. The play clearly indicates that innocence in man is not a natural and common state; it will be lost at the first opportunity, even for the perfect couple.

A quick glance at some of the plays not only reinforces the prevalent thematic patterns of the *Heptameron* but its very formal essence—ambiguity and dialogue.[34] Indeed, these

34. For additional themes common to Marguerite, see the following plays: the *Comédie des Innocents* which opposes *cuyder* (false truth) to *vérité* both on a religious and ethical plane and delineates the discrepancy between an ideal state and an existing situation; *L'Inquisiteur* which plays on the words *savant* and *voir*; *Trop, Prou, Peu, Moins* which contrasts *oreille* (a natural but faulty hearing device, related to the first two characters) to *corne* (an artificial hearing aid equally uncertain), and both, of course, bear upon the *bruit* frequently found in the *Heptameron*. This last drama can be considered the most literary one because of its highly metaphoric language and its ambiguity due to the multifaceted nature of words. Its characters, at the same time enigmatic and mythic, create a pervading ambivalence that brings to mind Bonaventure Des Périers's *Cymbalum mundi*.

plays actually do not present dramatizations of individuals and their condition; they are merely an exercise in dialectics, a debate on issues by means of dialogues and longer monologues comparable to the emotional declarations in the stories. Without a doubt, therefore, dialogue is a mode of expression proper and essential to Marguerite; it is a primary tool in the exchange of ideas and opinions following the tradition of the medieval debate and the Platonic symposium. In turn such a mode reflects Marguerite's fluid position; she dissects the truth, or what is thought to be the truth, and moves from one segment to another, from one vista to the next. Such a spatial and visual movement leads to a suspension of judgment, and it explains the innovative inclusion of the conversation-debate, the symposium, at the end of each story.

It would be misleading then to think that Marguerite in the *Heptameron* has forgone the use of dialogue, as some believe.[35] To begin with, each novella is composed of a story and a debate, and by virtue of the formal nature of this debate it contains a varying abundance of dialogue. In fact, Marguerite has unwittingly formulated her own definition of a novella: story plus debate; in her case then it would be deceptive to confuse short story or tale with novella. True, dialogue as a means of communication or as a character portrait technique, both of which also produce a certain dynamism in the narrative, does not abound in the stories themselves; she assigns this function to the debates. This relative scarcity, or better, economy, of dialogue in the tale itself does not necessarily reveal a narrative weakness; on the contrary, it can be argued that it is a studied element aimed at focusing more on the conversations of the debates and at deemphasizing dramatic components that may contribute to synthesis

35. "Elle en [dialogue] use peu: c'est qu'elle se préoccupe moins de la mise en scène dramatique de ses nouvelles que de l'étude des sentiments" (Jourda, *Marguerite d'Angoulême*, II, 973).

in the story. Attracting attention to a developed dialogue in the tale, which would tend to produce a coalescent meaning if communication took place, would in turn detract from the fragmentation effect that Marguerite wants to produce within the story and by means of the debate. Of course, dialogues do exist in the *Heptameron*, in the manner that critics expect them in order to judge the quality of a short story, but in a minor key.

This economy of dialogue in a number of tales is marked by only one word or a short sentence in direct-discourse form. Although its relative frequency can be attributed to a medieval narrative tradition such as the fabliau, which Marguerite continues in this sense, or to a formal reminiscence of even the *Decameron*, because Boccaccio can also sprinkle dialogue parsimoniously in his tales, the fact remains that Marguerite does so to suit her own purposes, which may coincide with the practices of some of her literary predecessors. But this rarity of dialogue does not amount to a defect, any more than it does in Boccaccio.[36] A one-word or a short-sentence dialogue takes on the role of a dramatic flash that momentarily gives the impression of meaningful synthesis but leaves waves of fluidity.

In the sixtieth novella the only word spoken is *Jesus*, which succinctly dramatizes the perversion of religious dogmas and rites that has dominated this tale: confession, extreme unction, marriage. *Miracle* is the only word spoken in the sixty-fifth tale, and it immediately brings into focus the dubious nature and ambivalence of religious practice and human credibility. Nothing else is needed for the specific intent of this novella; any additional dialogue would detract from it and shift the thematic emphasis. In the twentieth, the only dialogue in the tale, a one-sentence statement, summarizes the male protagonist's point of view when he discovers his so-called lady with the stable boy: "Ma Dame,

36. Cf. V. Branca, *Boccaccio medievale* (Florence, 1956).

prou vous face, aujourd'huy par votre méchanceté connue, je suis guéry et délivré de la continuelle douleur dont l'honnetteté, qu'à tor j'estimoie ettre en vous, étoit cause" (136). Naturally in a short tale this one restricted dialogue, a word or sentence, takes on significance since it stands for the synthesizing element which the ensuing debate will endeavor to disintegrate. In a longer tale, such an occurrence still has a similar effect; when an older gentleman comments "Monsieur, c'est trop" (XXVI, 190) upon seeing his adopted son kiss rather passionately his adopted mother, this short statement contributes immeasurably toward fixing for the moment a meaning to the story before arriving at the debate.[37]

If an extreme concision of dialogue momentarily fixes a truth, an interpretation, a more dynamic, extended form of dialogue becomes a vehicle for deception, for veiling the truth. Again Marguerite reverses the common usage of a narrative technique, for extended dialogue does not constitute a truthful means of communication in her eyes. A rather heavy dose of direct discourse occurs, for example, in the fifth tale, in which a "batelière" pretends to lead two monks aboard her ferry to paradise, but actually leaves them in the desert; they do not succeed in seducing her. Dialogue abounds in the twenty-third tale, which features a confessor's success with the lady of the house to which he is attached; here to a great extent the dialogue serves as a means of shielding the confessor's devious intentions. The same means of deception hold true in the forty-first tale; a Franciscan monk at first attempts verbally to break down a maiden's resistance by engaging her in a conversation dominated by the erotic and deceptive metaphor "corde cinte" (243).

Even when the dialogue form totally dominates a tale, as when it fills two out of four pages in the forty-ninth tale, the

37. For a further sample of one word or sentence dialogue, see novellas XLVIII, LI, LIX.

pseudo-symposium atmosphere created by the participation of several conversationalists still conveys the sense of a game played with truth. The male protagonists finally drop the mask of pretense, realize and admit they have all been tricked by the same woman. The dialogue here stands for an admission and realization of truth, and counterpoints an earlier dialogue during which each protagonist kept his mask on; the conversation also reinforces the central element of playfulness and preludes the gentlemen's vengeance:

> Ma prison, dit Hatillon, commença et fina tel jour. La miéne, dit Duraciel, commença le propre jour que la votre et fina et dura jusques à tel jour. Valuëbon, qui perdoit patience, se preit à jurer et dire: Par le sang Dieu, à ce que je vois, je suis le tiers qui pensoi ettre le prémier et seul. Car j'entrai et en sailly tel jour. Les autres troys qui étoient à table jurnt qu'ilz avoient bien gardé ce jurérent reng. Or puisqu'ainsi est, dit Hatillon, je dirai l'état de notre géoliére. Elle est maryée et son mary est bien loin. C'est cette la propre, répondirent ilz tous. Or pour nous mettre hors de péne, dit Hatillon, moy qui suis le prémier en roolle, la nommerai aussi le prémier. C'est ma Dame la Comtesse qui étoit si audacieuse, qu'en gangnant son amytié, je pensoi avoir vincu un Caesar. Qu'à tous les Dyables soit la vilaine, qui nous a fait d'une chose tant travailler. . . . Si aymeroi je mieus ettre mort, qu'elle demeura sans punition. [274]

In this instance, Marguerite exhibits a certain talent in orchestrating a long comic dialogue which derives its humor from the development of an obvious notion beyond the logical limits of its meaning, as Molière could do so well; and the sparkle of this sort of dialogue adds considerably to the swift movement of the tale. Since this multiparty conversation, producing the atmosphere of a symposium, takes place in a tale dominated by the spirit of physical love, it brings out an anti-Platonic thrust, especially in the light of the setting: "un banquet où ils faisoient bonne chère" (273).

Marguerite, then, explores, in the tales themselves, several dialogue techniques always related to the many faces of truth and falsity. When a sparsity of dialogue prevails, the occurrence of a single word or sentence in direct discourse makes its calculated presence all the more dramatic and underscores its irony and double-entendre or its momentary validity. An identical effect results from a slightly extended dialogue, a rapid, strategically located exchange between the chief protagonists. A frequent cruelty, a piercing intellectual superiority, and a humorous brilliance tempered by irony form the trademark of the very concise as well as the slightly developed dialogue. In all these, direct flashes of discourse and conversation fall under a weight of constraint; they are never characterized by a total freedom of action and thought; they never give the impression of being a genuine means of communication; they conceal much more than they reveal. At all times, a dialogue, irrespective of its length, brings forth the oscillation between an apparent truth and its opposite, between wearing and dropping a mask, until the debate at the end of the story delineates the Pirandellian concept of naked masks, the relativism of truth. Considered in this light, Marguerite adapts to her own needs the paucity of dialogue typical of the medieval *conte* and even to some extent of the *Decameron*.

Because of the inherent weakness of the conventional dialogue form, as Marguerite sees it, she opts for the Platonic dialectical format which allows for an exchange of views and avoids the fixity of a global ideological conviction. Her Platonic affinity explains the usual overwhelming presence of the debate following a relatively short tale as well as its still strong impact on a more developed story. And the reason for the relative sparsity of conventional dialogue in the tales themselves then becomes quite plausible. Since the opinions propounded in the debate fragment the story, turn it upon itself to produce a kaleidoscopic effect just as happens in Diderot's *Jacques le fataliste*, these conversations understandably take on Marguerite's own peculiar stamp; they constitute a prime factor promoting ambiguity.

However, in the midst of fluidity and fragmentation, the characters of the narrator-conversationalists in the debates provide a constancy and also an index of any evolution there may be throughout the *Heptameron*. By remaining faithful to, or even somewhat evolving within, their framework of beliefs and moral code, the debaters become the real protagonists of the *Heptameron*, who coordinate this fresco of human conduct. A dialogue then ensues from one novella to another; it leads to a concatenation from which emerges an all-embracing unity of the work. The final synthesis is not an absolute thematic one but depends on the studied movement between and among novellas and on Marguerite's effort to provide foretelling and echoing thematic patterns throughout the *Heptameron*. Indeed, a structural study will easily demonstrate this dynamic unity.

5. STRUCTURE AND MEANING

BRANTÔME, the raconteur-historian, relates that according to his grandmother, who was one of Marguerite's ladies in waiting, the queen of Navarre composed her novellas in her litter while traveling from place to place.[1] He means to depreciate the quality and craftsmanship of the *Heptameron*. Unfortunately, this opinion of his lingers

1. "Elle composa toutes ses Nouvelles la pluspart du temps dans sa retirée. Je l'ay ouy ainsi conter à ma grand'mère, qui alloyt tousjours avec elle dans sa lytière comme sa Dame d'honneur, et luy tenoit l'escritoire dont elle escrivoit, et les mettoit par escrit aussitost et habilement, ou plus, que si on luy eust ditté." Pierre de Bourdeille, seigneur de Brantôme, "Des Dames," *Œuvres complètes* (Paris, 1882), p. 226.

on, though it is nowadays less sharp and more cautious. Suppose it is true that there is an alternation, either in the first day alone or in the *Heptameron* as a whole, between a shorter and a longer novella, or between a tragic one and a more spirited one. Is this the kind of thing, after all, that would be taken to indicate noteworthy craftsmanship in an accomplished writer?[2] In a collection of tales, a framework derived from the meeting of ten individuals who propose to narrate a story a day each for ten days does not quite guarantee a tight cohesion among the novellas; there remains the impression of a juxtaposition without any inner connection. Is this not the case here?

Such apparent effects can be deceptive, and certainly they are not persuasive, because Marguerite does give her reader some rather precise indications of studied composition in her work. Again the conversation-debates provide major indications of interior links between novellas, especially as these links can be perceived in the Le Hir edition in current use. When the entire debate comes after the tale, as in previous editions, a segment of it frequently introduces the transition to the next story. But here in the Le Hir edition, some of the debate becomes an integral part of the novella that follows. Since the conversations are split between two novellas, this division sometimes lets us observe a thematic overlap. Further, among other indices, the prologue to the *Heptameron* gives clear evidence that Marguerite works with a plan

2. Cf. Telle, pp. 96–139, especially pp. 96–105; and Jourda: "Cette première journée offre à cet égard, un tout bien constitué. On ne retrouve pas dans les autres journées un mélange de liaisons et d'oppositions aussi marqué. La princesse, semble-t-il, s'est vite lassée du travail que lui aurait imposé pareille méthode. Elle se borne, lorsqu'elle le peut, à indiquer nettement que deux nouvelles se répètent ou s'opposent, et, quelque fois, se répètent en s'opposant" (pp. 2, 963). Only recently have some additional pages been written giving a glimpse into a subtle plan on Marguerite's part; see A. J. Krailsheimer, "The *Heptaméron* Reconsidered," *The French Renaissance and Its Heritage: Essays presented to Alan B. Boase* (London, 1968), pp. 81–86.

in mind which grows clearer as the writing progresses.[3]

The notion of a prologue or preface contains by its very position and definition a paradox because it has usually been composed after the partial or full completion of the work it precedes. Balzac, for example, wrote the preface to his *Comédie humaine* after most of this literary fresco had been published; although he may not have intended it at the outset, after viewing the various components in relation to each other he realized that a certain pattern, order, and meaning emerged from the collage of his fictions. Similarly Marguerite composed her prologue sometime after 1545, because in it she refers to "les cent nouvelles de Jan Boccace nouvellement traduite d'Italian en françoys" (p. 18), which were in fact translated in that year by Antoine Le Maçon, commissioned by the queen to perform this task. Of course, the prologue could have seen the light at any time between that date and 1549, the year of her death. At any rate, even by 1545 the great majority of the novellas had already been written, and the prologue therefore represents to a large extent a post facto composition that foreshadows and illuminates thematic patterns interwoven in the *Heptameron*.

The prologue introduces the themes of perfect love and its potential failure, pro- and antimonasticism, class superiority seen ironically, the relativism of judgment, and the multifaceted nature of human behavior in any given circumstance; and it dwells at some length on the art of the novella, its purpose and composition. The setting of the prologue, as is well known, is the spa of Cauterets in the Pyrenees and the flooding of that area due to the fall rains, which force a

3. The title of a recent study would indicate that it deals with the structure of the *Heptameron*, but actually it comes to a well-worn conclusion: "Marguerite interessiert sich dabei vor allem für die Psychologie ihrer Gestalten. Sie gehört besonders zu den Vorläufern des psychologischen Romans." W. Krömer, "Die Struktur der Novelle in Marguerite de Navarres *Heptaméron*," *Romanistisches Jahrbuch*, 18 (1967), 88.

group of individuals to seek refuge in a monastery. These baths become something of a microcosm of the *Heptameron*: "se trouvérent à ceus de Cauderetz, plusieurs personnes, tant de France et Espagne que d'autres lieus: les uns pour boire de l'eaue, les autres pour s'y bagner, et les autres pour y prendre de la fange" (11). Although geographically logical, the nationalities of the spa visitors also announce the predominance of France and Spain, as well as Italy, in the settings of the novellas.[4] The variety of activities that the visitors can engage in at the spa partially prefigures the ambivalence and relativism surrounding the meaning of each novella.

On the surface it would appear that Marguerite, queen of Navarre and sister of François I, advocates by virtue of her position a supremacy of the noble class: "Quand toute la compagnie oÿt parler de la bonne dame Oysille et du gentil chevalier Symontaut, feirent une joye inestimable, louant le Créateur, qui *en se contentant des serviteurs, avoit sauvé les maitres et maitresses.* Et sur toutes en loua Dieu de bon cueur Parlamente. Car long tems avoit qu'elle le tenoit pour tres-affectionné serviteur" (14–15). Taken out of context, the statement italicized by us could indeed substantiate an anti-lower-class attitude, but the ambivalence arising from the two different uses of *serviteur* definitely weakens a feeling of class superiority; one may even detect a sly smile. If God satisfies himself with servants to let their masters live and thereby allows Parlamente to have her own servant, Symontaut, it should not be forgotten that Symontaut also serves both his lady and God. In the final analysis, the masters are the real *serviteurs.* As in the novellas, social factors do not exist primarily per se but in function of human behavior and love relations.

4. Cf. V. L. Saulnier, "Martin Pontus et Marguerite de Navarre: La Réforme lyonnaise et les sources de l'*Heptaméron*," *Bibliothèque d'Humanisme et Renaissance,* 21 (1958), 593–94.

Marguerite's dual position toward monks is clearly announced in the prologue. First she depicts the Abbey of Saint Savin in a very positive light; here the abbot and his colleagues give shelter to the stranded travelers who have escaped the flood, and one of the monks helps them reach Notre Dame de Sarrance, the monastery where they will all meet to wait for the waters to recede. To reinforce this climate of charity and kindness, the setting is pastoral, idyllic, and biblical; later, shepherds also house the travelers and introduce them to a monk who will show them the way to the monastery (cf. p. 14). On the other hand, the abbot of Notre Dame de Sarrance fits the more traditional pattern of the monk in literature; hypocrisy and avarice dominate his character: "Mais luy qui étoit vray hypocrite, leur feit le meilleur visage qu'il luy fut possible . . . mais il n'y meit pas un denier. Car son avarice ne le permetoit" (15). Since the momentarily stranded travelers and spa visitors, the future storytellers and debaters, are to spend the next few days (ten, they think) in this abbot's monastery, it is not surprising that the monks in their stories reflect this experience as well as previous similar observations. Yet the debaters are careful to point out that a monk's depravity in the tales constitutes neither a rule nor an exception, as they must remember the Abbey of Saint Savin where they had first stayed and in particular the old monk helpful to them.

Almost from the very start of the prologue the stage is set for events along the notions of ideal and courtly love. Although initially the general description of the setting and of the protagonists' behavior follows the rules of the game, so to speak, the adventures encountered by these individuals, when considered on a metaphoric plane, and the identities and activities of husbands and *serviteurs* begin to cast shadows on the perfection of the tableau:

Il y avoit aussi en la compagnie des Françoys, deus gentizhommes qui étoyent alez aus bains, plus pour accompagner les Dames dont ils étoyent serviteurs, que pour faute qu'ilz eussent de santé. Ces gentizhommes icy voyans la compagnie se départir, et que les marys de leurs Dames les emmenoient à par, pensérent de les suyvre de loin, sans se déclarer. [12]

First husbands, then *serviteurs*, protect the ladies from highway bandits; one husband survives, Hircan, as well as the two *serviteurs*, Dagoucin and Saffredan, and the two ladies, Parlamente and Longarine. This divulgence of identities obviously allows Parlamente to be matched with Dagoucin and Longarine with Saffredan; the first couple, considering what will subsequently be learned about it, comes closest to the ideals of perfect or Platonic love, Dagoucin much more so than Parlamente; but the second couple cannot reconcile reality with idealism. Actually, Saffredan closes ranks with Hircan in advocating a rational epicurism tempered with a strong dose of cynicism. This kaleidoscopic range of individuals cannot form a homogeneous micro-society adhering to a code of idealistic values.

The hardships resulting from the flood and the adventures encountered by the future storytellers smack of allegory, and the use of the bear image, on two occasions, reinforces this philosophizing tone. Yet a certain emerging melodrama also produces a sense of parody of ideal love values. The two *serviteurs* coming to the rescue of their ladies are easily reminiscent of some of the scenes in mock epics such as the *Orlando furioso*:

Les deux gentishommes regardans aus fenettres, veirent les deus dames plorantes, et cryantes si for, que la pitié et l'amour leur creut le cueur, de sorte que comme deus ours enragez décendentz des montagnes, frapérent sur ces bandouillers tant furieusement, qu'il y en eut si grand nombre de mortz, que le demeurant ne voulut plus attendre leurs coups. [12]

Furthermore this particular passage introduces the metaphoric theme of the window, quite notable in the novellas. Then the reader learns that two other ladies, later identified as Nomerfide and Ennasuite, have escaped from the claws of a bear:

> Car les pauvres Dames à demye lieue de Peirchite, avoient trouvé un ours décendant de la montagne devant lequel avoient pris la course à si grand' hate qu'à l'entrée du logis, leurs chevaus tombérent mortz souz elles, et deus de leurs femmes, qui étoient venues long tems apres, leur avoient conté que l'ours avoit tué tous leurs serviteurs. [13]

In the background loom the flood and Fortune, and everyone must eat his share of "ce gateau" (13). This flood does not have the same broad metaphysical repercussions that Boccaccio's plague has in the prologue to the *Decameron*.

In her own prologue Marguerite limits her scope to faith and love; from the baths the protagonists will eventually reach the safety of the Abbey of Serrance, with its dubious abbot, and the interrelations among themselves indicate more than casual or fortuitous acquaintance. The journey to this abbey, itself not quite flawless, is fraught with danger, and few reach their destination.[5] The image of the bear, whether in a protective or attacking context, represents these dangers—specifically, passions.[6] With its literal and metaphoric occurrences, it becomes the icon that casts its shadow on and over the *Heptameron*. The verisimilitude it conveys —bears were native to the Pyrenees and posed a danger to

5. The wavering attitude toward a reliance on monasteries and monks in order to reach safety does not necessarily prove a traditional antimonastic feeling. It can just as well indicate an ambivalent acceptance of the existing religious framework: "s'il y avoit moyen d'eschapper d'un danger les moynes le debvoient trouver" (2).

6. The presence of this image may serve the same purpose as the sudden appearance of the three beasts before the pilgrim-sinner in the first canto of the *Divine Comedy*.

travelers—performs a function only on the literal level and should not obscure its allegorico-metaphorical meaning.

Marguerite carefully establishes the purpose of her novellas; they are to be a pastime. And in attributing this function to them, she reflects the dominant principle of the Renaissance *novelliere*.[7] She clearly states that the forthcoming novellas will serve as means to "adoucir l'ennuy" (15) and to avoid the "danger de devenir malades" (16). Both conditions result from losses of loved ones, losses of varying importance: "Chacun n'a pas perdu son mary comme vous, et pour perte de serviteurs, ne se faut desespérer, car lon en recouvre assez" (16). Again the concept of ideal love comes under fire, but above all, the stories are to assuage the sickness of love, that Ovidian concept, and make more tolerable the task of living. These functions of the novellas are a counterpoint to the therapeutic value of the baths at the beginning of the prologue: "qui sont choses si merveilleuses, que les malades abandonnez des médecins, s'en retournent tout guéris" (11); thus a curative purpose emerges for the novellas from the prologue and then pervades the work as a whole. But therapeutics and didacticism should not be confused; the former soothes and tempers, while the latter moralizes. Marguerite chooses therapeutics in her *Heptameron*; she guides, and leaves a margin of choice instead of instructing directly. In this particular healing value of a literary work we detect a pattern that recurs in Renaissance writers of fiction. Three years after Marguerite's death, Rabelais in the prologue to the *Fourth Book* advocates moderation and wishes for health, while posing the fundamental question at the end of the work, already answered by the very writing of the book, "comment haulser le temps," how to raise fair weather, how to pass time (chap. 65).

Thus the function of the pastime is rather clearly de-

7. The best study on this matter remains the one by W. Pabst, *Novellentheorie und Novellendichtung* (Hamburg, 1953).

lineated; but it is of the nature of pastime to reject uniformity and its very multiplicity announces the pluralism to be found in the novellas. When asked what kind of pastime she advocates, Oysille, the fundamentalist, opts for the Scriptures as a model of life:

> Mes enfans, vous me demandez une chose, que je treuve
> for difficile: de vous enseigner un passetems, qui vous
> puisse délivrer de vos ennuys. Car ayant cerché ce remé-
> de toute ma vie, n'en ai jamais trouvé qu'un, qui est la
> lecture des saintes lettres, en laquelle je treuve la vraye,
> et perfette joye de l'esperit d'ond procéde le repos et la
> santé du cors. [16]

To counteract this spiritual extreme, Hircan offers the materialistic and sexual viewpoint:

> Mais si faut il que vous regardez quelque passetems et
> exercice corporel . . . faut choisir quelque passetems qui
> ne soit point dommageable à l'ame, et soit plaisant aus
> cors . . . si je pensoie que le passetems que je voudroie
> choisir, fut aussi agréable à quelqu'une de la compagnie,
> comme à moy, mon opinion seroit bien tot dite. . . . [17]

Parlamente, i.e., Marguerite, refuses to accept either of these positions; she chooses a middle ground because of her temperament: "laquelle n'étoit jamais oysive ne mélancholique"; this character should once and for all dispel the plausibility of any quietist tendencies that critics have wanted to see in Marguerite, at least in the *Heptameron*. Parlamente-Marguerite propounds a pastime which has a much broader basis, applicable to as many as possible: "celuy qui doit ettre commun à tous" (17)—the novellas. And these novellas will hopefully be more beneficial than the "images, ou pater-notres" (17) that travelers bring back from pilgrimages, for they will reflect the multifarious experiences of life, and not some static spiritual abstraction or icon. Furthermore, the tales are not an absolute;[8] all are of equal value, "car au jeu nous sommes tous égaus" (19). No part is more important than the composite whole.

Marguerite seizes upon a most felicitous image, the bridge, which stands for the forthcoming act of storytelling and at the same time transmits the irreconcilability of fiction and reality; this latter meaning emerges, as it turns out, by accident. Because the flooding waters have destroyed a bridge connecting the Monastery of Sarrance across a ravine with the mainland, the *brigata* will spend the time needed to repair it narrating tales. The repair of the bridge then becomes the metaphor of storytelling. The bridge will link metaphorically the world of fiction, the monastery place where the stories are narrated, with the world of reality across the ravine, but because Marguerite never reached the end of her proposed work, the members remain forever in a world of fiction. However, in the novellas themselves they try to reconcile fiction and reality when as debaters, as individuals guided by the experiences of life, they dispute or agree with the actions of the characters. In this vein, Marguerite foreshadows Cervantes, whose Don Quixote wants to live in a world of fiction but is constantly forced back into reality. On the other hand, the unfinished bridge also brings the *Heptameron* closer to the *Canterbury Tales*: just as we will never know what would have happened if the bridge had been completed, if the full hundred stories had been written and its narrators had crossed back to the real world, so we will never know who would have received first prize if the pilgrims had returned to the inn.[9] This open-endedness, whether deliberate or accidental, not only provides a state of suspension and ambivalence, but above all asserts the hegemony of fiction over reality.

8. Cf. "si quelqu'un d'entre nous trouve quelque chose plus plaisante, je m'accorderai à son opinion" (18).

9. Cf. Krailsheimer, p. 92.

Specifically, on a metaphoric plane, the source of inspiration and fiction is the field where the narrator-debaters will meet to exercise their pastime:

> Tous les jours depuis midy jusques à quatre heures nous alons dans ce beau pré, le long de la riviére du Gave, où les arbres sont si feuilluz que le soleil n'y sçauroit percer l'ombre, n'y échaufer la frécheur . . . et ne faillirent pas à midy de se trouver au pré selon leur délibération, qui étoit si beau et plaisant, qu'il auroit besoin d'un Bocace pour le dépindre à la verité. Mais vous vous contenterez que jamais n'en feut veu un pareil. [18–19]

Because Marguerite gives a stylized and brief description of her meadow instead of any such luxuriant and detailed description as is found in the prologue to the *Decameron*, she has been thought to be taking an anti-Boccaccian stand, against the sensuous quality of his prose.[10] But such a critical stance makes things too simple.

Marguerite is not against Boccaccio; rather she has decided she will not write in the manner of her distinguished predecessor both because it will not suit her purposes and because she is wisely aware that she might not succeed if she tried. To begin with, this particular spareness of description prefigures the work as a whole, in which natural scenes have no place; but it does not follow that Marguerite, for example, takes a stand against a naturalism à la Rabelais or Montaigne. On the contrary, this scanting of details belongs to her style; she does not create a setting for her characters to move in, but pits them directly one against another to explore their motivations and helplessness against the face of their condition. In short, stylistically she is Pirandellian and not Balzacian.

In giving her definition of the novella, Marguerite will eventually fail to distinguish between theory and practice;

10. Cf. Delègue, p. 34.

she will not abide by some guidelines she propounds in the prologue. The ambivalence of her theoretical propositions allows her much leeway. In advocating the veracity of the forthcoming stories, she neither takes a stand against Boccaccio, as it may appear, nor does she actually pretend that every novella contains verifiable events in history, although she claims so: "délibérérent d'en faire autant, si non en une chose différente de Bocace: c'est de n'écrire nouvelle qui ne soit véritable histoire" (18). The key word is *véritable*—"real"; but it does not mean the same as *vrai*—"true." Although there may be a coincidence of the two adjectives in some novellas, Marguerite states that her tales are not outlandish; they have happened or can happen in life. And she differentiates herself from Boccaccio in order to give herself some distinction and not appear as a mere imitator. Even if they share the identical purpose of assessing the broad spectrum of human behavior, she will not wear, for example, his broad comic mask that distorts a fictional reality. In essence, when claiming authenticity or verisimilitude, Marguerite plays the perennial mystifying game of fiction writers, while at the same time she wants to convince the reader of the basic substance of life found in her novellas. Then unfortunately critics take her *véritable* literally and engage in the somewhat curtailing, if not sterile, game of the *roman à clef*, thereby denying the ascendancy of fiction, even if on occasion there is an historical basis in a novella.

Self-depreciation belongs to the bag of literary tricks a writer can use to avoid criticism or to bolster his position and merits; Montaigne was a masterly practitioner of this deceptive art. Again in keeping with a traditional technique of the novella genre, already noted in the case of that tempting bait, *véritable*, Marguerite lures the reader with her self-depreciation. Supposedly she will follow the advice of some in the royal family, including herself, who had first thought of this storytelling project as a pastime, and she will exclude from the category of narrators "ceus qui avoient étudié et étoient gentz de lettres. Car Monseigneur le Dauphin ne vouloit que leur art y fut mélé; et aussi de peur que la beauté de la rhétorique feit tor en quelque partie à la vérité de l'histoire" (18). First of all, Marguerite does not present these precepts as her own or the ones that she will necessarily follow, now that this group is about to embark on its journey of fiction. She was and is part of both groups, but the one composed of royal members did not materialize in their narrative endeavor, whereas the group she is with has done so. Even if one refuses to differentiate between the two groups, the attack against "la beauté de la rhétorique" still does not convince.

Those who consider this attack another censure of Boccaccio, specifically of his flowing yet chiseled syntax and style, do not seize upon the essential meaning of mystification and self-depreciation conveyed by this apparent slap at a specific concept of style.[11] Furthermore Marguerite herself will fall under a heavy rhetorical spell in the long and short declamations which her characters indulge in so often; i.e., she does not take her own advice. Given this discrepancy between theory and practice and the ambivalence resulting from which group is actually or supposedly advocating the hegemony of truth over art, it becomes clear that the anti-artistico-rhetorical statement cannot be taken at face value. Marguerite placates the reader in hopes of avoiding future criticism concerning the aesthetic weakness of her novellas, while quite aware that they have their own literary raison d'être.

The *novellieri* of the Renaissance are obsessed with Boccaccio as a model to emulate, but none really manages to equal him. Stylistically Marguerite's sentence does not undulate like Boccaccio's; it is either spontaneous and natural or it is contrived, and rarely chiseled. Instead her novella re-

11. Delègue, p. 32.

volves around an image or a patterned metaphoric language; there is little in her of manicured Flaubertian prose or the convoluted Proustian syntax or even the Senecan amble in Montaigne. Yet she has a consciousness of style, for a syntax of a distinct causal quality marks her prose; one need only observe the high frequency of causal conjunctions in her writing.[12] On the surface, such a syntactical characteristic may smack of simplicity and even carelessness; actually it integrates form and content. There are many shades of "because" in the novellas, since Marguerite above all is always asking herself "Why?"; she seeks the truth behind apparent contradictions and paradoxes in human behavior and studies the irreconcilability of fiction and reality.

At this point a further ambivalence, if not irony, mars the statement that art and rhetoric will be left out in order not to jeopardize the truth of the tale. Each story reflects a measure of verisimilitude, some more than others, but there is not just one "vérité de l'histoire"; inevitably the truth becomes fragmented either in the tale itself or in the hands of the debaters, or in both. And Marguerite knows it when she writes the prologue; therefore her smile pierces this veil of self-apology. Just as some irony emerges from her stance against art and rhetoric because it reflects rather a certain incapacity, a self-apology, than a conviction. Yet Marguerite the novella craftsman succeeds in her own way.

In the prologue the question of the interrelation rhetoric-

12. Cf. the cited article by A. Lorian; however, we do not agree with the conclusion, which reflects a reading itself contradictory to the purposes of such a technique stated by the author: "C'est donc un procédé stylistique en accord avec les tendances de la prose française de l'époque et correspondant à des besoins intellectuels et artistiques profondément ressentis par l'auteur. La technique est commode, mais sent un peu trop la contrainte de la logique et la naïveté de l'emphase; et, poussée à l'extrême, comme elle l'est dans l'Heptaméron, elle crée trop souvent une forte impression de monotonie, d'artificialité et de maladresse" (p. 119). We are not aware of this excess or artificiality; perhaps the author comes to this conclusion in order not to stray from the prevalent attitude toward Marguerite's style.

art-truth brings out the final matter of the persona and focuses on the purposely nebulous distinction between fiction and reality. As already noted, first some members of the royal family, including Marguerite, had wanted to compose short stories emulating Boccaccio's; now the present group, still including the king's sister, will undertake the task. Therefore, Marguerite in person remains the one constant and assumes the role of the omniscient narrator who will control and activate the fictitious narrator-debaters in the *Heptameron*. Thus in the prologue she presents herself as the pervading persona-narrator in the forthcoming novellas. Furthermore the dual composition of either group, both containing members of the royal family and other individuals, unspecified and therefore fictitious, ties in with the sense of historicity, of ambiguous truth, which Marguerite wants to give to the background of her novellas. She and her brother the king, as well as other historical figures, appear either directly or indirectly in a number of tales; their presence ostensibly gives a stamp of authenticity and authority to the novella. Yet the fiction submerges them, and the splintering effect of the debate erases the faint seal of history. Historicity does not quite become the vehicle for fiction that one finds in *Le Rouge et le Noir*, but the introduction in the prologue of historical figures and fictitious individuals as potential narrators and personae in the novellas announces the blurred demarcation line between fiction and reality, so pronounced in the *Heptameron*, in order to mute the clarity of an absolute truth.

Technically the prologue to the *Heptameron* is the prologue to the first day. The rest of the days have each its own prologue, but a much shorter one, never more than half a page. These additional prologues tighten and brace the exterior framework, but more important, they produce a relationship between themselves and the main prologue that reveals a dichotomy of the spiritual and the materialistic.

They also stress the integration of this dichotomy with literary creation, the consciousness of the abyss separating the ideal from the real. In fact, this consciousness becomes more pronounced as day follows day and one views the curve described by the successive prologues.

Whereas the main prologue orchestrates and announces the forthcoming themes of the work, the smaller ones are dominated by a spiritual atmosphere to which a preoccupation with the creative process is opposed. Oysille reigns at these daily preambles, mornings and afternoons, that bring together the other nine narrators. Her function both on a thematic and a metaphoric level had already been established in the main prologue; there when asked what her pastime was, she answered: "Pareillement avant souper, je me retire pour donner pature à mon ame de quelque leçon" (15). To stress the ascendancy of the spiritual, the image of *pature,* or some generic form of it, appears in each prologue, beginning with the fifth day, to denote the reading of the Scriptures: "ma Dame Oysille leur prepara un déjeuner spirituel" (242), "La Compagnie trouva cette viande si douce" (280), "Au matin ne faillit ma Dame Oysille de leur administrer la salutaire pature" (314), "prièrent ma Dame Oysille de leur donner la pature spirituelle comme elle avoit accoutumé" (357). Significantly when *viandes* had occurred in the third prologue, it had the literal meaning of food for the body, to be taken with moderation in order not to interfere with the impending task of storytelling (39).

In the prologues to each day, the dominance of spirituality remains, however, a matter of implicit or explicit emphasis. In the first four, it lurks in the background, but still pervades the *brigata*'s mood; whereas in the last four a detailed description of the Scripture readings is given. On the surface, then, one could argue for an apparent curve toward a dominance of the spiritual that would also purposely contrast with an increasing ferocity and depravity (cf. LI, LXX). Actually activities in each prologue revolve around a mixture of spiritual food and physiological or concrete food, the care for soul and body. Again the general prologue to the first day has a foreshadowing function; here Oysille, pure spirit, is opposed to Hircan, pure physical appetites, and Parlamente stands between the two. In the prologue to each successive day, the debater-narrators alternate between going to Oysille for spiritual food and eating to satisfy bodily needs, and afterwards preparing for the narration of tales, that is, figuratively going to Parlamente, who is Marguerite's persona. Parlamente incarnates a third kind of *pature*, the novellas, a mixture of spirit and body—of fiction and truth.

The rest of the prologues echo the prologue to the first day by making repeated allusion to the great care exercised to insure the quality and truth of the tales. Hence the figurative connotations of the antirhetorical stance taken in the general first prologue gain further validity. The stress placed on memory will at the same time continue the game on veracity and reveal the difficulty and attentive planning and rehearsal involved in the process of writing the novellas: "s'en alèrent diner ramentevans les uns aus autres plusieurs histoires passées" (II, prol., 80); "La messe oÿe bien devotement et le diner passé assez sobrement, pour n'empescher, par les viandes, leur mémoire, à s'aquiter chacun à son reng le mieus qu'il luy seroit possible, se retirérent en leurs chambres, à visiter leurs registres . . ." (III, prol., 139). This statement might even imply the consultation of a written or rough draft of the story as well as refer to memory. "Le diner achevé, s'en alèrent reposer pour étudier leur rolle" (IV, prol., 204); here we have the concept of a studied fiction. "Et apres alèrent diner, ramentevans cette vie apostolique [listening to the reading of Saint Luke]. En quoy ilz preindrent tel plaisir que quasi leur entreprise étoit oublyée" (VII, prol., 315). This remark again indicates the explicit emergence of spirituality in the second half of the *Heptameron* and almost displaces the attention given to the task of storytelling; even the form of *ramentevans*, first used in the prologue to the second day to express the recollection and practice of narration, occurs here in a biblical context. As a matter of fact, in the very same prologue to the seventh day, Oysille refers to the content of Saint Luke as "ces contes" (315). Obviously in Oysille's eyes the Scriptures are the only real, the only true tales worthy of man's attention, for they contain the best available *exempla*. By virtue of becoming "contes," the biblical readings are automatically contrasted with the novellas; the spiritual, idealistic framework is opposed to the fictionalized concrete experiences of life. And once again, the two do not and cannot coincide.

As the nature of the spiritual food becomes more specific, and therefore only in appearance more prevalent, some of its traces can be observed in the stories following the prologue of the seventh day.[13] The specificity of the biblical readings in the prologues thus acquires much more of a thematic structural function within the novellas of that day than an intrinsic importance in a supposed ascendancy of spirituality in the prologues. Even if the emphatic curve of spirituality in the prologues is one of explicitness rather than substance, this omnipresence throughout the prologues creates an embracing effect upon the novellas and a transparent veil that may attempt to mitigate the harshness, tragedy, and despair, the cruel and cynical whim found in the tales. Yet essentially the steadfastness of the religiosity, of this spiritual food, is broken down by the pessimism of the stories.

The prologues themselves demonstrate both the difficulty of maintaining a precarious balance between body and soul

13. In the prologue to the eighth day, the last one written, Marguerite further states that Oysille kept her audience longer than usual in order to finish the Book of St. John, begun in the prologue to the sixth day (cf. 280 and 351).

and the surge of one or the other in relation to creativity. Following the momentum of the first prologue and day, the second prologue expresses an eagerness on the narrators' part to proceed with the tales and their opinions about them. Then in the third prologue they are so enthralled by Oysille's readings that they almost fail to go to mass, but later they continue with "ce beau voyage" (139), the act of narrating novellas. By the beginning of the fourth day the narrators show signs of fatigue; they arrive late at Oysille's. Paraphrasing Saint Luke 14:20, they playfully excuse themselves: "J'ai une femme" (204).[14] This expression means that a pause was taken to satisfy bodily needs, sexual ones. Significantly enough, Hircan and his wife Parlamente are the last ones to arrive, and he chides her for her laziness. On a metaphoric plane, her lethargy stands for a loss of interest in sex, a momentary lack of inspiration, and literally a tiredness of the spirit. Oysille will try to remedy these shortcomings with appropriate readings from the Scriptures, and Marguerite-Parlamente will also help herself by renewing the narration of novellas.

In an otherwise total spiritual atmosphere, antimonasticism, echoing the first prologue, reappears in the fifth one; the abbot hopes for a rapid return to normality and access to the outside world, because he misses his "pelerines accoutumées" (242). Nothing interrupts the spirituality of the sixth prologue, but the ecstatic atmosphere reaches such a point in the seventh one that the narrators almost forget to proceed with the storytelling that waits on them. This lapse suggests a counterpoint to Hircan's and Parlamente's late arrival in the fourth prologue and illustrates the interrelation of literary creation and spiritual comfort or crisis. In the seventh prologue, the youngest of the group, Nomerfide, has to re-

14. Cf. "And another said, I have married a wife, and therefore I cannot come."

mind them that the inviting meadow awaits their return for more novella narrations. In the last prologue, Oysille may keep the group longer than usual; they may be enthralled by her readings and spiritual experience and retire to reflect upon it—"pour y donner ordre" (357)—but even at this stage some wish the bridge would never get finished.

Indeed the bridge, symbol of the gap between an earthly paradise and the outside world, and between fiction and reality, reappears in the course of the prologues. Its meaning and function echo those already set in the first prologue, for the bridge serves as a reminder of the ephemeral nature of the narrators' present condition and stands for the creation of fiction. Either by coincidence or design, the bridge goes unmentioned until the prologue to the fifth day, the point that would have marked the middle of the proposed work; some in the group dread its completion, which will mean a return to the real world: "Et Saffredan leur dit qu'il voudroit que le pont demeurat encores quatre moys à faire pour le plaisir qu'ilz prenoient à la bonne chère qu'ilz faisoient" (242). The absence of the bridge stands for an idyllic life conducive to creativity, and it implies that inspiration, here represented by the metaphor of the meadow, needs to operate in a calm climate, outside time and space, while drawing upon the harshness of experience. The other mention of the bridge, in the eighth, that is the last extant prologue, is a rather full one, the fullness indicating obsession with and fear of the impending end, but it provides the incentive to proceed with the task at hand; hence the construction of the missing bridge acquires the role of an urging muse. Although not originally so intended by Marguerite, the incomplete bridge voids the gap between fiction and reality within the framework of the *Heptameron*; the narrator-debaters will never have to cross back into the outside world and will remain in the comfort and security of their utopia, nurtured by the unchallenged scriptural readings. But their tales do reach the other teeming shore, embody the complexities and contradictions found there, and bring with them the inexorable irreconcilability of the two shores.

While the prologue to each day reflects and continues some key thematic projections of the main prologue to the first day, it also announces one or more levels of meaning particular to the novellas for its day. This Janus-like role underscores the cohesion in the *Heptameron* and attests to a careful, subtle, and preconceived planning, here within a given day. We need analyze no more than two days from this critical point of view to demonstrate the validity and potential of this interrelation between a prologue and the novellas that follow it, and to bring into clearer view another seemingly invisible framework. Let us then discuss the fifth day, the day that would have been the center of the work originally intended, and the seventh day, the last full day of the uncompleted French decameron as it stands. These two days will illustrate the system of structural ramification.

In a typical vein, the prologue to the fifth day offers the usual dichotomy of the ideal and the real, of the soul and the body, while presenting four themes or thematic metaphors that will pervade the day's ten novellas, either literally or with a reversed meaning from the original one. The first two themes belong to the spiritual realm; Oysille gives her companions the customary "déjeuner spirituel . . . pour fortifier le cors et l'esprit," and then they go "[s]'exercer à la contemplation des saintz propos" (242). The next two themes counterbalance the preceding two; Saffredan wishes it would take another four months to build the bridge "pour le plaisir qu'ilz prenoient à la bonne chère qu'ilz faisoient" (a further counterpoint to Oysille's activity), and the abbot wants his unexpected guests out of the way because in their presence "n'ausoit faire venir ses pelerines accoutumées" (242).

This last theme, the monks' lust, becomes the link to the day's first tale, the forty-first, whose purpose is to demonstrate that "l'aveuglement de leur fole concupiscence, leur ote toute crainte et prudente consideration" (242); here indeed a monk attempts to seduce a maiden in the confessional. The exploitation of this traditional situation aims as much at starting the day on an entertaining note as at moralizing and castigating the culprit. The forty-second novella mirrors and at the same time rejects the metaphoric meaning of the "contemplation des saintz propos"; the self-mortification, that is, the saintliness of a peasant girl resisting the advances of a prince is seriously questioned in this story, as is self-glorification, whether sought or not. The next novella, featuring the lascivious Yambique, whose life is spent in pursuit of "bonne chère" (257), echoes in reverse fashion the same nominal activity in the prologue. Yambique too had succumbed to a false glory: "[elle] avoit préféré la gloire du monde à sa conscience" (257). The forty-fourth novella returns to the corruption of the "cordeliers," who also seduce women with words by falsifying the meaning of the Scriptures, and thus it illustrates a perversion of the first theme, the abuse of the "déjeuner spirituel." A visual and again abusive "contemplation des saintz propos" occurs in the forty-fifth novella; a covetous married man goes out with a cooperative chambermaid "faire le crucefys sur la neige" (263) while we watch them. Here the question arises whether the wife who accepts her husband's behavior is really a saint.

The novella beginning the second half of the day recalls the tale introducing the same day, for both reflect the fourth theme of the introduction, the monks' lust. In addition, this forty-sixth novella, by stressing the untrustworthiness of Franciscans, also illustrates the reverse side of the first theme in the day's prologue; the monks serve their religious constituency a false and deceptive "déjeuner spirituel." The forty-seventh story takes a mundane view of the second thematic precept in the prologue, the "contemplation des saintz propos"; here the "amour parfait" between two men proceeds well until the wife of one of them interferes and jealousy sets in. If the wife's sustained patience gives her a saintly aura, the relation and the conversations between the two men convey a distorted view of ideal, saintly conduct. The forty-eighth tale reverts to the antimonastic theme; a friar goes to bed with a newlywed bride while the bridegroom still dances in the courtyard with the guests. This third tale within the same day about monastic concupiscence causes Oysille to exclaim: "Mon Dieu . . . ne serons nous jamais hors des contes de ces facheus Cordeliers? Ennasuyte luy répondit: Si les Dames, Princes et gentiz hommes ne sont point épargnez, il me semble que les Cordeliers ont grand honneur de ce qu'on digne parler d'eus" (271). The real target is not the monks, but man, no matter what mask he wears, whether a frock or a lace ruff and sword. And on this particular day, most specifically, vainglory and an ironic "bonne chère" are the prime targets: "Car l'habit est si loin de faire le moynne, que bien souvent par orgueuil il le défait" (271).

The end of the fifth day emphasizes the image of food, but in direct contrast to the "dejeuner spirituel" propounded in the prologue. The fiftieth novella deals with a woman who will not even with a single word acknowledge the one she loves until it is too late. The comments on this tale develop the food images in an erotic context and also as clear indications of vainglory (278). Then at the end of the day, words and food appear in a literal context, but not without metaphoric connotations that sum up and define the thematic precepts of the prologue: "Veppres oÿes, s'en alèrent souper autant de paroles que de viandes" (278). *Viandes* is both spiritual food and carnal appetites, while *paroles* stand for "saintz propos" and for storytelling—building the bridge, metaphorically speaking. The circle opened in the prologue is closed at the end of the day. Furthermore vainglory, before God, men, or oneself, emerges as the underlying theme peculiar to this fifth day. Marguerite takes care to weave her tapestry in such a way that the colors, the themes, are blended and counterpointed at the same time, while the backdrop, the underlying theme, takes on a pattern out of the mingled colors.

The seventh day again announces four basic tenets that will pervade the day's ten novellas. To begin with, Oysille gives the future narrators the usual "salutaire pature" (315), here in the form of readings from Saint Luke. The purpose of these readings is to draw a contrast for her audience between exemplary conduct and the corruptions of this life: "Ces contes la devoient ettre suffisens pour desirer voir un tel tems, et plorer la déformité de cettuy cy envers cettuy la" (315). However, spiritual deformities can be redeemed through divine grace accorded to those "qui en la foy la requierent" (315). And the Gospel of Saint Luke is indeed dominated by parables, including the notable Return of the Prodigal Son, which center on those who choose to err and then seek and see the light. The final thematic point counters with a recall to the business of storytelling, the realities of daily life, for the potential narrators have become too engrossed in the exemplary evangelical tales. In another instance of mystification, Nomerfide, the youngest of the narrators, has the task of issuing this call to order because she is one of the more mischievous individuals of the group and embodies a certain frivolity and earthiness. Once more the themes of the prologue offer contrasting chiasmas: "salutaire pature / nouvelle" and "déformité / grâce."

As the novellas will demonstrate, the dominating theme of the seventh day is to be that of deformation, moral disguise through the wearing of deceptive masks or clothes. The sixty-first tale, dealing with a wife who runs away with a canon, casts the line in this direction: "Voylà, mes Dames, comme les chesnes de saint Pierre sont converties par les mauvais ministres en celles de Sathan . . ." (320), but God's grace has the last word in the story: "Si est ce, dit Longarine, un péché

172

qui à grand' péne peut ettre si secret, qu'il ne soit révélé, si non quand Dieu par sa miséricorde le couvre en ceus qui pour l'amour de luy en ont vraye repentence" (320). The following tale points up the arbitrariness of God's grace and man's nudity before him,[15] but it particularly relates to the element of youth introduced in the prologue; a young wife, a "Damoyselle," with a much older husband, falls prey to the advances of a young man, a "june folatre."

In the sixty-third novella the stress again is on youth and deformation or dissimulation, both of a positive and negative nature. Through a subterfuge a young nobleman thwarts his young king's covetous moves toward a maiden and thereby cancels out the king's deceptive plan. This transmutability of man's actions leads to the next story on the "déformité" of perfect love, which theoretically is a "salutaire pature," but not when in man's hands. A woman overtests her suitor's motives until he gives up his good intentions and escapes to the refuge of the monastery, and perhaps God's grace. The uncertainty of motives and the misdirection of ideals bring about the tragic deformities of this life: "il y en a beaucoup qui pour cuyder mieus faire que les autres, font pis, ou bien le rebours de ce qu'ilz veulent faire" (329). This thesis of mutation offers the transition to the following tale. A woman in church thinks she is resting her lighted candle on the forehead of a statue, but finds to her surprise, when he wakes up shouting, that it is actually a sleeping man. The error brings forth a warning against distortions, willful or not: "regarder d'ores en avant à quel saint vous baillerez vos chandelles" (330). Before the altar of love, love of God or man, deformities will inevitably occur; for such deviations are inherent to man. Only a state of grace can remedy these inadequacies;

---

15. "Celuy qui n'est couvert par la grace de Dieu, ne le peut ettre, ny ne se sçauroit nyer devant les hommes. Et y en a maintes qui prenant plaisir à telz propos se sont bien lourdement coupées [trahies] . . . . Jamais femme ne fut plus étonnée que moy, quand je me trouvai toute nue" (321, 322).

otherwise the solution resides in the individual: "Par quoy ne faut juger que soy mesme" (331). The perennial theological dispute emerges, pitting free will against predestination, with no clear answer, since a natural propensity toward deformation weighs man down.

The second half of the seventh day shifts to a depiction of deformity that centers in a spouse's blind and foolish fidelity and trust. The sixty-sixth novella, in which a chambermaid discloses the existence of an affair in a household, provides the transition; in the discussion following it, Nomerfide, the one who in the prologue had urged the group to return to storytelling, reveals that a relationship exists between her and Hircan.[16] As a matter of fact this conversation is triangular; Parlamente and her husband, Hircan, duel until they bring about Nomerfide's confession. The rest of the novellas in the day will reflect Parlamente-Marguerite's questioning her own perhaps naive attachment to an unworthy Hircan. Fiction interplays with life.

In the sixty-seventh novella, a wife stands by her husband, guilty of disloyalty to his superiors, and both are sent to a deserted island; after his death, she protects his corpse from being devoured by beasts. Her eventual return to civilization rewards this doglike fidelity. The discussion brings out the themes of the prologue: divine grace and "salutaire pature" for the wife,[17] and deformities, the husband's and the wife's bestiality as Parlamente points out (335). The following tale continues to demonstrate the spiritual disfigurement caused by excessive love. A wife overuses an aphrodisiac in attempt-

16. "Et pensez vous, dit Nomerfide, que les hommes se soucyent qui le sache, mès qu'ilz viénent à leur fin [?] Croyez que quand nul n'en parleroit, encores faudroit il qu'il fut sceu par eus mesmes. Hircan luy dit en colère: Il n'est pas besoin que les hommes disent tout ce qu'ilz sçavent. Mais elle rougissant luy répondit: Peut ettre, qu'ilz ne diroient chose à leur avantage" (333).

17. "Dieu est aussi puissant de nourrir en un desert ses serviteurs, comme aus plus grans festins du monde" (335).

ing to regain her husband's favor and fails because of the overdose. The notions of *pature* and excess also relate this story directly to the prologue of the day. The sixty-ninth novella stresses again a husband's infidelity and deformation, and his wife's inordinate patience.[18] His illicit activities with the chambermaid are presented in the metaphoric act of sifting flour, and to protect himself from the flying bran he wears a hood which epitomizes his deformation. The disfiguring disguise becomes the thematic umbilical cord to the prologue. This act of sifting also echoes an implied reversed meaning of *pature*, suggested by the eventual purpose of the purified wheat.

As for the seventieth novella, quite obviously its basis is to point out man's animality, the duchess's gross desires toward the young nobleman, and the duke's murder of his wife upon discovering her abuse of his patience; these respective bestialities substantiate the prologue's premise. Oysille, the narrator of this lengthy tale, offers the meaning of the novella's "salutaire pature"; paraphrasing Saint Paul (I Cor. 1:32–35), she declares that one ought not to become a slave of worldly possessions, including human beings. In this particular novella, such a precept involves the following couples: duke / duchess, duchess / young nobleman, young nobleman / Dame de Vergy, Dame de Vergy / her little dog. Divine grace may be the answer for escape from man's deformities, but does the duke, sole survivor of the tragedy, at the end really reap its best fruit when he "passa sa vieillesse heureusement avec Dieu" in a monastery (354)?

On the seventh day, all novellas revolve around the concept of *déformité* announced in the prologue. The theoreti-

18. "... mais si y a il des femmes qui ont porté l'amour et jalousie patiemment. Ouÿ, dit Hircan, et plaisamment. Car les plus sages sont celles qui prennent autant de passetems à se moquer et rire des oeuvres de leurs marys, comme les marys de les tromper secrettement. ... Que dites vous, mes Dames, de cette femme [?] n'étoit elle pas bien sage de passer tout son tems du passetems de son mary?" (338, 339).

cal solution may lie in emulating the exemplary lives of the saints or in seeking out divine grace as an immunization to earthly defects. But the "salutaire pature" is also the corpus of novellas, and on this particular day the practical remedy offered to combat inevitable human affinities toward excessive love and materialism, both good and bad, is moderation. The stories then mean to redress deformation, not to substitute for it an ideal and thereby create an unresolvable polarity. Again as on the fifth day, the dominating surface theme, deformity, serves as a catalyst to precipitate a seemingly invisible thesis, moderation. Such a process can only attest to a deliberate design.

Indeed Marguerite takes care to develop a cohesion both within a day and in the projected decameron so that theme and structure are closely integrated. The novellas are the *pature* or *nourriture* that attempts to harmonize apparently irreconcilable elements, such as life and religion. The ends of the days, beginning with the very first one, are punctuated by references to the attraction of listening to the novellas at the expense of religion: "Car la dévotion d'oÿr la fin du conte étoit plus grande que celle d'oÿr Veppres" (79). Not only the narrators give in to this temptation; so too do the monks, the hosts of the group. The hidden presence of the latter is not discovered until the end of the second day; they are allowed henceforth to listen to the stories in the open, for they too can profit from the narratives: "Et, comme ceus qui aymoient plus leurs plaisirs que leurs oraisons, s'étoient alez cacher dans une fosse, le ventre contre terre, derrière une haye fort époisse. Et là avoient si bien écouté ces beaus contes, qu'ilz n'avoient point oÿ sonner la cloche de leur monastère" (138). Even after their presence becomes public, they will run late for vespers at the end of the third and sixth days. These occurrences are not meant to underscore the dichotomy between the profane and the spiritual, but rather to establish the benefit the monks can also derive from their exposure to the practical problems of life, to which they contribute measurably. The novellas therefore stand between the narrators and their ideals, between these monks and their depredatory behavior in the tales, and through their variable meaning offer themselves as a moderating and modulating force. And this added accent on an attempt to fuse the ideal and the ugly reality results from a conscious punctuation of references to seemingly blasphemous activities; this pattern in turn produces a structure.[19]

The cohesion that marks the *Heptameron* receives added impetus through the movement from one novella to another in a given day. It soon becomes clear that novellas are not juxtaposed haphazard or merely in antithetical patterns, but rather are connected by thematic or metaphoric links so that the progression is studied and not superficial. In the fourth day, for example, the word given in the prologue, "J'ai une femme" (204), acts as a transition to the first tale, in which a monk with the help of a band of retainers savagely takes possession of a woman after knifing her servants. The punishment these monks receive for their atrocious deed—they are burnt alive in their monastery—becomes the link to the thirty-second novella, in which an unfaithful wife is condemned to drink all her life from the skull of her former lover. Besides continuing to sound a macabre note, the point is made that punishment by death may not be the most effective retribution.[20] Then the unpredictable happens; at the end of the thirty-second tale, the husband does forgive his sinful wife, and this apparent miracle provides the link to the following novella. Here a priest pretends an immaculate conception for his pregnant sister, with whom he has had an

19. This presence of the monks in the *Heptameron*'s framework contributes to a concentric audience for the tales: the narrators, the monks, the readers.

20. "Par quoy la plus grand' punition que lon puisse donner à un malfaiteur, n'est pas la mor, mais de donner un torment continuel, si grand qu'il la fait desirer, et si petit qu'il ne la peut avancer" (209).

incestuous relation; this pretense reveals the link: "Aussi sous espece de miracle y a souvent des abus" (213).

The transition between the thirty-third and thirty-fourth novellas focuses on and plays with the concept of "bien entendre" (216). Unwittingly the sister confesses her crime when she swears upon a crucifix to her virginity: "Je pren le cors de notre Seigneur icy present à ma damnation, devant vous, Messieurs, et devant vous, mon frére, si jamais homme m'attoucha non plus que vous" (214); but the last clause gives her away, since one of her judges understood well the "m'attoucha." And so the thirty-fourth story, narrated to substantiate the belief that misunderstood words can be the cause of so much evil (216), presents two monks who think they are a butcher's intended victims when they overhear him tell his wife that in the morning he will be slaughtering one of his fat "cordeliers," his euphemism for pigs.

The animality of man provides the link between the thirty-fourth and the thirty-fifth novellas. The end of the former emphasizes man's inherent fall, from which he cannot recover no matter how much he tries: "Il n'y a nulle de nous, dit Parlamente, qui ne confesse que tous les péchez extérieurs ne soient les fruys de l'infidélité intérieure, laquelle plus est couverte de vertus et de miracles, plus est dangereuse à arracher" (219). In presenting the tale he is about to relate, the sardonic Hircan picks up his wife's cue and will set about to prove that "la nature des femmes et des hommes est de soy inclinée à tout vice" (219). Here a woman gives in too readily to her so-called spiritual love toward a priest and is cured by her husband's beatings; although both man and woman fall prey to some form of vice, the wife's straying receives the emphasis. Then the thirty-sixth novella pretends to carry forward the theme of the universality of vice—"je n'épargnerai homme, ne femme, à fin de faire tout équal" (225)—but actually the emphasis shifts to the husband's fatal punishment of his wife, who has gone astray with a younger man; he poisons her by forcing her to eat "une salade de telles herbes" (226). Although the surface continuation from the thirty-fifth to the thirty-sixth novella appears to be the universality of vice, the real link is found in the progression of the punishments husbands administer to their unfaithful wives and produces a dilemma when one tries to pinpoint the real culprit in the triangles.

The thirty-seventh novella aims at counteracting the pejorative light in which women had been depicted in the previous two stories. It falls to Dagoucin, the champion of the fair sex and ideal love, to correct this blurred image. Therefore his narrative focuses on a wife who, through her infinite patience and persistence, brings her unfaithful husband back to the fold. But most of the narrators in the discussion immediately question the wisdom and feasibility of the wife's patience and perseverance, and foremost among them, Parlamente declares categorically that she would not be capable of such virtues in the given circumstances (cf. 228). As a result, the verdict that Dagoucin pronounces, at the beginning of his narrative, on the preceding tale also applies to his own: "il ne faut point donner tant de louenge à une seule vertu, qu'il la faille servir de manteau à couvrir un si grand vice" (228–29). And this notion of excessive virtue as a vice becomes the link between the two novellas.

The image of cleanliness provides the transition from the thirty-seventh to the thirty-eighth novella. In the former, the wife had washed her husband's hands each time he returned from a visit to the chambermaid's quarters. In the latter, the wife takes one further step; she goes to the tenant farmer's cottage and cleans up the premises where her husband and the farmer's wife meet. When the husband finds himself in this artificial clean environment, and even drinks from a silver bowl brought there by his wife, he returns to the natural cleanliness of marriage. Yet in spite of these virtuous conclusions, man still feels a natural attraction toward cold and filth.

Although man's and woman's equality before the god of Vice seems to be the outer link between the thirty-eighth and thirty-ninth novellas, as stated by Saffredan, the narrator of the latter tale (234), the fundamental connection between the two and also with the immediately preceding stories is the proposition that if good common sense triumphs over evil spirits, man and woman still derive pleasure from sinning, and a return to the fold need not mean that a conversion or catharsis has taken place. The thirty-ninth novella then becomes a commentary on the preceding three tales. The narrative of the tale is actually quite short, only about a page; the action therefore assumes the aura of an allegory. A nobleman captures the ghost that haunts a house—a chambermaid who wants to scare away her masters so that she can continue unhindered her relationship with a servant of the household and they can have the premises to themselves.[21] The story itself may demonstrate the final triumph of reason over temptation, but the discussion following it, as usual, casts serious doubts on such an oversimple conclusion.

This questioning of reason or common sense, as opposed to allowing natural appetites their way, becomes the transition to the last novella of the fourth day. One of the last comments in the discussion to the thirty-ninth novella offers another link to the fortieth story: "tant plus le péché est grand, de tant plus il est plaisant" (235). In the last novella, a young lady secretly marries the one she loves, but when her brother learns of this secret marriage, he kills the new groom because

21. "Mais d'autant qu'est vitupérable l'intention de la chambrière, le bon sens du maitre est louable, qui sçavoit tresbien que l'esprit s'en va et ne retourne plus" (235).

his sister's act had not gained the family's sanction. This situation obviously pits natural genuine love against the mores and constraints of society. We find ourselves quite far from the reason / love dichotomy of the thirty-ninth tale, but in fact it is the hyphen between the preceding stories and the last one, which opposes the sister's true love to the brother's false reasoning.[22]

Not only is the fourth day held together by a network of interwoven inner links, but an echoing theme at the beginning and the end gives it a further cohesion, while the revelation, in the middle of the day, of the biblical passage read at the outset reveals the pervading tone within the novellas. The fourth day culminates with a praise of marriage that explains why most of its tales feature a return to conjugal union even after infidelities; at the same time this praise counterpoints the prologue's "J'ai une femme" (204), on which it now sheds a positive light as well. However, the discussion at the end of the thirty-fourth tale, by paraphrasing I Corinthians 1:21–29, unveils the dominant theme of the day—the perversion of sentiments:

Ne vaus ai je pas leu au matin dit Oysille, que ceus qui ont cuydé ettre plus sages que tous les autres hommes, et qui par une lumière de raison sont venuz jusques à connoitre un Dieu créateur de toutes choses, toutesfois pour s'attribuer cette gloire, et non à celuy dont elle venoit, estimans par leur labeur avoir gangné le savoir, ont été faitz non seulement plus ignorans et déraisonnables que les autres hommes, mais que les bestes brutes? Car ayans erré en leurs espritz, s'attribuans ce qu'à Dieu seul appertient, ont montré leurs erreurs par le désordre de leur cors, oublyans et per-

22. For a comparison of the fortieth tale with an antecedent in the *Decameron*, see my article "Ambiguïté chez Boccace et Marguerite de Navarre," *Boccaccio nella cultura francese* (Florence, 1971), pp. 557–65.

vertissans l'ordre de leur sexe, comme saint Paul aujourd'huy nous montre en l'Epitre qu'il écrivoit aus
Romains. [218–19]

Contrary to what Oysille the idealist states, Marguerite in
her novellas assigns to reason a two-faced nature because
some confuse reason with passion; but in its moderate state
reason does constitute the only mitigating force in the conduct of man, similarly "J'ai une femme" can be black or
white. The fourth day therefore becomes an excellent microcosm of the *Heptameron*; it fuses theme and structure and
attests careful composition and well-delineated metaphoric
patterns that repeatedly expose paradoxes and a resulting
ambivalence.

Looking at the most superficial outer structure of the
Heptameron, one could argue that it smacks of a scamped
job; after all, in the edition used here, Marguerite devotes
twice as many pages to the first four days (230 pages) as she
does to the last three (115 pages). One might conclude that,
pressed for time, she hurriedly attempted to reach the end of
the ten days, forsaking form and shortening the tales.
How does one explain, then, that the seventh day ends with
the second longest novella of the collection (16 pages), second only to the tenth novella (25 pages)? Although novellas
in the last four days tend to be somewhat shorter on the
whole, Marguerite never loses sight of a design and a cohesion within each day and within the *Heptameron*, not to
mention the structure of the novella itself, which has a bear-
ing on its very meaning, always fluid. Death cut short her
narrative endeavor, but fate has closely related the *Heptameron*'s open-endedness to Marguerite's own exploring and
shifting mind.

6. THE FICTION OF TRUTH AND THE TRUTH OF FICTION

At this point, one may wonder why Marguerite de Navarre, the writer and storyteller, has received at the hands of her critics for the most part a negative judgment. Repetition of adverse critical opinions accounts for such a stance much more than reevaluation.[1] Of course,

1. The negative statements are quite categorical, and on occasion paradoxical: "En réalité Marguerite est aussi peu que possible un écrivain, au sens où nous prenons ce mot: la forme, pour elle, ne compte pas. De là tant de récits traînants où rien ne frappe, où rien ne se détache de la trame d'un style diffus. La reine, sur ce point, manque tout à fait de métier: elle n'a jamais réfléchi aux ressources que pouvait lui offrir la prose comme la poésie; elle n'a jamais eu le souci du style. . . . Elle manquait totalement de génie esthétique. Loin d'elle les préoccupations stylistiques d'un Rabelais, d'un Ronsard, ou même d'un Marot" (Jourda, *Marguerite d'Angoulême*, II, pp. 978–79, 986). "Il est vrai: mais il faudrait enfin s'en aviser, l'*Heptaméron*, n'est pas, dans l'intention de Marguerite, une œuvre littéraire. Aussi bien, elle nous en avertit elle-même dans le prologue" (Febvre, *Autour de l'Heptaméron*, p. 206). "Margherita del resto non è e non si cura di essere un'artista, non ammette alcuna importanza alle sue occupazioni letterarie, ed è quasi completamente priva del senso della forma; tuttavia quando raconta e conversa questa intelligente gentildonna, tra le meglio informate, e le più rappresentative dell'epoca sua, non ha affatto bisogno di essere una scrittrice per scrivere eccellentemente" (Garosci, p. 189). "In the main, they [narrators] speak straight on, with no trace in either of the learned, even slightly pompous tone of Boccaccio. Their construction and syntax are linear: at times the line described is as long, as tortuous and as rambling as it often is in genuine talk, when one stops and starts, runs down hill into a morass of digressions, and then climbs painfully back to get a finger-grip upon one's principal clause, finally has to make up another, because the audience and the narrator no longer have the slightest idea what it was originally. . . . The method of composition here is agglutinative, a favourite with females be they queens or scullery wenches, who can never in any century see the harm in another relative clause" (Hartley, *Bandello and the Heptameron*, pp. 30–31).

As for the positive judgments, they are intuitive but vague: "La prose de l'*Heptaméron*, quoiqu'un peu délayée, est coulante, facile, naturelle, élégante, souvent animée par des saillies fines et d'ingénieuses comparaisons [cf. Jourda, "Il est rare toutefois que la Reine s'attache longtemps à colorer ainsi son style" (p. 971)]. C'est le langage de la bonne compagnie française avec la part de hardiesse qu'il comporte encore au XVIe siècle, mais déjà empreint de

she is not a stylist in the narrow sense of the word, as Flaubert, for example, is; she does not chisel meticulously her sentences nor does she claim to do so. But the absence of such a stylistic attitude does not imply failure as an artist; Balzac does not concentrate his efforts on syntax either. In the *Heptameron*, the novellas center on imagery, paradox, and structure. The language Marguerite uses is the language of ambiguity; the usual meanings of words disintegrate either through metaphoric projections or through paradoxes and contradictions. The harmony among words—syntax—matters less to her than the disintegration she imparts to the meaning of words because of the uncertainty she witnesses about her.

Of primary importance to Marguerite is the function of the novella as literature. In this matter she endeavors to create a harmony and continuity among the tales, with a particular consciousness of their proper length. Furthermore she poses the question of inspiration and the heavy responsibility of choosing one story over another in the search for an integrated whole. Above all, the novella attempts to bridge the gap between fiction and reality and even to eliminate the chasm between the two in order to give more validity to the fiction and demonstrate the multifariousness of reality. Finally the novella functions as a pastime, and in this capacity it amuses and elicits laughter, though the laughter is wry and often cruel; this concept of a *homo ludens* reflects Marguerite's latent pessimism.

Marguerite seeks order both in the world around her and

---

la grâce facile et délicate qui sera un jour son caractère distinctif" (Loménie, p. 687); "Le talent poétique de Marguerite n'intéresse guère nos critiques littéraires. Mais on continue de discuter sur la nature de ses idées religieuses" (Lebègue, "Le second *Miroir* de Marguerite de Navarre," p. 51); "C'est peut-être dans la construction de la phrase et dans l'ordre des mots que le naturel de son style apparaît le mieux: ses vers sont, à certains égards, plus proches de la langue parlée que sa prose, la langue de la *Navire* est moins 'artiste' que celle de l'*Heptaméron* . . ." (Marichal, *La Navire*, p. 233).

in her collection of novellas.[2] In the latter case, this concern manifests itself through an omnipresent sensitivity for harmonious composition. As a matter of fact, the word *ordre* surfaces more readily at the end of the *Heptameron* than at the beginning and occurs in an interplay with *mettre ordre, donner bon ordre,* and *donner ordre.* Parlamente set the tone in the comments to the sixty-fourth tale: "mais connoisçant sa mutation [of time] donnerez ordre à l'avenir" (316). And Marguerite herself in the very last story, on one of the very few occasions that she appears as a character, will seek to establish order: "Car à elle [Marguerite de Navarre] je conterai mon affaire, étant asseurée, que s'il y a ordre, elle le trouvera . . ." (362).[3] To *ordre,* Marguerite opposes *ordure.* The latter, occurring metaphorically as early as the eleventh novella, connotes the realm of base desires.[4] While on a moral plane, order means a happy marriage and spiritual health, and ordure means refuse and excrement, spiritual sickness and sexual degradation (cf. XXXVII and XXXVIII), on an aesthetic plane, order means harmonious composition, and ordure stands for disorder or chaos in composition, which Marguerite abhors. Of course, the queen of Navarre is much more explicit in her ethical judgments than in her aesthetic

2. Strangely enough, Jourda contradicts himself on this matter: "Au lieu de coudre les uns aux autres des récits sans aucun lien, elle s'attache à présenter ses nouvelles dans un ordre logique ou esthétique . . . Il y a dans l'*Heptaméron* un indéniable souci de la composition: Marguerite a voulu offrir au lecteur un livre médité, préparé, composé" (*Marguerite d'Angoulême*, II, p. 682); and then later "A-t-on le droit de parler de la composition de ces nouvelles? Est-il possible de découvrir en chacune d'elles un plan médité à l'avance? Il ne le semble pas. L'auteur, sans doute, dispose, et quelque fois fort très habilement, ses péripéties. Nous ne pensons pas cependant que la reine ait travaillé sur un schéma comparable à ceux que se tracent les romanciers modernes . . . Marguerite prend soin pour ne pas donner à son livre l'air d'avoir été composé, pour qu'il garde le naturel de la vie . . . la Reine cherche le naturel et la vraisemblance, même au prix de l'ordre et de l'élégance" (ibid., pp. 926, 931).

3. Cf. also novella LXI, 319; here *ordre* means formulating an equitable moral situation, sometimes with ironic counterpoints.

4. Cf. also novellas, XX, 136, 137; XXXVI, 230; LII, 285.

pronouncements; she speaks directly to the former and lets the *Heptameron* speak for itself in the case of the latter.

To Marguerite, order means balance, and she remains fully aware of the desirability of an equilibrium in the length of the stories between the first and the last days, and within a day. She warns the reader of the extreme length of the tenth novella; Dagoucin tells Parlamente: "ne craindez point à parler longuement, car il y a encores assez de tems pour dire beaucoup de bonnes choses" (54). And again at the beginning of the fifteenth novella, Longarine informs her audience of her forthcoming long tale.[5] Conscious of the lengthy first two days, Marguerite proceeds to reduce first the twentieth and then the twenty-second tale because it follows a rather long story: "Il seroit long à vous conter le discours de son amytié, la longue fréquentation qu'il eut avec elle, les voyages qu'il faisoit pour la venir voir. Mais pour venir à la conclusion . . ." (135); "Mais elle qui étoit sage avoit mis par écrit, tout ce qui est icy dessus, avec mile autres inventions que le Prieur avoit trouvées pour la decevoir, que je laisse à conter pour la longueur" (160). Of course, also implied in this regulating process is the writer's very conscious will to include this or that episode, a sign of careful composition. Finally, toward the end of the third day, Marguerite moves on to shorter tales to counterbalance the rather lengthy first two-thirds of the day.[6] What could be construed as unchecked narrative expansion is actually always under control and soon gives way to shorter novellas in order to achieve a more visible balance within the day.

Beginning with the sixth day, Marguerite calls our attention to the brevity of some of the tales about to be narrated: "Et combien que le conte qu'il aloit dire fut for court" (LIV,

5. "Si mon conte est un peu long, vous aurez patience" (104).
6. "L'heure les poussoit si for, que pour perachever la journée, et satisfaire à leurs propos, Symontaut fut contraint s'avancer de donner sa voys à Nomerfide, les asseurant que par sa rhétorique, elle ne les tiendroit pas longuement" (XXIX, 196).

292); "Je n'avoi pas délibéré, dit Nomerfide, de raconter une si courte histoire, mais puisqu'elle vient à propos, je la dirai" (LV, 294).[7] The presentation of the forthcoming lengthy seventieth novella marks one notable exception during the last days; because of its length, Oysille is reluctant to narrate it, but "toute la compagnie la pria de le vouloir dire et qu'elle ne craindit point la longueur" (340). It has not been noted that if in the seventh day the novellas are indeed somewhat short, they are so in order to allow for the very long last novella which will not then lead to an overinflated day. On the first day too, the first nine tales are relatively short to make room for a notable last one. In addition to this symmetry between the first and last full day, a further calculated composition becomes quite evident and achieves a global balance: the longer first days will be counterpointed by forthcoming shorter ones.

One significant evidence that Marguerite possesses a stock of novellas which she chooses to include only at a given time is the announcement or the projection of a story to be narrated at some future time involving the same set of characters as the one just told. At the end of the twenty-first tale, the famous Rolandine novella announces what will be the fortieth story: "Le père sachant cette piteuse nouvelle, ne la voulut point voir, mais l'envoya dedans une forest en un chateau qu'il avoit autresfois édifié, pour une occasion bien digne d'ettre racontée après cette nouvelle" (151).[8] Parlamente, the narrator of both tales, thereby opens the third day and closes the fourth. Later two successive novellas revolve around the same main character in order to delineate and

7. Cf. also: "Et pour ce qu'il disoit de sçavoir l'histoire au vray, qui n'étoit ne si longue ne si piteuse que le conte de Parlamente" (LXV, 330); "Le conte ne sera pas long, dit Ennasuyte" (LXVI, 331); Or donques, dit Nomerfide, selon ma coutume, je le vous ferai court et joyeux" (LXVIII, 336).

8. "Or puisque je suis pour mettre fin à la journée, dit Parlamente, et que je vous promi hyer vous dire l'occasion pour laquelle le père de Rolandine feit faire le chateau où il la teint si long tems prisonnière, je la vous vai raconter" (XL, 236).

focus on her wickedness. The fifty-eighth tale sets forth a damoyselle who tricks her lover; then the following novella, backtracking in time, depicts her capable of the same sentiments toward her husband. This form of repetition emanates, not from a narrative weakness, but from a desire to arrive at a kaleidoscopic view of an individual's conduct.

A writer in full possession of his narrative material sometimes likes to project events within a tale, or again, the narrative becomes a vehicle for his own premonitions. In this vein the last three novellas of the *Heptameron* substantiate an awareness of composition. In the seventieth, the young nobleman, upon revealing to the duke the identity of the woman he loves, "ala batir le commencement de son malheur" (347); then when the duke transmits the information to his own wife, "[il] luy jura que si jamais la révèloit à créature, elle ne mourroit d'autre main que de la siéne [husband's]. A quoy elle se condamna et accepta la punition" (349). The last two novellas bring with them the theme of death as it had not appeared before; they pose the question if "la méditation de la mor refroidissoit merveilleusement un cueur" (360). The stories themselves negate such an assertion; the discussions, as usual, are less categorical. The seventy-first tale depicts a man who seduces a chambermaid before the eyes of his dying wife; in the seventy-second, a dying monk who profits from his last living moments and from the sympathy they elicit, seduces several nuns. The tales, purporting to reflect "les plus grandes follyes" (358), play with lubricity *before* death. At the end the personal element rushes forth: "J'en ai assez veu de telles, dit Hircan, qui pleurent leurs péchez et rient leurs plaisirs tout ensemble. Je me doute bien, dit Parlamente, pour qui vous le dites. D'ond il me semble que le rire a assez duré et seroit tems que les larmes commençassent. Taisez vous, dit Hircan. Encore n'est pas finie la tragédie qui a commencé par rire" (362). Quite possibly, Marguerite may have known that the seventy-second novella could be the last one; in the face of death, the flesh (hers?) still lives.

By punctuating the *Heptameron* with overt allusions, Marguerite takes care to inform the reader that her novellas are not written or included impulsively but rather chosen because of their quality and in order to follow a structural and thematic plan. These references usually occur at the end of a day, on occasion in a prologue, in regard to the narrators' activities: "Le diner achevé, s'en alèrent reposer pour étudier leur rolle" (204). The narrators rehearse backstage, so to speak; as a result, the recited novellas reflect a distilled process, a meditated composition: "Le service finy s'en alèrent souper. . . . Mais par ce que l'un rompoit la parole de l'autre, on n'a peu retenir les contes tout du long, qui n'eussent été moins plaisans à écrire, que ceus qu'ilz disoient dedans le pré" (XL, 241).[9] In short, each narrator, i.e., Marguerite, has given careful thought to the novella finally surfacing above the others that never see the light. When Oysille, for example, narrates the forty-sixth tale about a monk's ruse to seduce a maiden, she seems to excuse herself for the poor taste of the story, but in fact she is saying that a novella's function depends on its intrinsic moral and aesthetic value as well as on its pertinence in a given thematic context: "Vous me faites souvenir . . . d'un conte que je n'avoi pas délibéré mettre au reng des bons" (364).

Quality relates to inspiration, and halfway through the proposed ten days, Marguerite pauses to assure the reader that inspiration will not fail her in the second half and to propose at the same time her ars poetica. Dating back to antiquity, the practice of calling upon the Muses to continue blowing into the sails of inspiration had become quite a

9. Cf. "En ce disant se levèrent et s'en alèrent à l'église, où ilz oÿrent Vèppres bien dévotement, et apres s'en alèrent souper devisans des propos passez, et rémémorans plusieurs cas avenuz de leur tems, pour voir lesquelz seroient dignes d'ettre retenuz" (XXX, 203). See also X, 79; XX, 138; LX, 314.

commonplace in the Renaissance. Marguerite follows the practice, but has no doubt concerning her ability to continue and endure, for inspiration will not fail her as long as she lives and can observe the life about her; however, this inexhaustibility of inspiration should not be correlated to facility:

> Dame Oysille leur dit . . . que les cinq journées étoient accomplyies de si belles histoires, qu'elle avoit grand' peur que la sysiéme ne fut pareille. Car il n'étoit possible, encor' qu'on les voulut inventer, de dire de meilleurs contes, que véritablement ilz en avoient recontez en leur compagnie. Mais Géburon luy dit que tant que le monde dureroit, se feroient tousiours cas dignes de mémoire. Car la malice des hommes mauvais est touiours telle qu'elle a été, comme la bonté des bons. Tant que la bonté et malice regneront sur la terre, elles la rempliront touiours de nouveaus actes, combien qu'il soit écrit, qu'il n'y a rien de nouveau souz le soleil. Mais nous qui n'avons été appelez au conseil privé de Dieu, ignorans les premières causes, trouvons toutes choses nouvelles, et de tant plus admirables, que moins nous les voudrions, ou pourrions faire. Parquoy n'ayez point de peur que les journées qui viendront, ne suyvent bien celles qui sont passées. [L, 279]

In a capsule form, this ars poetica centers on the thematic dichotomy *bonté / malice*, whose gray mixture pervades the whole *Heptameron*, and on its aesthetic counterpart *digne de mémoire / nouveau*.

The emphasis on the new brings forth the question so prevalent during the Renaissance of the relationship between inspiration and imitation. Where does one begin and the other end? In French, of course, the very word *nouvelle* means a new story, often drawn on an old canvas, as does the same word in the other two chief romance languages, *novella*. The genre of the novella flourished during the Renaissance,

beginning with the *pater familias*, Boccaccio, precisely because it embodied the imitation-inspiration complementary
dichotomy and allowed each writer to give evidence of his
creative narrative talent without claiming any originality for
the plot. The newness resides in the mode and in the didactic
purpose of the novella. Marguerite, like other *novellieri*, may
claim a complete originality for her tales, but this sort of
declaration is simply a mystifying literary device. In the one
novella whose model is flagrantly evident, the seventieth and
its medieval *Chastelaine de Vergi* antecedent, she reasserts
her ars poetica and the originality of her version, although
the weak linguistic argument she propounds reveals all the
more clearly a twinkle in her eye: "nous avons juré de ne rien
mettre icy qui ait été écrit. Il est vray, dit Parlamente, mais
me doutant à peu près du conte que c'est, il a été écrit en si
vieil langage, que je croi, hors mis nous deus, il n'y a icy
homme ne femme qui en ait oÿ parler. Par quoy sera tenu de
nouveau" (340).

If every novella is new, hence "digne de mémoire," it
attests an inspiration supported by a most fertile supply of
cases, stories, in society—again a conjunction of inspiration
and imitation. For every novella assuring Marguerite of yet
another jewel in her crown for posterity, several never saw
the light, that is, were deemed worthy to be forgotten. As a
result, one witnesses throughout the *Heptameron* an interplay between remembering and forgetting, on both the moral
and the aesthetic plane. Each story is the manifestation of a
willful act of memory, either spontaneous or by association;
contrary to what happens in Proust, unconscious or associa-
tive memory does not take precedence over conscious memory. But memory, as in Proust, does become the equivalent
of literary creation.[10] If not, it expresses historical immediacy,

10. Among numerous examples: "Veppres oÿes, alèrent souper, qui ne
fut tout le soir sans parler des contes qu'ilz avoient oÿs, et sans cercher par
tous les endroitz de leurs mémoires, pour voir s'ilz pourroient faire la journée

a literary ploy to connote veracity.[11] Or again, it combines the moral and the creative in denoting conscience: "Quand lon a pris grand déplaisir à l'oeuvre, lon en prend aussi en la mémoire . . ." (LXII, 322).

On a creative level, to forget remains an implicit concept, since it relates to the excluded novellas; in this context, then, it assumes a positive connotation because it automatically refers to inferior tales. However, on a moral plane forgetting occurs repeatedly to indicate a loss of honor, virtue, conscience, reason; during a husband's absence from home, a woman "oublya tant sa conscience, son honneur, et l'amour" (XXXII, 210). In fact, *oublier* is one of the ubiquitous words in the *Heptameron*, and its frequency gives further evidence of man's frailties.[12] Because man's propensity is to forget, Marguerite will remember, will write the novellas. Accordingly, *oublier*, for the most part, refers to the characters' moral lapse in the stories, and *rémémorer* or *mémoire* to the creating of fiction. Marguerite and her narrators immortalize man's lack of memory and thus attempt to reconcile fiction and reality; or perhaps the irreversible dichotomy between remembering and forgetting reflects the gap between fiction and reality.

Indeed, one of the more important questions Marguerite asks herself in the course of the *Heptameron* is what relation

---

aussi plaisante que la première" (X, 79); "je pense qu'elle recordoit quelque bon rolle" (XV, 104); "je n'en doi laisser perdre la mémoire" (XVIII, 172); "Et vous, Saffredan, demandez luy [God] pardon d'avoir rémémoré une si grand' villanie contre les femmes" (XX, 137).

11. "Je vous raconterai une histoire en laquelle je ne nommerai les personnes, pour ce que c'est de si fresche mémoire, que j'auroie peur de déplaire à quelques uns de leurs parens bien proches" (IV, 33); "Et à fin que par faute d'exemple ne metez en oubly cette vérité, je vous en vai dire un tresvéritable, et dont la mémoire est si fresche, qu'à péne en sont essuyez les yeus de ceus qui ont veu ce piteux spectacle" (LI, 281).

12. For just a very few instances of this word's frequency, see III, 28, 31; IV, 33; VI, 41; VII, 43; XV, 105, 106, 107; XVII, 114; XVIII, 124; XIX, 129.

exists between fiction and reality? and she answers it by blurring the line of demarcation between the two; she endeavors to construct concentric realms of fiction that cancel each other out; and she playfully alternates between artificially created concepts of fiction and reality. This question remains foremost in her mind because it demonstrates once again her refusal to accept absolutes and her will to settle instead for an exploratory flexibility both on an aesthetic and a moral plane, à la Montaigne. In addition, the blurring of this line of demarcation unsettles any simple Aristotelian notion of art imitating nature.

Most dominant is the world of the stories purporting to have happened. We know only, however, those the narrators (i.e., Marguerite) choose to tell. Then there is a whole world of stories and comments known only to the narrators: "se meirent à relever et poursuyvre les propos qu'ils n'avoient sceu achever dedans le pré, qui durèrent tout le long de la soirée" (XX, 138). It will never be known what impact this invisible fictional universe may have had on the printed tales or on the opinions held by the narrators in the discussions following each printed story. Although Marguerite dismisses the unknown stories as inferior, they still loom large in the immediate background, thanks to constant references to them; they shadow the concrete printed stories and acquire importance through their very absence. It is not mere conjecture to suppose that Marguerite's repeated references to another fictional world she chose not to include are meant to have a willful unsettling effect on the tales that are included.

The narrators create their own dual universe; they exist both as they function in the novellas they narrate and comment on, and within a world of their own. By virtue of this duality, the discussion figures at the same time as a reality and a fiction. When they comment on the stories, they break the spell of fiction, since they bring to bear on the tales the experiences of their own lives, a lived reality in relation to a limiting and rigid fiction. At times the narrator of a tale even remains a victim of a supposed true fiction—and Marguerite is thereby able to avoid fixed positions; in the eighteenth novella, for example, when the merits of the protagonist's actions are discussed, the narrator Hircan claims that he cannot answer how the character behaved in a given situation because he was not informed of it. This so-called ignorance reveals a contrived truth, the fiction of the novella. Then the character of a protagonist in a story can bring to light an antithetical trait in one of the narrator-commentators; in the discussion to the fifth novella, the ferrywoman's virtue is opposed to young Nomerfide's doubted virtue. Here the story as fiction sheds light and intrudes upon the narrators' private world, another level of fiction. This interplay among realms of fiction produces a prismatic concept of them; it transposes some into a reality in relation to the others.

The narrator-commentators' or participants' private world which emerges from the discussions reveals their rather intimate interrelationships. Its particular feature is that it comes into focus through an impressionistic technique; allusions and comments among the parties are strategically placed throughout the discussions in order to form a composite picture of a world of living characters who exist, contribute, and draw from the fictional universe created through the novellas they narrate. The portrait, character, and life of each participant have recently been carefully delineated and analyzed and need not be elaborated upon here, except for one or two salient examples:[13]

> Je le sçai bien, dit Parlamente, mais je ne lairrai pour cela desirer que chaqu'une se contente de son mary, comme je fai du mien. Ennasuyte, qui par ce mot se

13. See a recent dissertation by Régine Reynolds, "Les Devisants de l'Heptaméron: Contribution à l'étude de la pensée politique et sociale de Marguerite de Navarre" (The University of Texas at Austin, 1970), pp. 6–119.

sentit touchée, en changeant de couleur lui dit: vous
devez juger que chacune a le cueur comme vous, ou vous
pensez ettre plus perfette que toutes les autres. [XXXV,
224]

Si faut il, dit Nomerfide, que l'amour soit grande,
qui cause une telle douleur. N'en ayez point de peur, dit
Hircan. Car vous ne mourrez point d'une telle fièvre.
Non plus, dit Nomerfide, que vous ne vous tuerez
après avoir connue votre offense. Parlamente qui doutoit
le debat ettre à ses dépens, leur dit en riant: C'est assez
que deus soyent mortz, sans que l'amour en face batre
deus autres. [LXX, 356]

However, what matters in the context of our discussion is the
very presence of this parallel world that darts in and out of
the dominating fiction of the tales themselves and their ensuing discussions. The *Heptameron* then appears as a tapestry
in which patterns of fictional threads outline an additional
form within a clearer and broader design.

One last such pattern is the world of historicity. To impart
an aura of authenticity to the tales, Marguerite introduces
historical figures as either protagonists or sources of stories.[14]
In these capacities, the queen herself, her brother François I,
his wife Queen Claude, and unnamed noble personalities,
whom critics delight to identify, play roles in the tales. Numerous characters of low rank are also in the service of this
and that important royal or noble personage. History then
appears in the guise of fiction, or again, history produces
fiction with an inevitable interplay of reality and literature,
of true and false. The supposed private lives of individuals
become part of the public domain. Marguerite may make
every effort at historicity, at authenticity; she may place
many a novella in an historical setting which helps, for instance, to situate its time of composition (1542 for LVII).

14. "Je tien ce conte de la dite Duchesse mesme [Marguerite de Navarre]"
(LXXII, 362).

Yet this historicity is soon diffused into the fiction of the *Heptameron* as a whole and thus becomes a mere veil of verisimilitude and a narrative technique that will not usually have any aesthetic impact on the story itself. On the other hand, an historical fact or occurrence can provide the impetus toward the writing of a novella (cf. LXV), just as a "fait divers" in Grenoble gave birth to *Le Rouge et le Noir*, but such uses of history are to be considered much more creative accidents than vital creative forces.

Finally, by refusing to name historical figures—to protect them, she says—Marguerite suspends a story between fiction and reality. While aiming at authenticity, this historicity allows her to interrupt the spell wrought by fiction; supposedly facts and real settings are introduced in a narrative that by definition is fiction, in spite of all claims to the contrary. In juggling with levels of fiction, Marguerite arrives at an interchangeability of fiction and reality. She pursues this willful confusion in order to demonstrate the varying levels of truth, one as valid as another, or rather one complementing another. The different worlds of fiction she presents are also worlds of truth fragmented and encased one in another to form a whole or an attempt toward integrity.

The more Marguerite endeavors to tell the truth by means of so-called true stories the more she realizes its illusiveness and infinite variety. In the prologue to the *Heptameron*, she promises to tell only the truth; therefore, hardly a novella passes without a reminder of its "vérité" or its "véritable" character.[15] She ends up protesting too much the veracity of her tales, as if she needed to convince herself and the reader. Through their frequency, these protestations become much

15. The references to telling the truth are too numerous to catalogue here; suffice it to mention that in the very first lines of the first novella the narrator proclaims "et si ne dirai que pure verité," and toward the end of the *Heptameron* this reminder persists: "mais souviéne vous qu'il faut icy dire vérité" (LXIII, 323).

less a rhetorical device than an hypnotic force to play on the audience's gullibility. They also constitute another means of breaking the fictional spell; they supposedly remind the reader that the event actually happened—in case he wanted to think otherwise. One of the participants, Symontaut, finally undermines the whole edifice of truth: "Je croy, mes Dames, que vous n'ettes pas si sotes, que croire en toutes les nouvelles que l'on vient conter, quelque apparence de sainteté qu'elles puissent avoir, si la preuve n'y est si grande, qu'elle ne puisse ettre remise en doute" (XXXIII, 213). However, the levels of fiction—the novellas, the discussions and the private world of the narrator-commentators, the climate of historicity—all converge toward the creation of a truth that refutes absolutes by its very composite fictional nature, and pose the question of the function of fiction, here particularly of the novella.

In the past, critics have agreed on the function of Marguerite's tales; primarily the novellas have a didactic purpose. Jourda, on two different occasions more than thirty years apart, summarizes this prevalent opinion: "Amuser, sans doute, elle y pense,—mais c'est le moindre de ses soucis. Elle se propose d'atteindre un but plus élevé, d'instruire,—et c'est pourquoi elle cherche à distraire, sachant qu'il n'est meilleur moyen d'enseigner que de paraître de le faire. . . . Elle n'écrit que pour dégager de chacun de ses contes une conclusion pratique d'ordre élevé."[16] Doubtless Marguerite pro-

---

16. *Marguerite d'Angoulême*, II, p. 887; "*L'Heptaméron*: livre pré-classique," p. 136. Cf. "En fait ce n'est pas la qualité poétique, la tenue littéraire des œuvres de Marguerite qui nous retient: ce sont les idées qu'elles traduisent. Ou mieux les sentiments: je n'aime guère la formule 'idées religieuses', s'agissant de cette femme sensible et mystique, si peu théologienne et si peu dogmatique" (Febvre, p. 39). However, recently an American critic has taken a notable exception to this prevalent view: "*L'Heptaméron*, as a whole, is not a didactic work, nor is it so much a debate as an inquiry into human experience." Donald Stone, "Narrative Technique in *L'Heptaméron*," *Studi Francesi*, 11 (1967), 476.

claims that fiction exists as a function of truth, and in this regard, the discussions after the stories have a vital role in attempting to decipher it.

However, at the same time she remains perfectly aware that she is writing literature, by definition a product of the imagination, as well. To preclude any such consciousness would be comparable to stating that Montaigne cared primarily for the world of ideas and morals and had little concern for the craft of fiction. Her consciousness of form she must have derived in great part from her reading of and strong affinity for Boccaccio. Furthermore, the very genre of the novella contains inherently a fusion of "plaire et instruire," as every *novelliere* of the Renaissance well knew; he abided by this precept mindful that the novella is basically a pastime, but he did not shun literary glory. And Marguerite does not take exception to the rules that govern the genre she has chosen as a vehicle for her imaginative expression.[17]

If the novella has the function of a pastime, it is to elicit laughter, a broad laughter at first, followed by a more reflective laughter most of the time, because human nature hesitates to accept a strictly gratuitous glee. The novellas in the *Heptameron* do not lay claim to any Rabelaisian comic strain; they may contain a certain ribald current, but not the heartiness and verbal vitality found in the *Gargantua*. This basic dissimilarity does not mean that Marguerite and Rabelais do not have identical aims: to bear witness to the variety of human nature, to evidence helplessness before the contradictions promulgated by multifarious sources of human knowledge and its resulting ambiguity, to advocate flexibility and reason in religion, and a certain melancholy, if not pessimism, in the face of the human condition.[18] Marguerite offers

17. Again we refer the reader to the excellent book by W. Pabst, *Novellentheorie und Novellendichtung*, who analyzes the novella and its generic trait as a pastime during the Renaissance.

18. For this comic pessimism in Rabelais, which is beginning to surface in critics, see J. Paris, *Rabelais au futur* and M. Beaujour, *Le Jeu de Rabelais*.

tragic and comic tales, but both are merely the two faces of the same coin. What they have in common, however, is Marguerite's underlying smile, for irony pervades all the novellas, which reflect therefore a pessimistic view of man derived from his moral fall and from her observations of fragmented and irreconcilable components of society and thought. In this light, Marguerite foreshadows Montaigne, whose smiling shadowy presence stands behind every essay as he manipulates notions and mystifies the reader. He set the tone in "Au lecteur" when he advised us not to waste time in proceeding with the reading, just as Marguerite protested in her prologue that she would tell only the truth. What truth?

Irony pervades the *Heptameron* because the novellas persist in revealing the wide gap between seeming and being; it depicts man's noble actions as mere appearances for base motivations, or if truly noble the actions fail invariably. The world of fiction conveys these unveilings, and what parades as truth in the action of the novellas becomes illusion. The novella is meant to bring illusion, to mystify, but the reader must not be deluded; the tale casts shifting lights on the social structure, and Marguerite's smile peers through certain narrative techniques. In this context, superlatives have an important role. Most main characters, especially those of noble extraction, are depicted both physically and morally in a superlative vein; then in the course of their actions, or in the course of the discussions by the narrators, their perfect nature is reversed or seriously questioned in an explicit or implicit manner. The thirty-fifth novella offers a case in point: "En la ville de Pampelune y avoit une Dame estimée belle et vertueuse, et la plus chaste et dévote qui fut au païs . . . [et] un cordelier tenu de tout le peuple pour an saint homme, à cause de sa très grande austérité et bonté de vie, qui le rendoit maigre et palle, mais non tant qu'il ne fut un des beaus hommes du monde" (219, 220). In another instance, an ironic use of *beau* forms the basis of the twenty-third tale where it occurs at least ten times; here the double-entendre focuses on *beau-frère*, the handsome brother-in-law who incarnates evil, and not only in the eyes of his sister-in-law!

Irony in the guise of a smile or forced laughter reveals and even takes the place of bitterness. Values summarily and jocularly dismissed are not scorned, but regretted; again the narrator remembers best when the character forgets: "A l'heure sans avoir égard à l'obligation qu'il avoit à son maitre, ny à la maison dont étoit la Dame, sans luy demander congé, ny faire révérence, se coucha auprès d'elle, qui le sentit plus tot entre ses bras qu'elle n'apperceut sa venue" (IV, 34). Scorn needs no mask; it points an accusing or mocking finger through the use of the demonstrative adjective against the lustful monks: "laissant ces deus beaus frères aus désertz" (V, 39); "ces pauvres fratres voians venir si grand' compagnie" (V, 40); or against ordinary human beings, victims of their base appetites: "ce malheureus homme" and "cette pauvre fille" (XXII, 160).[19]

Onomastics leave no doubt about the irony intended in a story; a protagonist's name will provide a clue to the tone or the outcome of the action and thereby make the reader omniscient; hence the irony. A shortsighted husband who gets caught in his own trap is called Bornet (cf. *borné*); a nobleman who had been faithful to his loved one and finds her lying with a groom is called the Seigneur du Ryant (XX);[20] Bernard du Ha is the ham merchant who brings this product to sell to the ladies of the town (XXVIII); Yambique, the heroine of the forty-fourth novella whose name carries erotic connotations, has nymphomaniac appetites;[21] and Mar-

19. Need we say that these examples are only a mere sample.
20. This story, usually referred to as the tale of Giocondo, the happy one, appears as early as Ariosto, and later La Fontaine uses it too; but Marguerite by calling him "Ryant" avoids any subtlety before her French audience; cf. the Le Roux de Lincy edition of the *Heptameron*, IV, 256–60.
21. Significantly enough, Gruget the first editor and expurgator of the *Heptameron* changed Yambique's name to an innocuous Camille.

guerite puns with the metaphor of the fall and the name of the monk who gets kicked downstairs when discovered by the husband: "Monsieur de Vale, devalez" (XLVI, 264). Marguerite smiles on the surface but winces within herself. She does not deceive herself nor should the reader deceive himself by leaning more toward the bitterness than the mystification, or vice versa. Irony elicits and affects a dispassionateness which is a necessary ingredient in the creation of fiction.

An interrelation exists between irony and paradox; one derives inevitably from the other. The double level of the former and the dichotomy of the latter do not make choice easy for the reader and give flexibility to the author. By definition the novella is a pastime that attempts to elude the inexorable passing of time, and a means of attaining a measure of glory for its creator. This reach for immortality may not surface readily because the crux of irony is to hammer away at certain notions (here God, love, morals) while an essential by-product (literary glory) slips in the back door. Of course Marguerite would never make any explicit claim to earthly glory, as Ronsard unabashedly did. Even Louise Labé, that self-centered poetess, only implied, but strongly, a desire to be remembered by posterity.

The only instance in the *Heptameron* that the concept of time receives concentrated attention occurs in a sixty-eight-line poem, novella XXIV, in which the word *tems* appears twelve times. Terrestrial time, associated with suffering and healing, false happiness and true happiness, is opposed to heavenly eternal time, but the actions of the rejected nobleman turned hermit and those of the lady who overtested him are both questioned by the narrators; these individuals bemoan the protagonists' loss of opportunity for happiness and do not particularly extol the monk's new-found spiritual eternity. The emphasis on the tribulations of terrestrial time and the deemphasis of spiritual eternal life allow the novella itself to stand as a literary monument to eternity.

Following her propensity for dichotomy, Marguerite takes the language associated with literary creation and reverses its positive meaning in the tales. Although at first she may seem to produce a tension between form and content, she actually reinforces the fusion of the novella's functions to amuse and instruct. Even in the above instance, her apparent anti-terrestrial-time stance occurs in a poem that amounts to a tritely overworked antipoem, as do all poems in the *Heptameron*—and on purpose, we think.²² Only once in the framework does she refer to novellas as a pastime: "Après qu'ilz eurent diné, et un peu pris de repos, s'en alérent continuer le passetems accoutumé" (280). In the novellas themselves any mention of pastime or games has a negative connotation, since it implies idleness, waste, vice, ruse.²³ Similarly, acting or learning a part has positive implication in the framework, where the narrators spend their time in "étudier leur role" (204), but in the tales, an antitheater position, so to speak, is taken by means of a reversed use of a metaphor drawn from the religious stage; here a woman who had a secret relationship with a monk "jouoit son mistère" (XXIX, 196).²⁴

22. The lines are:

> J'ai par le Tems connu l'Amour d'enhaut,
> Lequel connu, soudin l'autre defaut.
> Par le Tems suis du tout à luy rendu,
> Et par le Tems de l'autre deffendu.
> Mon cueur et cors luy donne en sacrifice,
> Pour faire à luy, et non à vous service.
> En vous servant, rien m'avez estimé.
> Ce rien il a, en l'offensant, aymé.
> Mor me donnez pour vous avoir servie,
> Et le fuyant, il me donne la vie. [174]

23. Cf. XXIII, 168; LVIII, 304, 305; XLIX (in this novella, it is the basic metaphor).

24. The notion of the game is the central image of the fifty-ninth tale. The master of the house "ne sçavoit point de meilleur passetems, que de jouer au cent" (308); the maid "sçavoit son rolle par cueur" (307), and the shrewd lady "qui sçavoit sa maladie [her husband's infidelity] aussi bien que luy, luy demanda s'il vouloit qu'elle jouat son jeu. Il luy dit que ouÿ et qu'il reviendroit

Although one of the functions of the novella is to amuse, within the stories themselves Marguerite downgrades laughter. This position does not mean that there is a discrepancy between theory and practice; it simply separates the author's gloomy view of the world from any comedy a whole novella, the tale and the commentaries following it, may contain, because the story itself may still be quite hilarious. Her proposed theory of laughter reflects the one found in fabliaux and the medieval profane theater; an individual laughs at the expense of others: "Nous ne rions, dit Parlamente, pour oÿr dire ces beaus moz [obscenity]. Mais il est vray que toute personne est encline à rire, ou quand elle voit quelcun trebucher, ou quand on dit quelque mot sans propos, comme il avient souvent que la langue fourche en parlant, et fait dire un mot pour l'autre: ce qui avient aus plus sages et mieus parlantes" (LII, 286). Although as a matter of theory Marguerite also propounds the Aristotelian thesis that man is naturally inclined to laughter[25] and adds that *lapsus linguae* and *fatrasies* elicit laughter as well, in the stories themselves comic effects result from the superiority one protagonist feels over another; or the narrators may have the same sentiment upon hearing a colleague's tale. However, the frequent cruelty inherent in laughter in the tales does not find a counterpart in the narrators' laughing reactions.

The importance of laughter in the *Heptameron* has not been sufficiently noted. Direct references to it occur in more than a third of the seventy-two novellas. For the most part in the stories themselves, the protagonists' laughter has a demonic and didactic function, in the sense that Baudelaire defines it and that Pascal had earlier professed:

bientot . . . [elle] feit semblant d'avoir une tranchée [stomach ache] et bailla son jeu à un autre. Et si tot qu'elle fut saillye de la salle, laissa ses haus patins, et s'en courut . . . au lieu . . . où elle ne voulut que le marché se feit sans elle" (308).

25. Cf. the identical principle enunciated in "Aux lecteurs" at the beginning of the *Gargantua*: "Pour ce que rire est le propre de l'homme."

Le rire est satanique, il est donc profondément humain. Il est dans l'homme la conséquence de l'idée de sa propre supériorité; et, en effet, comme le rire est essentiellement humain, il est essentiellement contradictoire, c'est-à-dire qu'il est à la fois signe d'une grandeur infinie et d'une misère infinie relativement à l'Etre absolu dont il possède la conception, grandeur infinie relativement aux animaux. C'est du choc perpétuel de ces deux infinis que se dégage le rire.[26]

Meanwhile the audience of the narrator-commentators laughs at the tales in the Aristotelian sense, for laughter is a natural and spontaneous reaction; here it has a salutary and physiologically beneficial effect: "La nouvelle ne fut pas achevée, sans faire rire toute la compagnie, et principalement ceus qui connoiscoient le seigneur et la dame de Sedan" (XLIV, 259). This audience even asks for and looks forward to comic novellas: "Et ceus qui étoient délibérez de dire quelque folye, avoient desià le visage si joyeus qu'on espéroit d'eus occasion de bien rire" (138). Its members appreciate, then, the stories according to the traditional precepts of the Renaissance novella: a form of amusement, but not to the detriment of meaning. This particular audience separates the didactic purpose of the story from its comic aim; whereas in the tale itself, laughter and meaning are integrated to depict a certain cruelty and reflect a dismal view of society.

The two opposite notions of laughter not only demonstrate Marguerite's affinity for paradox and dichotomy but contain essentially the crux of her *angoisse* and her attempt to resolve it through a shifting fiction. A parallel opposition occurs between a story and its discussion. The tale in more or less fixing the action of the protagonists achieves a degree of integrity, while its veracity and historicity gain the status of fiction; therefore, action, truth, and fiction become amal-

26. C. Baudelaire, "De l'essence du rire," *Œuvres complètes*. Bibliothèque de la Pléiade (Paris, 1954), pp. 716–17.

gamated in an apparent dispassionate manner. But the discussion fragments the integrity of the tale, and in so doing, asserts itself over the story. The discussion then, being itself a fiction composed of narrative voices, is cast against the true fiction, the tale. Fiction clashes against fiction, just as the truths of the discussion clash against the truth of the tale. The integrated tale becomes dubious when the disintegrating discussion takes on the veil of truth. This reversal of role produces, not a mutual elimination, but a complementary fiction, the total novella: story and discussion.

To recreate a multidimensional world of human appetites a unilinear narrative does not suffice; it must be joined by another fiction that produces the prism of truth. And the cells, each a total novella, added one to another, constitute a fictional honeycomb, the *Heptameron*. Then the contradictions and similarities within the total novella and from one novella to another lead to a composite fiction that hardly differentiates truth from fiction. Although not integrated, truth and fiction merge and interchange roles in the *Heptameron*. The creative act of writing springs from the very failure of this integration.

7. CONCLUSION

THERE has never been any question of placing Marguerite de Navarre among the foremost prose writers of French literature. Such a classification would be both erroneous and pointless. Yet Marguerite has a mastery of the craft of the novella, and once and for all, it must be emphasized that the function of her novellas is not simply or principally didactic, because in them form and content are fused. A distinctive metaphoric language of love and deceit emerges from the *Heptameron* and reveals the ambiguity fundamental to this book. The global structure of the *Heptameron*, developed in the prologues and the ends to each day and in the thematic concatenation from one novella to another, further demonstrates Marguerite's ambivalence and bears witness to a careful composition and a conscious design. Quite by themselves, these metaphoric and structural fusions of form and content suffice to elevate the novellas from mere rhetoric to accomplished literature.

The *Heptameron* is marked by an all-pervasive concept of dichotomies which in turn leads to the notion of diversity. A given viewpoint is introduced only to be immediately set in contrast with its opposite, and within this spectrum there exist variables of reason and moderation. The language of love, derived from the Platonic, Petrarchan, courtly, and biblical traditions, applies to spiritual relationships as well as to physical desires; this conflicting duality aims at showing up pure spirituality and pure animality—both are impractical and blind positions—and favors some intervening point along the polarized gamut of spirit and body. In their attempt to thread the maze of human conduct, the novellas expose an unremitting duplicity and deception behind man's motivations and actions. Therefore love and truth fail. To convey this failure, Marguerite forges her own language by imparting contradictory meanings to identical words and images.

The conversations of the ten narrators that follow each novella are a distinctive feature of the *Heptameron*. The conflicting opinions they project do not allow for a synthesis of the novella they discuss. Their role is quite the contrary —to reveal a tale's many facets and to interpret and focus on key words and metaphors; in this way, the narrator-commentators are the book's first and best-informed critics. Even when at times the commentaries border on digressions, they actually function as thematic and structural links to the next novella. They create their own brand of fiction, involving the narrators' personal experiences and relationships, and pit it against the fiction of the story proper; a further dichotomy then carries over to the realm of fiction.

Buffeted by a world of paradoxes and contradictions and tossed on a sea of doubt, no wonder Marguerite de Navarre exhibits signs of pessimism, even cynicism, through some of the narrators. But not despair. The exploration of the human condition inevitably produces such a reaction; indeed, her reaction is, if anything, rather mild. The *Heptameron* delineates the limits and power of human judgment and knowledge. True to the Renaissance spirit, it refutes absolutes in the face of a multitude of equally valid choices. In a Baudelairian vein, the novellas proclaim that perfect Good on earth will never return; man will not recover from the Fall; in the *Heptameron*, just as later in Laclos's *Les Liaisons dangereuses*, flawless virtue succeeds on very few occasions. The tragic essence distilled from the novellas is the impossibility of determining the exact nature of vice, virtue; truth, falsehood; guilt, innocence; spiritual and physiological desires. Pascal's wager would offer the best solution, but from Marguerite's vantage point, few take it, although she fervently advocates it.

The narrator-commentators laugh heartily at each other's tales, but the protagonists within the tales exhibit a cruel laughter of superiority toward one another. Although the reader perceives the pessimism filtering through the characters' behavior, he remains puzzled, mystified by the fluid propositions and partial solutions offered by the novellas. The frequent discrepancy between the purposes stated at the outset and at the end of a story and a widespread irony contribute further to this fluidity. Thus monolithic didacticism fails, and the resulting multifarious moralizing proves to be more dilute than effective. Only the novella itself stands immutable and impervious to time and strengthens our faith in the permanence of literary creation, even if Marguerite chooses not to admit it. These novellas, which she sets before us as an instructive and entertaining pastime, are meant to be remembered with posterity.

The *Heptameron* offers one final paradox in relation to Marguerite's other works, especially her poetry. Owing to its intense lyricism, the poetry at first glance seems to reflect a polarized mind, fleeing the corrupt earthly domain to take refuge in the perfect divine realm; *Chansons spirituelles* can be used best to illustrate such a polarization, and so can *La Navire* and *Les Prisons*, though less well. However, future studies on the poetry may well minimize this flight and stress the *angoisse* emanating from the lyrics, in the Villon tradition. The poetry will emerge more as a search—which fails—for meaningful values in life rather than an escape from it. Marguerite's plays, because of their dialectical nature—similar in this point to the commentaries after the novellas—reflect more clearly the Socratic method and wisdom found in the *Heptameron*. In essence, Marguerite's works, and the *Heptameron* foremost, explore the human condition and discover no foolproof practical solution, even in faith, nor any behavioral code that man will conform to; after all, one fundamental purpose of life is to develop in man a proper pattern of life on earth, no matter how difficult such a process may be. And each man, devoured by varied appetites, will have to formulate his own pattern somewhere between perfect Good and absolute Evil.

Selected Bibliography

1. Basic Editions of Marguerite de Navarre's Works

L'Heptaméron. Ed. Félix Frank. 3 vols. Paris: Liseux, 1879.
L'Heptaméron des Nouvelles. Ed. MM. Le Roux de Lincy and Anatole de Montaiglon. 4 vols. Paris: Eudes, 1880. Slatkine Reprints, 1969.
Les Marguerites de la Marguerite des princesses. Ed. Félix Frank. 4 vols. Paris: Librairie des Bibliophiles, 1873. Slatkine Reprints, 1970.
Les Dernières poésies de Marguerite de Navarre. Ed. Abel Lefranc. Paris: Colin, 1896.
La Navire; Ou Consolation du roi François I à sa sœur Marguerite. Ed. Robert Marichal. Paris: Champion, 1956.
L'Heptaméron. Ed. Michel François. Paris: Garnier, 1960.
Théâtre profane. Ed. V. L. Saulnier. Geneva: Droz, 1963.
Nouvelles. Ed. Yves Le Hir. Paris: Presses Universitaires de France, 1967.
Œuvres choisies. Ed. H. P. Clive. New York: Appleton-Century-Crofts, 1968.
La Coche. Ed. Robert Marichal. Geneva: Droz, 1970.
Chansons spirituelles. Ed. Georges Dottin. Geneva: Droz, 1971.

2. Critical Studies

Andon, James. "Contribution à l'établissement d'un tableau social du peuple français dans la première moitié du XVIe siècle. Portrait des devisants dans l'*Heptaméron* de Marguerite de Navarre." *Bulletin de l'Association Guillaume Budé,* 26 (1967), 293–301.
Arlan, Marcel. "Une cour d'amour." *Hommes et Mondes,* 5 (1948), 399–418.
Auerbach, Erich. *Zur Technik der Frührenaissancenovelle in Italien und Frankreich.* Heidelberg: Winter, 1921.
Bambeck, Manfred. "Religiöse Skepsis bei Margarete von Navarra?" *Zeitschrift für französische Sprache und Literatur,* 77 (1967), 12–21.

Brockmeier, Peter. "Das Privileg der Lust. Bemerkungen zur Darstellung der erdischen Liebe im *Heptaméron*." *Germanisch-Romanische Monatsschrift*, 49 (1967), 337–53.

Coulet, Henri. "Marguerite de Navarre." *Le Roman jusqu'à la révolution*. Collection U. Paris: Colin, 1967. Pp. 121–28.

Delègue, Yves. "Autour de deux prologues: *L'Heptaméron* est-il un anti-Boccace?" *Travaux de linguistique et de littérature publiés par le Centre de Philologie et de Littérature Romanes de l'Université de Strasbourg*, 4 (1966), pp. 23–37.

Deloffre, Frédéric. *La Nouvelle en France à l'âge classique*. Paris: Didier, 1967.

Ely, Gladys. "The Limits of Realism in the *Heptaméron* of Marguerite de Navarre." *Romanic Review*, 43 (1952), 3–11.

Febvre, Lucien. *Autour de l'Heptaméron: Amour sacré, amour profane*. Paris: Gallimard, 1944.

Ferrier, Janet. *Forerunners of the French Novel: An Essay on the Development of the Novella in the late Middle Ages*. London: Manchester University Press, 1954.

France, Anatole. "La Reine de Navarre," *Le Génie latin*. Paris: Lemerre, 1917. Pp. 11–36.

François, Michel. "Adrien de Thou et l'*Heptaméron*." *Humanisme et Renaissance*, 5 (1938), 16–36.

Frappier, Jean. "La Chastelaine de Vergi, Marguerite de Navarre et Bandello." *Mélanges de la Faculté des Lettres de Strasbourg*, 2 (1946), pp. 89–150.

———. "Sur Lucien Febvre et son interprétation psychologique du XVIe siècle." *Mélanges d'histoire littéraire (XVIe–XVIIe siècle) offerts à Raymond Lebègue*. Paris: Nizet, 1969. Pp. 19–31.

Garosci, Cristina. *Margherita di Navarra*. Turin: Lattes, 1908.

Gelernt, Jules. *World of Many Loves: The Heptameron of Marguerite de Navarre*. Chapel Hill, N.C.: University of North Carolina Press, 1966.

Hartley, K. H. *Bandello and the Heptameron: A Study of Comparative Literature*. Melbourne: Melbourne University Press, 1960.

Jeffels, R. R. "The Conte as a Genre in the French Renaissance." *Revue de l'Université de Ottawa*, 26 (1956), 435–50.

Jourda, Pierre. "Récents écrits sur Marguerite de Navarre." *Revue du Seizième Siècle*, 11 (1924), 273–88.

———. *Marguerite d'Angoulême, Duchesse d'Alençon, Reine de Navarre (1492–1549). Etude biographique et littéraire*. 2 vols. Paris: Champion, 1930. Bottega d'Erasmo Reprint, 1966.

————. "La dixième nouvelle de l'*Heptaméron*," *Mélanges de philologie, d'histoire et de littérature offerts à Joseph Vianey*. Paris: Les Presses Françaises, 1934. Pp. 127–31.

————. "L'*Heptaméron*: Livre préclassique." *Studi in onore di Carlo Pellegrini*. Turin: Società Editrice Italiana, 1963. Pp. 133–36.

————. "La première nouvelle de l'*Heptaméron*," *Mélanges d'histoire littéraire (XVIe–XVIIe siècle) offerts à Raymond Lebègue*. Paris: Nizet, 1969. Pp. 45–50.

Kasprzyk, Krystyna. "L'Amour dans l'*Heptaméron*: de l'idéal à la réalité." *Mélanges d'histoire littéraire (XVIe–XVIIe siècle) offerts à Raymond Lebègue*. Paris: Nizet, 1969. Pp. 51–57.

————. "La Matière traditionnelle et sa fonction dans l'*Heptaméron*." *Mélanges de littérature comparée et de philologie offerts à M. Brahmer*. Warsaw: Editions Scientifiques de Pologne, 1967. Pp. 257–264.

Krailsheimer, A. J. "The *Heptaméron* Reconsidered." *The French Renaissance and its Heritage: Essays Presented to Alan B. Boase*. London: Methuen, 1968. Pp. 75–92.

Lebègue, Raymond. "Les Sources de l'*Heptaméron* et la pensée de Marguerite de Navarre." *Comptes-rendus des séances de l'année 1956*, Académie des Inscriptions et Belles-Lettres (Paris, 1957), 466–73.

————. "De Marguerite de Navarre à Honoré de Balzac." *Comptes-rendus des séances de l'année 1957*, Académie des Inscriptions et Belles-Lettres (Paris, 1958), 251–56.

————. "La Femme qui mutile son visage (*Heptaméron* X)." *Comptes-rendus des séances de l'année 1959*, Académie des Inscriptions et Belles-Lettres (Paris, 1960), 176–83.

————. "Réalisme et apprêt dans la langue des personnages de l'*Heptaméron*." *Actes du colloque de Strasbourg: La littérature narrative d'imagination*. Paris: Presses Universitaires de France, 1961. Pp. 73–86.

————. "Le second *Miroir* de Marguerite de Navarre." *Comptes-rendus des séances de l'année 1963*, Académie des Inscriptions et Belles-Lettres (Paris, 1964), 46–56.

Lefranc, Abel. "Les Idées religieuses de Marguerite de Navarre d'après son oeuvre poétique." *Bulletin de la Société de l'Histoire du Protestantisme Français*, 46 (1897), 7–30, 72–84, 137–48, 295–311, 418–42; 47 (1898), 68–81, 115–36.

————. "Le Platonisme et la littérature en France à l'époque de la Renaissance." *Grands écrivains de la Renaissance*. Paris: Champion, 1914. Pp. 63–137.

————. "Marguerite de Navarre et le Platonisme en France." Ibid., pp. 139–249.

Le Hir, Yves. "L'Inspiration biblique dans le *Triomphe de l'agneau* de Marguerite de Navarre." *Mélanges d'histoire littéraire de la Renaissance offerts à Henri Chamard.* Paris: Nizet, 1951. Pp. 43–61.

LoCicero, Donald. *Novellentheorie: The Practicality of the Theoretical.* The Hague: Mouton, 1970.

Lomazzi, Anna. "Recenti interpretazioni della 'Châtelaine de Vergi.'" *Studi di Letteratura Francese,* 2 (1969), 268–73.

Loménie, Louis de. "La Littérature romanesque: La reine de Navarre et l'*Heptaméron* d'après de nouveaux documents." *Revue des Deux Mondes,* 40 (1862), 651–87.

Lorenzetti, Paolo. "Riflessi del pensiero italiano nell'*Heptameron* di Margherita di Navarra." *Athenaeum* (Pavia), 4 (1916), 266–308.

Lorian, Alexandre. "Intensité et conséquence dans l'*Heptaméron* de Marguerite de Navarre." *Neuphilologische Mitteilungen,* 63 (1963), 106–19.

Luzio, Alessandro. *Le nozze di Margherita di Navarra.* Bergamo: Istituto Italiano d'Arti Grafiche, 1912.

Meylan, Edward F. "La Date de *L'Oraison de l'âme fidèle* et son importance pour la biographie morale de Marguerite de Navarre." *Modern Language Notes,* 52 (1937), 562–68.

Mignon, Maurice. "L'Italianisme de Marguerite de Navarre," *Les Affinités intellectuelles de l'Italie et de la France.* Paris: Hachette, 1923. Pp. 116–77.

Pabst, Walter. *Novellentheorie und Novellendichtung.* Hamburg: Cram, De Gruyter, 1953.

Paris, Gaston. "La Nouvelle française au XVe et XVIe siècles." *Mélanges de littérature française du moyen âge.* Ed. Mario Roques. Paris: Champion, 1912. Pp. 627–67.

Pellegrini, Carlo. "Riflessi di cultura italiana nella prima opera di Margherita di Navarra." *Cultura Moderna,* 2 (1930), 967–83.

Picco, Francesco. "Margherita di Navarra." *Donne di Francia e poeti d'Italia.* Turin: Lattes, 1921.

Rasmussen, Jurgen. *La prose narrative française du XVe siècle; étude esthétique et stylistique.* Copenhagen: Munksgaard, 1958.

Rat, Maurice. "L'Amour courtois et l'*Heptaméron* de la reine de Navarre." *Revue des Deux Mondes* September 15, 1966, 227–36.

Redenbacher, Fritz. "Die Novellistik der französischen Hochrenaissance." *Zeitschrift für französische Sprache und Literatur,* 49 (1927), 1–72.

Renaudet, Augustin. "Marguerite de Navarre, à propos d'un ouvrage récent." *Revue du Seizième Siècle,* 18 (1931), 272–308.

Renier, Rodolfo. "La Margherita delle principesse." *Svaghi critici.* Bari: Laterza, 1910. Pp. 263–81.

Reynier, Gustave. *Les Origines du roman réaliste.* Paris: Hachette, 1913.

Sainte-Beuve, C.-A. "Marguerite de Navarre." *Causeries du lundi.* Paris: Garnier, 1850. VII, 434–54.

Saulnier, V. L. "Marguerite de Navarre: Art médiéval et pensée nouvelle." *Revue Universitaire,* 63 (1954), 154–62.

———. "Martin Pontus et Marguerite de Navarre: La Réforme lyonnaise et les sources de l'*Heptaméron.*" *Bibliothèque d'Humanisme et Renaissance,*" 21 (1958), 557–94.

Simone, Franco. "La Présence de Boccace dans la culture française du XVe siècle." *Journal of Medieval and Renaissance Studies,* 1 (1971), 17–32.

Söderhjelm, Werner. *La Nouvelle française au XVe siècle.* Paris: Champion, 1910.

Sozzi, Lionello. "Boccaccio in Francia nel Cinquecento." *Il Boccaccio nelle cultura francese,* ed. Carlo Pellegrini. Florence: Olschki, 1971. Pp. 211–356.

Stefel, A. L. "Die Chastelaine de Vergy bei Margaret von Navarra und bei Bandello." *Zeitschrift für französische Sprache und Literatur,* 36 (1910), 103–115.

Stone, Donald. "Narrative Technique in L'*Heptaméron.*" *Studi Francesi,* 11 (1967), 473–76.

Strohl, Henri. *De Marguerite de Navarre à Louise Scheppler: quelques étapes de l'évolution de la piété protestante en France.* Strasbourg: Librairie Evangélique, 1926.

Telle, Emile V. *L'Œuvre de Marguerite d'Angoulême, reine de Navarre, et la Querelle des Femmes.* Toulouse: Lion, 1937.

Tetel, Marcel. "Une Réévaluation de la Xe nouvelle de l'*Heptaméron.*" *Neuphilologische Mitteilungen,* 72 (1971), 563–69.

———. "Marguerite de Navarre et Montaigne: Relativisme et paradoxe," *From Marot to Montaigne.* Lexington, Ky.: University of Kentucky Press, 1972. Pp. 125–35.

Tilley, Arthur. "The Literary Circle of Marguerite de Navarre." *A Mis-*

cellany of Studies Presented to L. E. Kastner. New York: Cambridge University Press, 1932. Pp. 518–31.

Toldo, Pietro. *Contributo allo studio della novella francese del XV e XVI secolo.* Rome: Loescher, 1895.

——. "Rileggendo il novelliere della Regina di Navarra." *Rivista d'Italia,* 26 (1923), 380–405.

Vernay, Henri. *Les divers sens du mot "raison" autour de l'œuvre de Marguerite de Navarre, reine de Navarre (1492–1549).* Heidelberg: Winter, 1962.

Welter, J. Th. *L'Exemplum dans la littérature religieuse et didactique du moyen âge.* Paris: Guitard, 1927.

Index